Joining the Sisterhood

SUNY series in Modern Jewish Literature and Culture
Sarah Blacher Cohen, editor

Joining the Sisterhood

Young Jewish Women Write Their Lives

Edited by
Tobin Belzer
and
Julie Pelc

State University of New York Press

Published by
State University of New York Press, Albany

For information, address State University of New York Press,
90 State Street, Suite 700, Albany, NY 12207

Production by Judith Block
Marketing by Jennifer Giovani

Library of Congress Cataloging-in-Publication Data

Joining the sisterhood : young Jewish women write their lives / [edited by] Tobin Belzer
and Julie Pelc.
    p. cm. — (SUNY series in modern Jewish literature and culture.)
    Includes bibliographical references and index.
    ISBN 0-7914-5861-X (alk. paper) — ISBN 0-7914-5862-8 (pbk. : alk. paper)
    1. American literature—Jewish authors. 2. American literature—Women authors. 3.
Jewish women—United States. 4. Young women—United States. 5. Jewish
Women—Poetry. 6. Young women—Poetry. I. Belzer, Tobin. II. Pelc, Julie. III. Series.

PS508.J4J65 2003
810.8'09287'089924—dc21   2002045256

10 9 8 7 6 5 4 3 2 1

With gratitude for their love and support,
we dedicate this book to:

Kayla Leah Jacobson Sanchez
and
Grandma Jean Belzer Simon Cohen

Contents

Acknowledgments

We gratefully acknowledge Sarah Blacher Cohen, whose support has been invaluable in all areas of our book's production. Thank you to James Peltz and Judith Block at SUNY Press, for their vision to see this project through to the end. Thank you to Chanel Dubofsky, Neil Keikover, and Riqi Kosovske, for helping with the essential details. And thank you to the gifted young women whose writing graces these pages.

We are extremely appreciative of the financial support this project received from the Lucius N. Littauer Foundation. We also want to express how much our lives have been enriched by wonderful relationships at many institutions and organizations during the process of creating this book: Brandeis University; The Hadassah International Research Institute on Jewish Women; Hillel: The Foundation for Jewish Campus Life; Joshua Venture: A Fellowship for Jewish Social Entrepreneurs; Kol Isha Leadership Seminar of the World Union of Jewish Students; Tufts University; Washington University in St. Louis; and the Wexner Foundation. Finally, thank you to our mentors, friends, sisters, parents, and allies, whose love has kept us in life, sustained us, and enabled us to reach this joyous occasion.

Julie Pelc and Tobin Belzer
Los Angeles, CA

Introduction

Nourish beginnings, let us nourish beginnings. Not all things are blest, but the seeds of all things are blest. The blessing is in the seed.

These lines were written by Muriel Rukeyser, a politically active, passionate Jewish American woman whose poetry and life spanned the twentieth century. As young Jewish women in the twenty-first century, we find deep meaning in her words. If the blessing is indeed "in the seed," as Rukeyser suggests, then we believe that this anthology is our seed. In it, we plant the spirit of struggles, celebrations, and our stories.

This anthology is a window on the lives of young Jewish women, in their own words. Through poetry and personal essays, these authors describe the paths they have taken in their search for both personal and universal truths. None of these journeys takes a linear route. Each woman is affected by a multiplicity of influences, inspirations, and frustrations as she tries to determine what it means to be Jewish and female in the twenty-first century. The negotiation of identity illustrated throughout the essays and poetry in *Joining the Sisterhood* is age-old and is also unique to this generation of Jewish women.

In the pages of this anthology, each author reflects upon her process of growth and development, and upon the choices she makes about her life and future as a Jewish woman. These young authors write about rejecting, reclaiming, and wrestling with Jewish tradition and history. They write about their bodies, and reveal their experiences of abuse and healing. In these pages, young women write about their philosophies, their politics, and their dreams. They share lessons they've learned from their travels across continents and cultures. They discuss their relationships with Jews and non-Jews, men and women.

Their roles—as daughters, sisters, lovers, and wives—are described and analyzed. They write about their passions: about dancing, storytelling, and singing. They record their struggles with self-esteem and self-criticism. And they acknowledge the many influences—mentors, books, communities, friends, and families—that brought them to where they are today.

Though many of the challenges facing young Jewish women today are not new, our stories and experiences represent major shifts in the landscape of Jewish and feminist history. We grew up enjoying the achievements and advances made during the Jewish feminist movement. Ours is the first generation where women can serve as executives and professionals in both Jewish and non-Jewish workplaces. For many young Jewish women, bat mizvah ceremonies are common. Naming ceremonies, often called "Brit Bat," now welcome baby girls into the Jewish covenant the way their brothers have always been welcomed. *Lilith: The Independent Jewish Women's Magazine* has been available since most of us could read. The modern State of Israel has been an assumed and constant presence in the world throughout our lives. We grew up knowing that women can be rabbis, and have come to learn that Orthodox women can be feminists.

Unlike our predecessors, we have access to a large body of literature by and about Jewish women, which has grown steadily throughout our lives. In the last thirty years, a proliferation of books and articles has emerged addressing issues surrounding Judaism and gender from across academic disciplines and in almost every literary genre. In our lifetimes, feminist scholars have sought to redress the inadequacy of Jewish history, which generally failed to include Jewish women's thoughts and experiences, or only included them circuitously. Biographers are reshaping history by uncovering Jewish women's untold life stories. Theologians are adding women's voices to the study and critique of religious doctrines. In addition, Jewish women's experiences and beliefs have been expressed in ethnographies and social histories.

It is a crucial historical moment to add *young* Jewish women's voices to this process of personal and social change. The authors in *Joining the Sisterhood* offer an early glimpse at the powerful ways in which we will be able to impact the Jewish future. Today, there are young Jewish women who engage in almost every aspect of religious and cultural Jewish life, yet our unique perspectives have remained largely invisible. Technology has availed young Jewish women with unprecedented opportunities for virtual and actual global cultural exchange, yet a 1995 study by The National Commission on American Jewish Women made young Jewish women (ages 21-35) one of their foci, because so little is known about this population. While Jewish organizations have recognized the need for engagement and outreach to this group, they continue to talk *about* young Jewish women, rather than *with* us.

Like our predecessors, we, as young Jewish women, are eager to tell our stories. From Jewish culture, we learned the invaluable lesson of communal memory by means of oral and written storytelling. Our sacred texts were passed down from one generation to the next, relying almost entirely on the artful discipline of storytelling. Jewish history teaches us that storytelling is a way of explaining our origins, sharing our beliefs about the world, and connecting us to one another. It is also the way in which we pass the torch of tradition onto the next generation.

Storytelling is also our inheritance from the discipline of feminism. From feminist discourse, we learn that sharing one's truth can be a tool for personal empowerment and social change. As feminist poet and activist Audre Lorde writes in her book, *Sister, Outsider*:

> Each of us is here now because in one way or another we share a commitment to language and the power of language, and to the reclaiming of that language which has been made to work against us. In the transformation of silence into language and action, it is vitally necessary for each one of us to establish or examine her function in that transformation and to recognize her role as vital within that transformation (Lorde, 43).

By writing about our thoughts and experiences, the young Jewish women in this anthology are planting our seeds firmly in the soil of both feminist and Jewish traditions. In this spirit, we join the sisterhood of women who work toward justice in their homes, synagogues, and communities: who tell their stories to illustrate the ways in which the personal and the political intersect in their lives. We join the sisterhood of Jewish women who recognize the vital need for their stories to be told. We honor the generations of women who came before us, and we honor those who walk beside us. And we provide a glimpse into our own lives and subcultures, setting the stage for our futures.

Joining the Sisterhood was born from a collaboration between two friends who shared a common vision. This project is based on our conviction that young Jewish women's stories provide a vital contribution to modern Jewish history, and that the very process of telling our stories is empowering. As such, the story of our collaboration and the creation of this anthology is precious to us.

We met in 1996, when we were participants in Kol Isha, the Young Jewish Women's Leadership Seminar sponsored by the World Union of Jewish Students. For one month, we toured Israel with twenty other young Jewish women from around the world. As we traveled through the country, we shared stories about the unique joys and challenges of growing up Jewish and female. We discovered that each of us, in her own way, had struggled to find a community that would honor and celebrate her identity as a Jewish woman.

Throughout that summer, we shared resources and discovered that we were connected across space and time through the books we had read. As avid readers and writers, we lamented the dearth of writing by young women in the quickly growing canon of Jewish women's literature. Our discussions helped us to realize that the time had come for our generation to join the sisterhood of Jewish women writers. We compiled *Joining the Sisterhood* as a form of activism. We heeded the guidance of Rabbi Nachman of Bratislava, who once said, "[She] who is able to write a book and does not write it is as one who has lost a child." We resolved to become midwives, and together, we created a forum for young Jewish women's autobiographical writing.

The anthology we envisioned would highlight the thoughtful, complicated, and provocative lives of women in our generation. It would include the voices of young Jewish women from diverse cultures, religious denominations, political viewpoints, and sexual orientations. It would bring forward their thoughts and experiences through autobiographical essays and poetry.

As editors of such an anthology, our first challenge was to find these women and their communities. We sent an open call for essays to Jewish Studies departments, Women's Studies departments, and Hillels at colleges and universities across North America. We solicited writers using both Jewish and feminist magazines, journals, newspapers, e-mail lists, and web sites. We also contacted more than forty national Jewish organizations and over a hundred feminist bookstores in the United States and Canada. The response was overwhelming.

Reading the submissions from young Jewish women across North America felt like a continuation of the exchange of life narratives that we had begun in Israel. Often, something in one author's writing would remind us of another essay or poem. We became matchmakers, connecting women across the United States and Canada, who shared life experiences or reflected on common themes. In collecting the essays our deep belief in the value of telling stories has redoubled.

We selected essays and poetry that complemented each other, and contributed to our image of *Joining the Sisterhood* as a cross-section of young Jewish women's experiences in North America. We did not endeavor to create a wholly representative sample, but we attempted to bring as many diverse voices to the conversation as possible.

We are a highly mobile group, and staying connected with one another throughout the process of writing and editing this anthology was an ongoing challenge since the contributors live in cities and towns throughout the United States and in two Canadian provinces. Our ages range from 16 to 33. Some of us have finished our educations, while others attend high school, college, graduate programs, and rabbinic school. We are scientists, environmentalists, artists, activists, storytellers, and teachers. We are gay and straight; single, divorced, and married. Since authors come from different ethnic backgrounds, we use different words and pronunciations to express our Jewish ethnic identities, reflecting our Ashkenazi, Sephardi, and Mizrahi cultures. This is the first publication for some of the contributors, while others will include this among a long list of their other literary accomplishments.

From both the poetry and prose, the impassioned voices of the next generation distinctly resonate. Each piece in *Joining the Sisterhood* describes the experience of being young, Jewish, and female from the author's own unique vantage point. Yet, in each poem and essay, there also exists a spark of universality.

The anthology is divided into three sections: "*Ruach:* Ourselves in Relation to Others and the Environment"; "*Nefesh:* Ourselves in Relation to Our Bodies"; and "*Neshamah:* Our Emotional and Intellectual Selves." *Ruach, nefesh,* and *neshamah* are Hebrew words that describe the spirit or soul. Each term evokes a subtle meaning: *ruach,* which means "wind," is associated with the sources of spirit outside of ourselves; *nefesh* means the physical state of being alive; and *neshamah,* meaning "breath" or "soul," speaks to the vitality of our emotional and intellectual lives. While every essay is imbued with elements of each type of spirit, we have categorized the pieces according to the type of spirit that is voiced most prominently by each author. The poems too, are categorized according to this method, and are tucked between the essays, like hidden jewels that are waiting to be discovered.

The essays and poetry in "*Ruach*" offer glimpses into the lives of women as they navigate both Jewish and secular worlds. *Ruach* is the "wind" that connects our internal selves with the external world. Authors delve deeply into their negotiation of identity in response to their social environment. They write passionately about their struggle to understand their place in the world in relation to their beliefs about politics, history, North American culture, and the organized Jewish community.

In "Bais Yaakov Girl," Eve Rosenbaum writes about her journey toward, and then away from, religious observance in reaction to her family's embrace of right-wing Orthodox Judaism during her early adolescence. She charts this path through her experience as a "Bais Yaakov girl," to her awakening in college, when she finds her way back to the woman she was meant to become.

Leah Berger writes about her political commitments to humanistic causes, and her personal revelations about Judaism and God in "Ground Contemplation Prayer." Her journey takes her to the redwood forests of California and to the deserts of Arizona, where she describes the sanctuary she finds in nature, as she struggles to find wholeness amid a social world that favors the categorization and compartmentalization of identity.

In "Singing Praises," Shoshana M. Friedman, the youngest essayist represented in the anthology, writes about growing up as part of a Jewish Renewal community. She writes about how her love of music enabled her to expand her world, while drawing upon the supportive foundation of her family and community.

In "God Lives in the Himalayas," Leanne Lieberman describes the places she travels—both literally and metaphorically—on her search for God. She laments her childhood experience of Conservative Judaism, where God was rarely mentioned, and she begins a spiritual quest. Her exploration of Asian countries and traditions, her studies in a liberal Orthodox yeshiva in Jerusalem, and her relationship with her non-Jewish boyfriend all factor into her journey, which ends where it began: with her family.

Professional storyteller Vered Hankin, writes about how her life has been influenced by her strong sense of place in "Where the

Mountain Touches the Sky." Her journey carries her through experiences in Israel, Kansas, and New York. Her discovery of feminism, her experience of anti-Semitism at her college sorority, and the healing work done after a debilitating car accident, all lead her toward a greater understanding of her place in the world.

The final essay in the section is that of Charlotte Green Honigman-Smith, whose journey occurs in relation with, and in reaction to, the organized Jewish community. In "*Mazel:* The Luck of the Irish," she writes, "According to decades of prediction, statistical research, and inspired sermons—I am not supposed to exist. I am the Jewish and Jewishly committed daughter of an intermarriage. My Ashkenazi mother and Irish-Catholic father raised me in a Jewish home."

Charlotte describes her lifetime of Jewish observances and commitments, her year of rabbinic school in the Reform movement, and her passion for social justice work—all supported and inspired by her Irish-Catholic father's religious commitments. Throughout her essay, she describes her struggle to find a place for herself within the organized Jewish community that would honor and respects all parts of her life and history.

In the second section of the anthology, "*Nefesh,*" the authors write about their journeys as related to their physical and spiritual health. They describe their processes of identity formation and self-exploration as they explore their sexuality, their religious observance, and as they begin healing from emotional and physical pain. By providing a glimpse at how these authors relate to their bodies, this section gives voice to the standards of beauty and success that many young Jewish women use to measure their self-worth.

In "Blessings in Boxes," Gabrielle Kaplan-Mayer describes how her practice of wearing the *tefillin* ultimately resulted in a decision that profoundly changed her life, her health, and her understanding of a chronic illness that she has lived since childhood. She writes, "I thought about my *tefillin*, of the way these ancient brown boxes connect to my body, how they fit, and what richness they bring me . . . so why not an insulin pump that could help to lengthen my life?" Her religious observance enabled her to create a life for herself based upon the marriage between her health and her experiences as a Jewish woman.

Clara Thaler, in "At Home in My Own Skin," describes her process of growth from girlhood to womanhood with attentive details toward which rites of passage were celebrated and which were ignored. She attributes her renewed interest in her Jewish identity to her ultimate acceptance of her body, and to her lesbianism.

In "Who Is a Jew?" Loolwa Khazzoom writes about her experience of growing up in a biracial, Mizrahi Jewish home. She is adamant in her refusal to compartmentalize any aspect of herself, as she skillfully articulates her encounters with sexual abuse, racism, sexism, and anti-Semitism. In this essay, she affirms her commitment to her Jewish and feminist identities, as she struggles to find a place where she can honor her multiple identities in both body and spirit.

Jessie Heller-Frank's awareness of the connection between mind, body, and spirit was awakened in Israel. In "When You're Looking for G-d, Go Home," she shares the story of her transformation from a secular Jew who was raised without a strong Jewish identity or community, to a baalat teshuvah, who finds meaning in observant Jewish life. She writes about how her transformation affected her relationship with men, her body, her community, and her conception of God.

In "A Woman of Valor, Who Can Find?" Julie Pelc describes her discovery of a healing spiritual practice, after a debilitating repetitive strain injury in her hands halted the pace of her previously hectic life. Through a dance methodology called "Five Rhythms," she finds a way to honor the rhythms of her body and soul, and is able to reconnect with the Divine presence on the dance floor.

In the final section of the anthology, "Neshamah" the authors write about their pleasures and struggles surrounding life cycle events. Essays highlight the way in which young Jewish women deal with issues such as marriage, divorce, sexual orientation, and dating. This section provides insight into how young Jewish women navigate the personal, social, and familial norms of growing up in North America.

In "Chutzpah and Menschlekeit: Negotiating Identity in Jerusalem," Caryn Aviv juxtaposes her own experience of marriage, divorce, and coming out as a lesbian with her doctoral research in Jerusalem. While conducting her research about the dating patterns of young American immigrants, she discovers the complicated interplay between gender, religion, sexuality, and the rules of interpersonal relationships among young American Jews living in Israel. She describes the social scene, Shabbat observances, norms of heterosexuality, and the role of formal and informal matchmakers in the Jewish community. She also relates her own painful feelings of invisibility and isolation as a queer Jew in Jerusalem.

Lynne Meredith Schreiber, in "Meeting in the Middle," describes how her relationship with a Catholic man eventually led her to live an Orthodox Jewish lifestyle. She describes interactions with both

Jews and non-Jews that challenged her to define her own beliefs. She struggles to find her own religious voice amid the many pulls to compromise some aspect of her identity and to "meet in the middle." In the process, she discovers her Jewish identity.

In "Ira Glass, Where Are You?" Tobin Belzer juxtaposes her fantasy of her perfect Jewish man with her real-life experience of being young, Jewish, and single. Using a sociological lens, she writes about the many stereotypes attached to singlehood in the twenty-first century North American Jewish community. She describes Aish HaTorah's widespread Speed Dating program, and the craze of on-line dating. Throughout her essay, she affirms her beliefs about feminism and the social construction of sexuality, while acknowledging the contradiction in her desire to exclusively date Jewish men.

In "Stepping Eastward," Daveena Tauber describes her early perceptions about Jews, family, and money, which she learned while growing up in a commune in rural California. She relates her culture shock when she moves east for the first time. She struggles with class and cultural differences as she searches for a home on the East Coast that reflects her vision of what it means to be a Jewish woman.

This section ends with "Making Love on the *Deutsche Bahn*." Ruth A. Abusch-Magder touches upon issues of family history, memory, and feminist scholarship in the context of her time living and studying in Germany. As a grandchild of Holocaust survivors, she reflects on how her familial experience affected her attraction to, and repulsion from, the subject of the *Shoah*. She records her experiences as a young, pregnant, Jewish woman living with her husband in a country filled with associations from her childhood landscape. In doing so, she illuminates her own internal struggle to make meaning of her history and to cope with the past while continuing to dedicate herself to living life in the present.

Together, the essays and poems in this anthology illustrate the inspiring ways in which young Jewish women are joining and creating sisterhoods in every corner of their lives. We are using our strength of spirit to transform our environments, our intimate relationships, and ourselves.

We are eternally grateful to each of the authors whose story is printed in the pages of this anthology. Each invested her time, emotional energy, and faith to help us create *Joining the Sisterhood*. We draw strength from them and from the generations of those whose lives and words proceed our own. We believe that this book is a bridge connecting one generation to the next. With this anthology, we offer our stories as a legacy for the Jewish women who will follow. We pray that they will find the strength, courage, and inspiration to tell their own stories and define for themselves what it means to be a young Jewish woman.

References

Rukeyser, Muriel. "Elegy of Joy." *The Green Wave: Poems.* Garden City, N.Y.: Doubleday, 1948.
Lorde, Audre. *Sister, Outsider: Essays and Speeches.* Trumansburg, N.Y.: Crossing Press, 1984.

1
Ruach

Ourselves in Relation to Others and the Environment

1

Bais Yaakov Girl

EVE ROSENBAUM

You would never believe where I come from. Standing next to me at a club, you would think: standard downtown Manhattan, punk rock wanna-be with middle class leanings, just drove in from the burbs, rich daddy buying her black shit-kicker boots. And you would be right.

Yeah, I'm from the suburbs: half hour north of Manhattan, straight up the Palisades Parkway. When you see the sign for New Square, you know you're going the right way. Head past the churches into downtown Monsey, *Ir Hakodesh*, "the New Jerusalem." This is where I live. Where I live with my parents, one brother, and one sister.

But this is not where I really come from. I come from someplace three thousand miles away. Los Angeles: home to plastic personalities, drive-by earthquakes, and the largest collection of Jews outside the New York metropolitan area. Within one of the largest cities in the world, there exists a religious Jewish community that prides itself on its very denial of all that LA represents. By keeping secular influences out, this community remains strong and pure and untouched. They teach their children to remain separate; they tell themselves they will be safe if they remain apart. It is closed to outsiders. And once, I wanted to be part of this community with all my heart.

I come from the San Fernando Valley: home to Valley girl culture, Ventura Boulevard consumerism, and all that is meant when people speak of LA-inspired hedonism and self-indulgence. The Valley is nothing like people imagine; there's nothing like it in the world. Take a half-hour drive from one end to the other, and you'll pass the houses of movie stars, gang-infused apartment buildings, and dirt roads leading to secluded horse farms. Once, all of this land was citrus groves, and before that, desert. In-ground sprinklers turned it into a paradise where anything can happen. Where dreams of stardom can inspire genius and where a girl can grow up surrounded by poverty and luxury, anarchy and religion.

This was my life. I was barely conscious, yet aware of everything. To me, there was no difference between staying at home and watching television with my best friend, or going to shul on Shabbos and looking over the *mechitza* at the boys in the men's section. I grew up in a city that was still learning how to contain its diverse sense of self. And I had trouble containing mine.

When we first moved to the Valley from New York, we lived in an area where the biggest claim to fame (whispered hurriedly behind notebooks by third-grade girls) was that Kirk Cameron, star of *Growing Pains* and the dreamiest guy ever on television, lived nearby. I went to public school. I walked there every morning and walked home every afternoon, stopping to talk with the crossing guard on my way. I petted the horses at the nearby horse farm, and tried not to step on the cracks in the sidewalk, because we all knew what would happen.

After school, I took horseback-riding lessons and thought that one day I would own horses and be the most graceful rider. I acted in plays. I was in *Cats*, and I played the Tin Man in the *Wizard of Oz*. I took dancing lessons, karate, piano, guitar, and violin, but I never practiced. Eventually all my lessons ended because my parents weren't convinced that I really wanted them.

On Saturdays, I played elaborate games with Barbie dolls at my best friend Becky's house. Sometimes our dramas would last all weekend. We created characters, plots, and background stories for each doll. When we finished, we rode our bikes to the park and bought ices or cookies from the nearby bakery. Becky's father added laugh tracks to television sitcoms at the NBC studios, and I thought that was just the most amazing job ever. My father only owned clothing stores and racehorses; not so exciting.

Becky was Jewish but her family bought a Christmas tree every year. We didn't. In my family, holidays meant sitting around the dinner table with my cousins from Granada Hills (the rich side of the family). We drove to temple, and I sat with my parents. I wasn't allowed to move and was not allowed to play outside with the rest of the kids.

Sometimes my father went to Friday night services. He invited the whole family, but I was usually the only one interested in joining him. Typically, we were late. My father wouldn't want to walk in when we were late, so he took me to the movies or to Tower Records. I loved going to temple, since we hardly ever got there.

I knew that something forbidden was going on, because when we phoned our grandparents back in New York, we had to be careful with what we said. One time, I was telling my grandmother that we went to the petting zoo on Saturday. My father grabbed the phone away from me, explained that I was confused, mixing up the days, and that I really meant Sunday. My grandparents were religious. If they knew we weren't, it would have made them sad, my father said. So we pretended.

On the High Holidays (the days when we had to go to temple whether we wanted to or not), our temple rented out the auditorium of a church nearby to accomodate the hordes of once-a-year Jews. My father said this made him sick: on the holiest days of the year we were praying in a church. When I was in the sixth grade he finally got frustrated and moved our family to a community where the only temple was a religious one. He told me that I would be attending a Jewish day school in the fall. My grandfather died that year. My father went to the funeral in New York, and when he came home, he said that we were becoming religious. And he meant it.

I gave up my Saturday softball league, my favorite sleep-away camp, and all of my nonreligious friends. We moved to another part of the Valley. I threw away my jeans and my short-sleeve shirts. I bought long skirts.

At first, I was just playing along, but at some point during junior high, I realized that I wanted to devote my entire life to religion. I decided that my education at a Jewish day school wasn't enough for me. I didn't know enough; I didn't know anything. I was years behind the rest of the girls in my class. I could barely read Hebrew and I kept making embarrassing mistakes. I wanted to know everything. I wanted to be perfect: in my faith and in my practice.

I asked people to call me "Esther," my middle name, like Esther from the Purim megillah. I thought she was really cool, because she saved the Jews. She saved our entire nation. She knew exactly who and what she was supposed to be. I thought: I can do that. If my name sounded like everyone else's, I thought I could be like them.

When I turned twelve I had my bas mitzvah. My father's mother flew in from New York. She was already sick, but she was very happy that her granddaughter was religious. I was making her proud and I knew it. I didn't have to hide things from her anymore. This is it, I thought. I know how I'm supposed to be.

She died a few months later, which made my desire for religion intensify. My parents were surprised. Before, they had to pull me along into faith, kicking and screaming. Now I was pulling them.

After my grandmother died, my father told me that years before, she had almost died. He had prayed harder than ever, and had begged God to let her live. *Let her live,* he cried, *at least until his first child's* bar *or* bas mitzvah. I hadn't been born yet. She got sick again while still in Los Angeles, and died soon after getting home. I couldn't wait to get married and have a daughter who I could name after her. I felt like I was part of something larger than myself.

At school, I heard about a place called "Fairfax," where I could truly devote my life to religion. It was straight through Coldwater Canyon, over the mountains, and just off of Melrose Boulevard. Sometimes, my family would take trips into the city to see the street filled from one end to the other with Jews and Judaism, bookstores, music stores, kosher pizza, bakeries, butchers, Hasidim, and *Misnagdim.* Every time we made the trip, my head would spin.

In the Valley we were religious, but our Judaism was sandwiched between guitar lessons, midnight movies, and weekend trips to the mall. I was religious but I had a past in the Valley that wasn't. I wanted to forget who I was before, to make a clean break, and to rebirth myself as a girl who knew her purpose in life. I wanted something written in stone and signed in blood. I was convinced I could only get it in the city.

In the city, girls wore knee-high socks and did everything they were told. I wanted to be these girls. I wanted to wear kneesocks, and get married at eighteen, and always know exactly how my life would turn out. I wanted concrete assurance that if I led my life the right way, I would be pure and happy and content. I would go to heaven; I wanted to make damn sure of that.

When it was time to choose a high school, there was only one choice I would consider: Bais Yaakov. It was five minutes from Fairfax, and affiliated to hundreds of other Bais Yaakovs all across the country. There was only one other girl in my class who was going there. Everyone else chose less restrictive schools. But I wanted to go to Bais Yaakov.

Every two years, the Bais Yaakov girls put on a show called "Song and Dance." To me, the Bais Yaakov girls were all talented and perfect and sweet and wonderful. I thought if I went there, I could become one of them. I would turn into a genuine Bais Yaakov girl just from

being around them. I thought that living in the city and going to Bais
Yaakov would be the most wonderful thing in the world. I wanted to
have my head filled with pure thoughts and good deeds and prayers.
I wanted to be in the show, and I wanted to marry a rabbi.

People warned me that I would never truly fit in there. It was a
different world over the hills. In Los Angeles, all the girls were the
daughters of rabbis, and would end up marrying rabbis. Everyone lived
within a ten-block radius, went to the same elementary school, and
had known each other forever. I didn't believe them.

Over the summer, a girl who was going to be in my class at Bais
Yaakov in the fall invited me to spend Shabbos at her house in the
city. I was nervous: it was the city; it was Bais Yaakov. I didn't want
to blow it.

My mother drove me to the city on Friday after school, and dropped
me off with a bottle of wine and a bouquet. Leah's house was nothing
like my house in the Valley. It was the most beautiful house on a
block filled with beautiful houses. It was just as gorgeous inside. It had
a three-room guest suite, several housekeepers, and a pool enclosed by
gardens and trees for privacy and modesty. Their living room was
draped in white and was extremely clean, even though they had five
small children.

I helped Leah set the table. When we dressed for Shabbos, she put
on kneesocks while I watched, jealous. My parents wouldn't let me
wear kneesocks. Hers were white cotton with lacy designs and stopped
just below the knee. She had a drawer full. She asked me if I wanted
to borrow a pair. I said no; I wore tights.

On Saturday we walked to shul. It was the most beautiful sanctuary I had ever seen. Inside, women in expensive suits prayed like
they really meant it. Leah and I sat beside them. When I prayed, I
really meant it. I felt like I belonged. After lunch, Leah and I walked
to her best friend's house where their eighth-grade class was getting
together for a summer reunion. Leah thought it would be a good way
for me to meet everyone before school started. I was nervous. I barely
said anything. They asked where I was from, and why they had never
seen me around. Leah said, "She's from the Valley." They said "oh,"
as if that explained everything. I didn't say much; I just listened. I
smiled. I laughed when I was supposed to. I was having the most
wonderful time. I couldn't wait to be a Bais Yaakov girl.

I told my new friends that I was really from New York and that
my father was from *Satmar*, and that I really was religious, just like

them. I didn't tell them that my family didn't become religious until I was twelve, or that my family was nothing like theirs. To be different was a sin, and to not be religious from birth was the worst sin of all.

The day of the entrance exam, I wore my longest skirt and my shirt with the longest sleeves. I didn't own kneesocks yet, so I wore slouch socks and pinned them to my slip so they wouldn't fall down. I thought I was so cool. I was going to be a Bais Yaakov girl. I had an interview. The principal spoke to my parents.

My parents ordered uniforms for the school year: a gray pleated skirt, a white or blue oxford shirt, a sweater, and a vest. That was it. I had a gray skirt from junior high that still fit (which was the most important thing to my mother), but I was convinced it wouldn't be long enough. I didn't want to be the only girl in school with a skirt that came only to midcalf. I would be laughed at. I would be shunned.

We went to the uniform supply place. We ordered a skirt that came to half an inch above my ankles. My mother was not happy—mostly because of the extra cost—but also because she said it looked stupid. I would have gotten it longer, but I didn't want to push it. When the skirt came in the mail, I put it on and wore it around the house for the next few days with my socks pulled up.

In September, I began traveling an hour and a half into the city to go to school. During *davening* the first morning, I sat at a table in the back of the auditorium with some rabbis' daughters. No one really knew me, but I was a great actor. The principal spoke and then did a roll call. We sat in the back and made jokes. I was shaking from nervousness. I reassured myself that it was OK. I was OK. I could do it.

Ninth grade was easy. We memorized the capitals of every state and country, and learned how to write a thesis statement, which I had learned years before. I was failing all of my Hebrew classes, but it didn't matter, since the Hebrew teachers passed everyone anyway. I was becoming a Bais Yaakov girl.

I made friends. I started staying in the city for Shabbos, at the houses of rabbis and their daughters. We went to the old age home and sang. We baked cakes for the Sukkos party and for the Hanukkah party and the teachers' birthdays. We told jokes in study hall, made fun of our gym instructor, and made four science teachers quit in less than three months. I was fitting in. I was a *Bais Yaakov* girl. I could fake it as well as anyone.

We wondered who would be the first in our class to get married. It would be Chayale, everyone said. We talked about babies and arranged matches and motherhood. I told my father that I wanted to get married at eighteen. He said: "Even unattractive boys want to marry beautiful girls. Maybe you're being a little unrealistic."

Walking to Faigy's house after school one Friday, she looked at my ears and said, "I wonder if long earrings are immodest." I took them off. I never wore them again. I stopped listening to the radio, because a good Bais Yaakov girl listens only to Jewish music. I started reading only Jewish books. I wore my skirts to the floor and socks to my knees.

Faigy said, "Esther, I've never seen you upset. I've never seen you cry." At school, I was always smiling. I always made sure that everything stayed within the boundaries I had established for myself. I was busy controlling myself at every moment.

At home my parents were beating me. I never told anyone. I was too embarrassed. It would mean that my family wasn't perfect. The only thing I wanted to be was perfect. Our teachers said that respect for our parents is the most important virtue. We learned that even if a parent beats a child, the child is not allowed to strike back. I sat in class, listening. And I sat there when they were hitting me. I wanted to be perfect.

In the ninth grade, I met Sharon. She was Lubavitch, or really a Sephardi from a Lubavitch junior high. We were inseparable. In typing class, we sat in the far corner of the room, and instead of working on the lessons, we typed lists of the supplies we would need when we were launched on the space shuttle. We read Shakespeare, boycotted frog dissections, watched movie after movie, and played geography games that lasted eight hours.

Sharon was from the Valley, like me. Her parents liked me because I was a good influence on her. She had a secret boyfriend who I hated. Not because Bais Yaakov girls were not allowed to talk to boys (which we weren't), but because he didn't treat her well.

During the floods that winter, we walked to the drugstore about a mile from her house. We waded in our uniform skirts through knee-high water to buy Clear Pepsi, potato chips, and trashy novels. Her mother said we were crazy. We spent the LA riots together, huddled around the TV as the city burned down around our school. With Sharon, I felt like I didn't have to pretend. I could almost be myself. Maybe after we'd been friends for a while, I thought, I could drop the act all together.

Things were changing. I was falling asleep during *Chumash* class. I was barely able to understand the teacher's daily lectures, which were conducted entirely in Hebrew. I started writing poetry. I turned the radio back on. Sharon and I traded tapes at recess, wrapping them in lunch bags so no one would see. We made up code names. I was Tam, like a Tam Tam cracker, the kosher version of a saltine, and she was Sam, because of her initials: her real name was Sharon Ahuva Margalit. We called radio stations and requested songs over and over again while we worked on biology projects or studied for *Navi* tests.

I was tired of pretending that I knew what was proper and appropriate for me to know, and that I didn't know other things that would supposedly corrupt me. I was tired of pretending to be interested in conversations that bored me silly. I wondered if my new friends would talk to me if they knew who I really was, if they knew what I thought about while my mind wandered during class.

I had always wanted to be an actor, but pretending everyday was exhausting. I wanted to be myself, to talk about things that interested me, like books and movies, politics and music. I could only do that with Sharon. We would sit in an empty classroom during lunch and talk about everything.

One day, during *Chumash*, our teacher said that a lot of religious people don't like to associate with *baalei teshuvah*, those who are not born religious. They don't want their children to be around them. "Who knows what those people might say at the Shabbos table when invited for dinner," she said. "Who knows what kind of influence they might have?" I was a *baalat teshuvah*. I had spent Shabbos at the houses of the biggest rabbis in the city. What if I was a bad influence? What if they knew? I wanted to scream.

I wanted to raise my hand and say something, but then everyone would know that I wasn't the person I said I was. I would never be the kind of girl everyone thought I was. I didn't have an impressive family name. I couldn't trace my ancestors back two hundred years to the greatest rabbis of Europe. I lived in the Valley (which was an unforgivable sin under any circumstances). I watched television. Sometimes I wore my uniform shirt untucked. And worst of all, my socks constantly fell down.

In the ninth and tenth grades, girls were allowed to wear pull-up socks that came to the knee. They were not, under any circumstances, allowed to fall. Our principal walked the hallway between classes, looking at girls' legs to make sure our socks were in their full, upright position. One day, mine happened to be falling down.

When I left the house that morning, I knew they were going to be trouble. The elastic was breaking. But they were my last clean pair, and my car pool was waiting, so I wore them anyway. I hoped that the principal wouldn't notice, since my skirt practically fell to the floor. Of course he noticed. As I was walking back from *davening* with Sharon, he pulled me aside and told me to follow him.

In his office, he leaned back in his chair for a minute, thinking. I was uncomfortable. I was missing class, failing anyway.

He said, "Esther I thought you were a good girl. I thought you were a good Bais Yaakov girl."

I had thought so too. I thought I was being a good Bais Yaakov girl, so I didn't say anything while he told me that good Bais Yaakov girls always kept their socks pulled up. He said that he was disappointed. He made me buy a pair of stockings from the secretary. I left his office in tears. Everything I had changed about myself meant nothing when my socks fell down.

The next time I was called to the principal's office I didn't cry. I didn't cry when he told me to stop watching television, or when he told me that I wasn't who he thought I should be. I didn't crumble. I walked out of his office and found Sharon and we laughed. He hated both of us. We weren't changing for the better, we weren't improving, and we weren't becoming Bais Yaakov girls.

In those days, it was Sharon who was the Bad Girl, even more than I was. It was Sharon who wore short skirts and talked to boys and ate Milk Duds at the movies, even though they weren't kosher. I was tired of being the good influence. In class, our teacher told us women weren't allowed to work. We shouldn't go to college. We were supposed to graduate from high school and get married. Maybe, after our children were grown, she conceded, we could be teachers or nurses, but only if our future husbands gave us permission. Our teacher told us to listen to everything our husbands said. She said that we shouldn't go shopping unless we asked our husbands. She said we should not do anything without permission. I thought: "You've gotta be kidding." I started looking around for out-of-town colleges. I was fourteen.

Sharon and I laughed together in class at how crazy everyone else was. We were going to travel all over Europe and spend summers with her relatives in Paris. We were going to talk to strange men and

we were going to move to New York and be famous. I would be a
writer and she would be a doctor. We laughed because everyone else
would be housewives like their mothers, and they would envy us and
our fantastic lives.

Sharon and I went to the Los Angeles County Museum of Art just
to stand for hours and hours in front of our favorite painting. It was a
painting of two girls, one with light hair, one with dark hair, playing the
piano. "That's us," Sharon said. It was a Renoir but we didn't know. We
didn't care. All we knew was that it was a painting of us. We were like
the girls who played the piano when everyone was telling them to stop.
We were going to play the piano as loud as we could.

We didn't want to be like everyone else. We had guts and everyone
in class knew it. We weren't afraid to get up at Song and Dance and write
our own drama skit and say what we thought. We weren't afraid to leave
school during free periods, walk a mile to the mall to see a movie, and
hitch a ride back to school before anyone knew we were gone. We
weren't afraid to tell people they were wrong. We had plans. We knew
where we were headed, and we were going there together.

Sometimes at night we would get dressed up in our best "on the
town" outfits. We begged our parents to drive us to City Walk, the
new shopping mall in front of Universal Studios with the coolest
stores and restaurants. It had a movie theater and bars. We went to
bars and ordered strawberry daiquiris without alcohol (when asked for
ID), and tried to look like adults. We congratulated ourselves for how
gutsy we were. We knew that if anyone saw us, we would be kicked
out of school. We were dangerous, living on the edge.

But then everything changed. Later that summer, I moved with
my family to New York. That same year, Sharon moved to Denver to
get away from her parents. They were beating her up, she said. They
left her with bruises. She would get out, she told me, even if she had
to kill someone to do it. She felt like I deserted her. She said: "You
left me here with no one. You left me in Bais Yaakov with no one like
me." We tried writing letters. We spoke every once in a while. We got
caught up in our new lives.

Both of us changed as well. My family was now living in a more
religious community. I bought sandals. I didn't want to live the rest
of my life based on three years of religion that weren't all that great.
I stopped believing everything I was taught. I realized that I'm not
who I thought I was. I stopped wanting to be Esther. I asked people
to call me "Eve."

I left high school after the eleventh grade to start college. There was no point in staying there. I wasn't paying attention in Hebrew classes anyway and my parents felt they were wasting their money. I was more than happy to leave. I was sixteen.

When Sharon was sixteen, she was living in a dorm room at Bais Yaakov in Denver. She didn't want to be a doctor anymore. She stopped wanting to be the girl playing the piano. She wanted to get married and have children. She wanted her own apartment, so she wouldn't have to live with her parents. She would do anything to get away from her parents.

Two years later she was married. When my parents said that I should get married too, I argued with them. I told them I was too young. I said, "Just because my friends are getting married doesn't mean that I have to." I told them that I wasn't ready. But they convinced me to go out on a date. We went miniature golfing. I thought: never again.

I didn't tell my parents that I was having serious doubts about everything. They wanted me to study in Israel for a year. I wanted to go away to college. They wanted me to participate in the community. I wanted to get as far away from the community as I could. I didn't want to tell my parents the truth. I didn't want to disappoint them, so for a while, I kept pretending.

When I finally told them that I wanted to be a writer, and that I didn't ever want to get married, my father called me a femi-Nazi. He told me that I didn't really understand Judaism. He told me that as a woman, I had the privilege to bear and raise children, and that this was the most important job I should ever hope to have. I should feel honored to give birth to sons and daughters who would follow in their ancestors' footsteps and to live their lives according to the laws of Torah.

I went away to college. Three hours by car, but really a million miles away. I lived in an apartment on campus with people who weren't ashamed to be themselves. They were vegan and feminists, goths and animal rights activists. We sat around the kitchen table painting our nails black, blasting the patriarchy, and eating pasta. I had never met anyone like them. It finally felt OK to stop pretending.

Sometimes I ate in the kosher kitchen on campus. I met Jews who considered themselves religious, even though they wore pants and spoke to boys, went to movies and listened to the radio. I usually preferred the company of people who were upset by the status quo, people who wanted to change the world. It wasn't enough to just

change myself. The world also needed fixing. I went to poetry readings, hung out in coffee shops, and started a feminist literary magazine. I found others like me. There were others who were tired of
pretending.

I graduated from college at twenty and moved back to Monsey. I
wanted to dye my hair purple and pierce my nose. My father said, "Do
it and don't bother coming home." When my sister grows up, she
won't be allowed to go out of town for college. It's my fault, she told
me, because of the way I turned out.

Sharon got married and had two babies, one following the other,
with not enough time in between for her body to heal. When her
second baby was two months old, Sharon came to New York for a
friend's wedding and stayed at my house for the weekend.

We played games and read Shakespeare, went shopping, and ate
pizza. She asked about my books. She didn't understand my posters
and wondered who Courtney Love was. I'd discovered punk rock and
postmodernism, poetry and politics. Sharon had learned how to be a
housewife. I didn't understand her either.

While she nursed her daughter, we spoke about our futures. She
told me she wanted a big family, and could picture having twelve kids.
I told her I was applying to doctorate programs; that I would be in
school for at least five more years. I was moving away, just waiting for
acceptance letters. She said, "You need to get married."

Sharon was no longer the girl who wanted to sit next to me at the
piano and loudly pound the keys. Now, she sings lullabies. I sat next
to her on the couch, watching her mouth move as she sang her
daughters to sleep. I could barely hear her song.

She left Sunday afternoon and we took pictures at the airport. We
cried. We hugged. She said, "I'll miss you." I said, "I'll miss you more."
I drove home through the Village. I listened to Patti Smith.

2

Questions

MELANIE LEITNER

The pagan rituals now
hold very different names—
microscopy, spectrophotometry, splicing.
Is my lab bench doubling as my altar?
If I reach deep inside
will I find that the pillar of fire
leading me through the moral desert
I inhabit
blazes with the word *Knowledge*
where once read The Lord?
Have I faith in nothing more
than my own stumbling mind?
Is it good science to cling to the unfounded
hypothesis of the soul?
How can I refuse to accept the findings
of 3,000 years of study,
although indeed the earth is neither flat
nor the center of the universe?
Am I kneeling in supplication
before myself?
Or merely rising above the vestigial needs of
long-forgotten eras?
Is the appendix of the human psyche
named religion?
Or is there something deeper,
a Why? More profound than any How?

3

Ground Contemplation Prayer

LEAH BERGER

It is an amazing feeling to stand next to a redwood tree, better yet, to climb inside of a hollowed-out trunk. The first time I did, I felt at peace, protected; it was a sanctuary to my own wildness. I was an ant, traveling ancient ground on the bark of a magnificent journey called a "tree." I knew nothing of the threat of logger's saws, had no concept of the history of our country's rapidly diminishing forests. I did not know that a Jewish man named Charles Hurwitz had acquired "ownership" of the last remaining unprotected old growth redwoods, and I did not know that he was cutting them down and liquidating his workers' pension funds in order to pay for his crimes in a savings and loan scandal. Perhaps I was not quite ready to know.

It was *Tisha B'av*, the day of the "exile," the *galut*. It was a perfect time for a group of Jews to gather in the forest to pray. *Tisha B'av* is about memory. It is the day when we remember how it felt to have a collective sacred space, before our people were scattered around the world. Our memories are of sacred spaces that no longer exist. For many Jews, *Tisha B'av* commemorates the destruction of the First and Second Temples, and also acts of discrimination and destruction toward our people throughout our collective history. We remember the desecration and bombing of modern synagogues, the pogroms, Kristallnacht, our exile from Spain, and the experience of slavery in Egypt. We must remember, so that it will not happen again. We must remember, so that we can purge ourselves of the things that we cannot change. And we must remember so that we will strive to change the things we can. We cannot move forward without taking the time to look back.

26

When I think about how often the Jewish people have been forcibly displaced, I better understand my own feelings of displacement in the current culture. I better understand my desire to preserve and restore land. The *galut* has spread our people to the far reaches of the globe. For centuries, our temples have been destroyed and our prayer books burned. We have learned to adapt to other cultures, sometimes by choice and too often for survival. In our dispersal, there is always a loss, even when something is gained. If we do not acknowledge the loss, then it continues to eat away at our culture, our livelihood, our inner being.

When you look up into the Headwaters Forest from Fisher Road, at Pacific Lumber's property, you can see the bald spots where the trees have been clear-cut. Stumps lie like headstones on a cemetery hillside to the east. Further north, the steep hill has turned brown. The salmon-spawning habitat that once marked this watershed is down to a mere 3 percent of its original size.

Within the two hundred thousand acres, which are privately owned by the Maxaam Corporation (the parent company of Pacific Lumber), lie the last six groves of unprotected old growth redwood forests remaining on earth. Fisher Road has been well traveled by both Pacific Lumber employees and environmentalists over the past several decades. The protesters have been as diverse as the flora and fauna in this rain forest; they have risked arrest to traverse these hills, sit in these trees, talk with loggers, and perform sacred ceremonies.

Our group was also trespassing in protest, but our numbers were much smaller than the thousands of protesters who were recently arrested for crossing the gate to Pacific Lumber's property. We had no major press coverage to bear witness if cops or Pacific Lumber employees harassed us. We were simply a small group of self-identified Jews who were there to pray.

As I walked through the gate and entered the lumberyard, I could see the rest of the group up where the road turned. To get there, I had to pass rows of neatly stacked, downed redwoods that stretched for what felt like the longest quarter of a mile I'd ever traveled. I imagined the downed pillars of the First and Second Temples in Jerusalem as I took in the sight of these logs. The trees, whose origins dated back to the time of the Second Temple, were now being reduced to the same tragic fate. I paused to wipe the sap from one trunk, as if to dry the tears it shed for its fading life. It is devastating to consider the extent of the massive destruction that has incurred in such a relatively short time.

We sang "*Avinu Malkeinu,* Our Father, Our King," and I found myself searching for a counterpart in my mind. "*Immeinu Malchateinu,*" I echoed, "Our Mother, Our Queen." We moved in a circle on Maxaam's property—death row for the ancient redwoods—and we prayed. Our plea was for the immediate protection of the groves and their linking corridors that would ensure safe passage for the creatures that make the forest their home. This is why my friends and I made the journey out of the desert to the northwest woods of California. We came to mourn and to pray, to call forth the spirit world's attention—if no one else's—to the corporate plundering of these forests.

My first image of the spirit world came from my mother. She told me: "God is in everything. God is in a flower, in a blade of grass." I shifted my gaze from the shaft of light cast onto the tiled kitchen floor of our duplex, out through the screen door toward the backyard. I spent the rest of that morning visiting with the daffodils, the trees, and the butterflies; I watched god in motion, felt the pulse of life and basked in the glow that surrounded all that was now also named god.

I did not think to ask about god in later years as we prayed in shul each Saturday or studied in Hebrew school. It was not a safe place to ask such a question. We were to pray facing an altar that held a sacred Torah from which only men could read. We were to learn how to say god's name, how to say King, Lord, and He, the father of Abraham, Isaac, and Jacob. The synagogue was where my feet hurt from standing, and where I grew bored and sleepy from the artificial lighting and sterile quiet of wall-to-wall carpeting. What can a child learn about herself when the prayers are either proscribed or silent?

Public school was no different. It was simply another religion. While standing to recite the Pledge of Allegiance every morning in elementary school, I wondered to myself: whose god? To pledge my allegiance to the stars and stripes meant praying to a god who looked like Uncle Sam. There was no dialogue in such prayer, just a background of white noise from the drone of politicians, religious fanatics, and from the static of the TV screen. *Kavannah,* the "intention" behind the act of prayer, was lost in the melting pot of monoculture. Diverse voices—which could inspire and heal—were silenced. I struggled to access a space within myself to nourish my spirit and to give voice to my prayers.

It has taken me years to come full circle and to understand the gift of that moment with my mother. Of course, my mother was right; it is a miracle to see a rock of many faces, a flower in bloom, a tree's leaves turning colors. These are the mysteries of the universe. They are far more vast and infinite than the intellectual dichotomies of science or the long-winded biblical competitions of Judeo-Christian tradition. What she shared with me had to do with cycles and senses. She listened to the ancient wisdoms carried within her.

This makes sense to me. Relating to the earth has always felt more tangible than relating to someone or something that I cannot know inside of myself. I feel incredibly powerful connections between the earth, Judaism, and the mother line. It is amazing to me that through the strength of my mother's spirit, her connection to the earth survived in spite of the dominance of patriarchy. I now believe that she was invoking the "Great Mother of the Grove," Asherah, whose story predates temple worship and who was silenced in subsequent years of patriarchal tradition. Asherah was the goddess of the trees, worshiped by ancient Hebrew women who traveled long distances in the heat of the desert sun. I imagine their inspiration to celebrate the presence of life when they stumbled upon an oasis. Their bodies, no doubt, took on the shapes of the trees that shaded them as they prayed, swaying in the wind with arms stretched out in dance and song. Images of Asherah were carved into wood and clay and placed outside of temples up until the destruction of the Second Temple by the Romans in 70 C.E.

Translating these stories into a cosmology has helped me make sense of my roots and sustained me in the work that I do. As both a writer and a Jewish woman, I am acutely aware of the ways in which gendered language has been used to perpetuate patriarchy within most cultures. I ultimately believe that God and the earth are neither masculine nor feminine, but spirits of creator and creation. Gender classification has served as an arbitrary construction to make sense of the biological differences within the species. It has also been used to establish a hierarchy of power and control. Reclaiming lost heritage is a powerful way to restore equilibrium where such imbalance has occurred. Bringing forth names for a god like *Shechinah*, and the even lesser known *Rachameima* (a wonderful weaving of the words *compassion, womb,* and *mother*), opens new pathways of meaning for those who feel disconnected from the Jewish tradition and spirit because of gender exclusion. I believe that Shechinah is a transformation of the once revered Asherah. Though rarely mentioned in most traditional forms of prayer, Shechinah's presence has been reclaimed and honored by many Jews as the complement to *El* or *Adonai*. She is the light or voice within, the small whisper of creation that speaks through the darkness. I envision the light of Shechinah as I strike the flame to light the Shabbat candles each week. She is the eternal flame that burns within each person as we pass down our traditions *l'dor v'dor,* "from generation to generation." She is the same burning energy churning deep within the earth that has sustained life on this planet for millions of years.

In college, I took a course on the politics of the Holocaust, taught by one of the only openly Jewish feminist professors at Kalamazoo College in Michigan. In class, she asked us: "How many of you have ever had a secret hiding place?" Instinctively, I raised my hand. Though I didn't have a picture in my mind. I knew that my secret place existed. The other students were confused. Did she actually mean a place where no one else goes? "Never mind," she said, nodding at me slowly, "if you have to ask, it doesn't apply." I was one of the only Jewish students in the class.

My grandfather was born in Russia. He came to this country at the turn of the century, when he was still a baby. We didn't find the documents until after he died. He lived seventy years, and his children never knew that he was not born on this continent. I continue to wonder what propelled him to keep this aspect of his identity a secret. "I think he was ashamed," my grandmother told me. When he was in college, he belonged to a Jewish fraternity with mostly German Jews. They were already second-generation immigrants and many of them were assimilated and well-to-do. He was ridiculed and called a "kike" because of his accent. Before he proposed to my grandmother, he confessed his secret, fully expecting her to turn him down because he was born in Russia. My grandmother always encouraged him to tell my mother and her sister, but he refused. He wanted to keep moving forward, Why look back?

Sometimes we forget because it is too difficult to remember. Perhaps my grandfather wanted to forget his Russian roots to take away the pain and shame he experienced growing up. I understand this. As a child a neighbor's son in a swimming pool sexually molested me. I told my friends immediately afterward, and they made fun of me. My shame increased, and I pushed the incident to the depths of my memory. Years later, I began to write and the story spilled out of me onto the pages of my journal.

I didn't share my experience publicly until I participated in a "Take Back the Night" march in college. Like Tisha B'av, the march is a ritual that helps us remember the violation of sacred spaces—of women's bodies. We sang, marched, and chanted to remember and reclaim what had been taken from us, without our permission. Our stories were both personal and universal. When shared, they become part of a greater healing process.

Recently, I read my poetry at a Counter Columbus Day celebration in Tucson. I talked about the experience of having to hide a part of myself to feel safe. As I spoke to the audience, I realized how much my writing speaks to indigenous people's experiences of relocation and racism. I realized that I was describing that hiding place when I raised my hand that day in the Holocaust class. It is the place where the truth is stored, where it is okay to be whole and to remember. It is a place where I stored my attractions to women for years. It is the place where it is okay to look back, while at the same time moving forward. It is the space where my voice in writing originates.

The stories in the Torah are the lifeline of the Jewish people. Likewise, the forest canopy is a living protective layer that ensures the survival of thousands of species that reside on this planet. Like the Torah, old growth forests are integral to our survival in a world of ever-depleting natural resources and rampant consumerism. Rabbi Nachmanides wrote: "Torah does not permit a killing that would uproot a species."

In the past two hundred years, the ancient forests in North America have declined by 97 percent. At least seventeen endangered species live in what remains of the ancient redwood forests. These animals, along with over sixty other birds, fish, mammals, reptiles, and plants, are considered indicator species. Their declining numbers indicate the level of harm that has already occurred in the ecosystem. Such numbers are fair warning: if a few trees are cut from the forest, it can sustain the loss. Clear-cut the forest, and the forest is lost forever.

Animals and plants are not the only ones to feel the loss of these ancient trees. Native peoples of the region have also felt the impact of white settlers. The Wylaki, Nongotl, Nomlaki, and Sinkyone peoples have experienced a decline in population and traditional culture due to raids, slavery, relocation, and disease brought by white settlers. The struggle continues today, as tribes fight against the damming of local watersheds, which prevent native salmon from spawning.

As a survivor of physical and sexual abuse, I understand what happens to the earth's abundance when it is taken, and when it is taken by force with no basic respect for life. I am angry and I continue to mourn the loss of safe and sacred spaces.

My first few years in Tucson were spent foraging through the forest of my identities, and trying to integrate all of the new information I was learning about corporate power. I balanced my time between working for an environmental organization, and answering crisis calls at a domestic violence shelter. During that time, I researched the southwestern willow flycatcher, a small bird listed as an endangered species since 1995. The birds' habitat was being destroyed in favor of cattle grazing and the construction of new roads and dams throughout the Southwest. It was my job to find out just how quickly the flycatchers' numbers were dwindling.

One biologist told me a story about a lone flycatcher living under a bridge slated for expansion on the Mojave River. The bird's chances for survival were so severely minimized by the loss of its habitat that it resorted to singing its mating call in the quiet hours of dawn, rather than during its natural daytime hours. Like an activist gone underground, the flycatcher learned to adapt for its call to survive.

Speaking the truth often feels like the flycatcher's lone cry for connection in a forest of concrete and buzzing lights. It is easy to feel powerless in the dominant, mainstream, patriarchal culture, where identities are fragmented and truths are rarely told. We each have our own his/herstory of harm, our own self-destructive desires that mine, plunder, bulldoze, and clear-cut our diversity of identities.

It is no surprise that this fractured state of consciousness is present within the environmental movement, as well. I often feel that my internal identities are stretched thin as I attempt to be whole in a world that would rather see me categorically packaged. I feel pressured to choose between my identities as a feminist, a bisexual, an environmentalist, and a Jew. It is from the earth that I have learned to love all life. From the earth, I have learned to honor the cycles of the seasons, to replenish the garden of my spirit, and to flourish. The earth continues to provide, despite violence, hate, greed, and division. I've become a stronger person because I've learned to persist and resist and remain whole.

I've learned that abuse begets abuse unless a new vision is planted and a new rhythm felt. Standing in a circle of Jewish protesters on Maxaam's property on *Tisha B'av*, I felt a sense of wholeness and completion. We do not "own" the redwoods. Nor do we have the direct historical connection to the land that indigenous peoples of the Northwest might share. But just as we never owned the trees that gave us food, shelter, and sustenance in the desert of Canaan, we can recognize trees as a source of life. They connect us to our ancestors who for centuries sought shelter from the desert sun. I have lived in the desert for seven years: first the Negev in Israel, now the Sonoran bioregion of the Southwest. I, too, am familiar with dry places and the struggle of spirit. I invoke another name for god, *Ein Hayyim*, the "fountain of life that never ends," as I pray for water to restore the depleted soil.

Remembering the harms committed against the Jewish people helps me to put the actions of Charles Hurwitz and the Maxaam Corporation into historical context. To take the time for prayer that day, in that place, put the cutting of those forests within the context of Jewish sacred spaces. We mourned the cutting of those forests within the context of the destruction of other Jewish sacred spaces. We dedicated our Tisha B'av service to prayer, ritual, learning, and solidarity with the trees.

My work with communities of indigenous resistors in the Southwest reawakened me to the importance of *kavannah* in my life. At first, this work was limited to political activities and meetings dedicated to maintaining these peoples' rights to traditional sacred sites and to their spiritual connection to the earth. During their religious ceremonies, we stood in a circle and elders offered prayers in their native language: prayers for the earth, the ancestors, and the people involved in the resistance.

In these circles, speaking one's own truth with intent and purpose was honored. Truth was welcomed as a form of energy with the power to transcend the immediate barriers of the struggle. I began to recognize prayer as the first step toward change. For me, this change has been both internal and external. If I am not fully present within myself, my words are empty and the meaning of my activism is lost.

The Hebrew word for "place," *makom*, is also a word for the creator. My mother taught me that every place is sacred, every valley, every mountain, and every tree—all are homes to creation. Our bodies are homes to heart, mind, and soul, just as a mother's womb is home to her child. It is this sense of sacredness of all life, the sense that the creator is a place inside of us, which keeps the thread of tradition alive in me. Traditions are the common thread weaving in and out of the dominant culture, and despite the dominant culture. I believe that it is our collective responsibility to carry a sense of sacred place, *Makom*, within us wherever we go.

The mitzvah of *Tikkun Olam* calls us to repair the world. This obligation holds each person responsible for mending the universe because we are all connected. I carry a sense of responsibility to the world community, the greater *kehilah,* to do what I can to create a sustainable future. We must retell our stories, revive the cultural values that have been lost over the centuries, and hold one another accountable for our actions.

When I entered the redwood forests to pray on Tisha B'av, I carried a deep sense of awe in my heart and an appreciation for the trees that are left standing. I carried a deep sense of responsibility to care for this living planet. Our prayers planted the seeds for future action.

> *Avinu Malkeinu, Immeinu Malchateinu*
> *choneinu v'aneinu, ki ein banu ma'asim.*
> Creator please forgive us
> for what we have not done.
> We permitted the earth to turn to asphalt,
> to cover the dryness which once held
> the wetness of her womb.
> We have ignored water,
> the earth's life indicator.
> Answer us, though there is still work to be done.
> Forgive us, for we are still trying to mend the earth.
> Bring justice and peace,
> kind blessings, new love,
> and saplings and saplings
> and saplings,
> breaking new ground,
> pushing through asphalt,
> breathing in the power
> of your name.

Reference

Nachmanides. 13th century Spain. Commentary to Deuteronomy 22:6.

4

Singing Praises

SHOSHANA M. FRIEDMAN

My parents tell me that the Sh'ma, the "call to listen," was the first sound I heard as I slipped from my mother's womb into my father's waiting arms. Every night when I was growing up, my father or mother sang those words to me while I snuggled under my flannel comforter. They would hum a few words of praise for my daily accomplishments, kiss me softly, and leave the door open to let in a yellow line of light.

Around the time of my birth, my parents founded B'nai Or, the first Jewish Renewal community in the Boston area. At the same time, my father began working at Kolbo Fine Judaica, a gallery of Jewish books and gifts. Each of these events has profoundly affected my Jewish experience.

As a child, I would wander around Kolbo, noticing the varied textures of challah plates, honey and apple sets, and *hannukiot*. When I got older, I helped out occasionally, dusting, vacuuming, and folding white cardboard boxes for the seder plates, mezuzahs, kiddush cups, and jewelry. I straightened and unpacked books, checked and filed invoices, and deposited money in the bank across the street. For these odd jobs, Dad paid me a few dollars. Sometimes, I would pick up lunch for my dad and the other employees. When I returned from buying food, I would find a book and a comfortable corner where I could eat a quiet lunch and read.

Throughout my childhood, my dad brought home new prints to hang in our living room, and new books for my sisters and me. When I was twelve, I had read practically every book on the young readers' shelf. From these novels, I gently learned about the horrors of the Holocaust, about shtetls and ghettos, about New York City's Lower East Side, and about other American Jewish children.

On Shabbat, my dad led services at B'nai Or, where I received a very unOrthodox taste of Judaism. The Jewish Renewal movement was started by a group of young Jews who had come out of the human-istic movement of the sixties and seventies. They wanted to incorpo-rate those experiences with their Jewish identities. The synagogues of their youths had left them cold and longing for something more spiri-tual. Their longing for a more personal connection with Judaism motivated, among other things, the creation of B'nai Or in Boston.

In the years before my birth, people joined my parents in living rooms and Sufi centers. They sang, danced, and davened in English and Hebrew. And they experimented with ways of bringing meaning to their Judaism. Later, the growing congregation began to rent space at a Masonic temple for their monthly services. My earliest memory of B'nai Or is watching the shadows cast by candlelight on the slanted ceilings, as I lay on the pillow-strewn floor. The lobby smelled of warm candle wax and incense. Soft singing lulled me to sleep.

When I got older, I lingered in the lobby with the adults before services. My mother circled her arms around me as she chatted with other mothers. Young children clung to their mothers' flowing skirts and birkenstocked feet. We could hear my father's guitar strumming, signaling the beginning of services. I followed my mom inside, and settled on the floor, leaning against her knees in the middle of a circle of folding chairs.

At services each week, the lights are dimmed and the congrega-tion grows quiet. In the summer, the fans spin slowly, as if they too are preparing to usher in Shabbat. Adults sway and sing, forgetting their weekday selves, as Dad leads us in *niggunim*, the "wordless melo-dies" of Ashkenazi Jews. Still singing, everyone makes their way over to a table to light candles in brass candlesticks. I nudge my way to the front, to stand next to my father.

He instructs the congregants: "Parents, find your children. Those of you without children, bless the child within." I stand beside him with my sisters, Ariel and Mia, and we burst with pride to be his daughters. I am careful not to bump into his radiant guitar, which seems to sing, even without the touch of his callused fingers.

I reach out my arm to light a candle. As flame kisses wick, I think of my extended family or a special teacher or a wish for a better world. When all of the candles are lit, my father tells us to "bring in the light as many times as you need to, until you really feel Shabbat enter your soul." A hundred hands reach toward the candles, making circles in the air above the flames, pulling the light inward. I open my eyes wide and stare at the flames, so that I can still see the light when I close my eyes to sing the blessings.

My father leads the service with his *tallis* draped over his shoulders like a royal robe. "This is not consumer Judaism," he reminds us. "Here, everyone sings . . . if you don't know the words, just la la la." As we chant, I hear my own voice amid the sphere of sound. My heart understands these wordless melodies, even when my mind does not. As I've grown older, my harmonies have become more daring, syncopating rhythms and deviating from the melody. I am at home in that circle of voices.

Shabbat services are held twice a month. On other Friday nights, my family celebrates in our dining room. We set the table with my great-grandmother's bronze candlesticks from Russia and Dad's modern blue ceramic kiddush cup. Our challah is covered, waiting to be blessed and divided into clumps by eager hands. We turn off the lamp, allowing the candlelight to cast curious shadows over the familiar room. We send light to relatives, friends, and people in need. I wash my face in the glow: once for myself, once for everything I love, and once for the whole world.

Every week, my parents bless us. They put their hands on our heads and recite the ancient prayer invoking the matriarchs. Dad shapes his hands in the sign of the *Cohane*, forming seven windows of light and blessing between his fingers. Mia insists on blessing Dad, since he is not included in the blessing for girls. She reaches up to his head, and I chant the blessing for boys while her lips try to follow the strange sounds.

Occasionally, a few of us have a hard time sitting through the long blessings. One week, to entertain us, my mom put her napkin on her head, a fork in her mouth, and a glass to her eye. Solemnly, each member of my family followed her example, giving one another suspicious glances through the tinted glass. "It's an ancient Babylonian custom that I decided to revive," Mom explained, after the last amen. "In a hundred years, Jews will be wondering why they put their napkins on their heads during the kiddush. No one will be able to figure it out."

According to my calculations, I had heard the Shabbat evening kiddush approximately 832 times by my sixteenth birthday. I love to sing the rich syllables and chords of kiddush with my family. We experiment with harmonies and styles. We imitate my great-grandfather's thick Ashkenazi accented chanting, or improvise operettas or doo-wop.

After kiddush, my sisters and I uncover the challah, which is warm from the microwave. "Touch the challah or touch somebody who's touching the challah," one of us says, and we sing *Ha-Motzi*, the blessing over bread.

The most beautiful Shabbat days are those spent walking in the country or singing with friends to the strumming of a guitar. More often, however, my Shabbat observance ends after dinner on Friday night. Saturday morning is a parade of soccer games, orchestra rehearsals, socializing with friends, and homework. When my life gets especially hectic, I find myself longing to be more observant. I want to receive the full gift of Shabbat, a sacred place in time.

My Jewish education officially took place at an informal school organized by the families in our community. There, I learned the Hebrew letters, Jewish songs, and holiday rituals. But my family life has been my most effective form of Jewish education. We celebrate ancient customs and also fashion new ones of our own.

Every year, my sisters and I each make our own *hannukiot*. Six *hannukiot* sit on waxy place mats on the coffee table in the living room. There is one for each member of my family, and one for the Jews in the world who are not free to light Hanukkah candles. Each night, we dedicate the new candle to a quality, a dream, or a goal. We sing Hanukkah songs in five part harmonies, taking turns with the guitar and song sheets.

To prepare for Passover, my family composes a script, which we use to tell the story of the Exodus at our seder table. With the help of my dad and his guitar, the kids at the seder perform an original play. We take a few midrashic liberties in our version of our people's liberation from slavery.

Every year, we update the script to include current political jokes, new melodies, original props and costumes. Our story includes Pharaoh's boom box, and a hockey stick that Moses uses to part the Red Sea. There is a fire extinguisher that Moses carries into the Sinai Desert, and a talking Bush that says "Hey Moses, read my lips; go back to Egypt."

Our telling is always a musical. We adapted the Beatles' classic, "You're Gonna Lose that Girl" into a solo for Moses, who tells Pharaoh: "You're Gonna Lose those Jews." The song "Help!" became the cry of the Israelites on the shore of the Red Sea. Our seder table rocks.

Becoming a bat mitzvah was also an opportunity for me to cre-
atively and spiritually celebrate Judaism. Like most kids who have the
ceremony, I learned about Torah, services, and history. But in addition
to the usual preparation for my rite of passage, I was able to integrate
my identity as a young Jewish woman with my new status of "adult"
in the Jewish community with a creative ritual.

My mother and our close family friend, Julie, created a ritual
called a *Bat Shechinah*, meaning "daughter of the indwelling, feminine presence of God." The ceremony took place on the Saturday
morning before I was called up to the Torah. My mother invited ten
women friends, Jews and non-Jews, to participate. I was nervous at
first, but my mom reassured me. "You don't have to respond to all of
it; just be open."

In the golden sunlight of late afternoon, we gathered in my backyard on a picnic blanket. Each woman was assigned a quality, which
corresponded to the spiritual gift she could best give: friendship, humor, body, joy, courage, Judaism, healing, creativity, wisdom, and
balance. Each woman presented me with a symbolic gift and blessing.
I received poems and letters, rose water and a pomegranate, a Miriam's
cup, and smooth stones. Each woman added her gift to a basket,
which my mother and sisters had decorated with beads and ribbons.
As the basket began to fill and overflow, the women too, began to
overflow with emotion.

Jewish rituals are often marked by physical acts, like dipping the
body into the waters of the *mikvah*, wrapping the leather straps of
tefillin around the arm and head, or experiencing the visceral effects
of a fast. At my Bat Shechinah, the attending women decorated my
hair. They brushed and braided it, and then tied it with ribbons.
While ten pairs of hands poured their maternal energies onto my
head, we sang about the Shechinah. They sprinkled flower petals over
me and wove blossoms into my braids. I relaxed into the sensation
like easing into a hot bath. I became a communal work of art: the
result of many hands and breasts and hearts. When I saw my reflection,
I thought of fairy queens and the woods of Vermont, where my family
spends our summers.

Months before my bat mitzvah, I wove and sewed my own *tallis*.
I made it from lavender cotton, and attached two woven panels on
each end. One symbolizes Creation, represented by the sun and moon,
a tree, a whale, and a rainbow. The other depicts Vermont, with the
sun setting behind mountains and a lake where my sisters and I swam

every summer. I tied three of the four *tzitzit* on the corners of my *tallis* with my family. At my Bat Shechinah, the circle of women wrapped and tied the fourth. My *tallis* represents my love for my family and community, and my love of Judaism and the earth.

My *kippah* is from Tibet, and was given to me by an old Israeli friend of my dad's. The circle of women each wrote a short message on the interior part of the head covering. At the end of the ceremony, Julie said, "Look around you, Shosh. Know that this ever-expanding circle will always be here, singing and dancing around you."

Before I read from the Torah at my bat mitzvah ceremony, the women who were present at my Bat Shechinah danced into the sanctuary and presented me with my *tallis*. As I said the blessing, they wrapped the shawl around me like the wings of Shechinah.

At my bat mitzvah ceremony, I felt connected to a legacy of our four-thousand-year-old history. While standing on the *bimah*, singing my Torah portion, I felt my circle of women expand to include a nation that has survived despite incredible odds. I realized that I am testimony to the strength and hope of generations of Jews: we were slaves in Egypt; expelled in the Inquisition; and victims of pogroms and the Holocaust. As a Jew who is loving and living Judaism, my existence proves that persecutors throughout history have ultimately failed. I am one strand of thread in the collective Jewish *tallis*, a part of the intricate tapestry.

At my sister Ariel's bat Shechinah, I was one of the ten women in her circle. I helped to decorate her hair with petals and ribbons, and I cried as I watched her accept her blessings. As my offering to her, I wrote a poem and pasted childhood photos of the two of us to a large poster board. This gift now hangs over Ariel's bed.

Becoming a Bat Shechinah was an incredible gift. A circle of women gave me their support and unconditional love, a circle of women who are connected across time to those who danced and sang with Miriam on the far shore of the Red Sea. That circle accompanies me wherever I go.

The winter of my freshman year in high school, my chorus learned Handel's *Messiah*. I had sung sacred Christian music before, but the songs had been in Latin, so I was not exposed to the overtly religious language. But with Handel's piece, the meaning of the lyrics was clear, since he wrote his masterpiece in English. I struggled with the idea of singing music that proclaimed "The kingdom of this world has become the kingdom of our Lord and of His Christ, and He shall reign forever and ever."

At first, I got through the Messiah rehearsals by singing "rice" instead of "Christ" and "cheese sauce" instead of "Jesus." As rehearsals progressed, my dad expressed his ambivalence about my participation. He told me that it would be difficult for him to hear me sing Christian messages of love and peace, when church doors of amnesty had slammed in the faces of Jews all over the world and throughout history. I expressed my concern to the conductor, who explained that the Messiah is a way to say "Yippie, God!" in any language or religion.

As the concerts approached, I tried to look at the experience as an opportunity to learn about another culture, like a research project for school. But music is emotional. The shivers that ran down my spine were entirely different from the detached feeling of reading about a foreign country. Finally, my mom suggested that I think of Christ "not as a person, but as a beautiful energy that is not specific to one religion or another."

At the performance, as we sang "Unto us a son is given," I felt the spirit of celebration in the song. I struggled with the intense joy that washed over me when the audience stood during the last chords of the Hallelujah chorus. In that moment, I understood that music speaks to a part of us that is deeper than religious differences. Just as I cannot fully embrace every one of Judaism's teachings, neither can I reject every aspect of Christianity. Indeed, sacred Christian music is among the most glorious choral music I have ever performed.

After the performance, I continued to think about the inherently political choice I'd made. Non-Jewish neighbors and friends have attended our Shabbat dinners and Passover seders, witnessed the lighting of our Hanukkah candles, and eaten in our sukkah. We welcomed the opportunity to share our traditions with them, and they always responded graciously. But as a Jew in a predominately Christian environment, I believe that my participation in Christian activities has more complicated implications.

To me, Judaism is like an island in the middle of a vast ocean. When the ocean tides go out and the island's land mass enlarges, there is an immeasurably small effect on the ocean's size. But when the tide rolls in and covers the beaches of the island, the land is in danger of eroding and losing itself to the sea. My role as an identified liberal Jew is to swim in the sea, ever mindful that I must also protect my inheritance, my island.

The summer before my senior year in high school, I was part of a group of twenty-two singers who attended a performance camp. We spent two weeks living and rehearsing on a remote island off the northern coast of Maine. We sang in the fields and pine forests, read poems around the campfire, and ate wholesome, home-cooked meals baked in the completely solar-powered, family-built house. We used energy from the sun to cook, and rainwater to wash and drink. Using outhouses and compost allowed us to complete the natural cycles of life. Each day, as we stood in the shade of the forest, breezes from the leaves blew air into our lungs. Transformed into music by the magic of the human voice, our breath returned to the trees and sent the leaves dancing again.

On the first Friday night of camp, I was one of three identified Jews who signed up to cook dinner. The last time I had baked challah was when I was three years old. I remembered how the dough felt in my hands, and how to make the braid, but I could not remember the recipe. We spent our Friday morning break frantically and fruitlessly searching through cookbooks. We almost gave up, resigning ourselves to bake braided Christmas bread, but Liat called her aunt and scribbled down a simple challah recipe. By the time we began assembling ingre- dients on the round wooden table, there were eight of us. As we measured flour and added spoonfuls of yeast and cups of sugar our conversation turned to Shabbat. We shared stories about our own families' traditions and explained, to those who didn't know, about the Jewish Sabbath. As always, we could not keep our voices from singing, but this time we did not turn to the familiar pieces that we were working on as a group. Instead, the songs "Hiney Ma Tov," "Shabbat Shalom," and "L'cha Dodi" tumbled from our mouths. As we waited for the yeast to feed off the sugar, I taught a two-part niggun, which I had learned at B'nai Or. Our voices blended naturally with our bread making, as if the recipe had called for singing. Eight pairs of hands rhythmically molded and smoothed the unborn bread. We braided the loaf and left it to bake during our afternoon rehearsal.

As the sky's colors faded into twilight, the entire group gathered into the kitchen. I set two stout candles on the table, filled a mug with apple-apricot juice, and covered our challah with my blue bandanna.

"Shabbat is a sacred moment in time," I said to the small circle of teenagers and camp leaders in the kitchen. It was the first time I had ever led the Shabbat rituals, and my father's voice echoed in my mind. I felt myself sitting at my dining room table at home, raising the kiddush cup that my community had given me when I became a bat mitzvah.

My voice resonated, naked without the group but strong with tradition, as I sang the blessings over the candles and the "wine." I imagined myself at home, and could hear my sisters' harmonies in my head. I envisioned the flames dancing on top of my great-grandmother's candlesticks. I felt their rings of light flowing over forest and highway and ocean until they merged with the glow in the camp kitchen. "It's a gift from God," I continued, "a time of joy and acceptance, and a time for singing."

The eight challah makers began to sing our baking *niggun* and, as in our rehearsals, other voices joined as they caught the melody. I shook my head in wonder as the tiny room on an island off the coast of Maine filled with the rich harmonies of my little congregation's wordless round.

Before uncovering the challah, one of the camp leaders (who is not Jewish), suggested that we each say what we are thankful for, as they do in his family and, incidentally, as we do in mine. My Jewish friend and I squeezed each other's hands, melting in the tangible sweetness of the moment, and overwhelmed by what had developed from our small idea to bake a braided bread.

I called out the familiar refrain, "Everyone touch the challah or touch someone who's touching the challah!" As I sang the blessing over the bread, individuals from eighteen different states and five different religions connected with each other through our loaf, which we'd kneaded with music and seasoned with thanksgiving. As we broke the challah and savored each chewy mouthful, I whispered the *Shehechianu.* "Thank-you God, for enabling me to reach this moment."

5

God Lives in the Himalayas

LEANNE LIEBERMAN

I was fourteen, and as usual, I was complaining about having to go to shul. My brother was trying to convince me that I needed to go, because "God said so." I squelched his argument by announcing that I didn't believe in God. My brother turned pale and called for my father. "Tell Leanne she has to believe in God," he cried. My father shuffled his feet around, looked embarrassed, and finally mumbled that I could believe in whatever I wanted. My brother was probably scarred for life, but I felt relieved. I felt like I had been released from something I didn't understand. I didn't see any reason to believe in something I couldn't prove.

Aside from the glaring lack of theological discussion in our home, I had a solid Jewish upbringing in the Conservative movement. My Jewish education emphasized family, *gimulut hasidim* (acts of loving kindness), and volunteer work. My parents practiced a cultural, rather than theological form of Judaism. Somehow, our blessings, prayers, and study seemed disassociated from God.

I enthusiastically became a bat mitzvah, but I was more concerned about the food, the presents, and performance, than I was about becoming an adult. It was definitely *not* a spiritual rite of passage. Like most everyone I knew, I was reluctant to participate in Jewish life after my bat mitzvah. I had other interests, and shul was not cool.

Unfortunately, my family and community still expected me to say kiddush on Friday night, attend Hebrew high school, and participate in the youth group. But no one explained how I would benefit from being Jewish. I learned that it was good to be Jewish to "continue the tradition," which I knew meant "don't marry a non-Jew." I didn't understand the point of keeping traditions alive for the sake of tradition. It felt like I was supposed to be Jewish because the Nazis killed us. My education felt like a bad combination of guilt and nostalgia.

No one mentioned that being Jewish would be good for my *neshamah*, my "soul," or that God was there to help me. And I was an insecure fourteen-year-old; of course I needed help. My youth group, United Synagogue Youth (USY), taught strong values, but didn't offer the spiritual instruction that I needed. Maybe it was the choir in the eaves of my synagogue that made me think of God as The-All-Powerful-Big-Guy-In-The-Sky.

When I observed my Christian friends' prayer circle at high school, I finally realized that religion was related to God in a spiritual way. I was amazed (and somewhat uncomfortable) by the intensity of my friends' relationship with Jesus and with each other. When I prayed, I chanted words that I could barely understand. I felt lost among the Hebrew and the complex liturgy. My Christian friends had an open dialogue with God, and with each other—in English. In USY, we didn't talk about God as our savior or our friend. Instead, we talked about how to help other people, what was ethical, and what we could learn from Maimonides.

When I decided to go to university, I moved away from our relatively small Jewish community in Vancouver to Montreal, which has much larger population of Jews. I was amazed by how easy it was to distance myself from Judaism. I ignored Shabbat, forgot about Yom Kippur, and didn't bother keeping Pesach.

Despite my conspicuous lack of interest in Judaism, I somehow decided to spend my third year at Hebrew University in Jerusalem. My parents warned me about terrorism, but they were also concerned that I would become religious. Several of their friends' daughters had returned from Israel as observant Jews. They cautioned me not to let myself be brainwashed into that trap. I considered it highly unlikely.

My first year in Israel was a profoundly unreligious experience. I never went to more than a handful of services. When I did go to shul, I didn't pray. I didn't learn any new prayers or study any biblical tractates; I just attended. But occasionally, when I participated in Shabbos dinners, I really enjoyed a sense of peace, and appreciated the cyclic nature of the holiday.

Israel didn't feel like home, or even like a holy place. It was historically interesting, but I didn't feel like I was walking on the ground of my forefathers and mothers. The first time I went to the Kotel, I was filled with an incredibly empty feeling. I knew the place was supposed to mean something to me, but it didn't. I cried at the wall because I felt no connection to it.

When I started to learn about Israeli history in my courses at Hebrew University, I began to feel more attracted to places like the Kotel and Masada. But I was still hesitant: I didn't want to think of the land as my people's or mine. I knew it was also an important homeland to other religious groups.

During that year, I also took a Women's Studies seminar, which made me reconsider my understanding of Jewish values. It was a noncredit night course taught by a religious woman named Gila. She was an ex-American who always wore a headscarf, long skirts, and sandals with socks. Gila was a *baalat teshuvah*, a returnee to the fold, a reborn Jew. In class, she unfolded the mysteries of the religious laws of *snioot* (modesty), dating, menstruation, and sexual relations.

Growing up, I had almost no direct contact with people who observed traditional Jewish law. I had heard rumors that made religious practice sound outdated and cruel: you had to have sex through a hole in the sheet, and you weren't allowed to even look at your husband while you were menstruating. Those stories didn't reflect my own Jewish experiences, but they made me feel alienated from Judaism anyway.

Gila explained the evolution of the laws of blood impurity, of *tahor* and *tameh*, and how they are usually mistranslated as "clean" and "unclean." I started to see how others could value these practices, but I wasn't convinced that avoiding all contact with men during menstruation truly "affirmed a woman's cycle and her spirituality." Still, having time to yourself when you're menstruating seems like a good idea to me (especially if you're feeling crappy).

I was fascinated by Gila's description of Orthodox dating. I learned that when an observant young man or woman is ready to get married (and their rabbi or mentor has also decided they are mature enough), a series of dates is arranged by go-betweens. The couple meets in a crowded place, and for a few hours, they talk about themselves: what they want for the future, what kind of lifestyle they hope to enjoy. There is no premarital touching, or even hand-holding. Orthodoxy maintains that physical contact makes it impossible to focus on whether that person would be a good mate, because desire takes over. To ensure that marriage partners will have similar interests and goals, touching is avoided until after marriage. The rules of dating are meant to safeguard against relationships that will lead to heartbreak.

Gila's teaching was particularly vivid to me once my Canadian boyfriend dumped me when I returned from Israel. The thought of facing a Montreal winter, my last year at school, and graduation made me feel lost. I started to think more seriously about what I learned in Gila's class and remembered the peace I felt during my Shabbat experiences. I started to wonder whether Judaism had a place for me, a place where I could enjoy the quiet of Shabbat. I loved the idea of a place that would prevent me from becoming involved in relationships that weren't going anywhere.

My best friend, who I had gone to Israel with, returned to Canada as an observant Jew. She had fallen into the trap our mothers warned us about. Though no one else was particularly thrilled about her new life choice, she seemed extremely happy. She was a whole lot happier than I was.

I'm embarrassed to admit that I had the potential to become a *baalat teshuvah* myself: I was lost, vulnerable, and searching. I actually considered going to yeshiva. My parents and friends thought I was crazy. Ultimately, I changed my mind: studying at a yeshiva sounded like an interesting experience, but I still felt alienated by the Jewish concept of God, and by the claim that Jews are the chosen people.

Instead, I embarked on a trip that evolved into a three-year adventure of travel and teaching through Asia. I never intended it to be a spiritual journey, or an inquest into Buddhism. I just wanted to see the world.

I spent most of my time in Japan. I saw some incredibly beautiful temples and shrines, but it is the most godless place I've ever been. Because of the strict separation of church and state since World War II, most Japanese know very little about religion. Consumerism and hard work seem to have replaced spirituality. The majestic temples and giant Buddhas piqued my curiosity.

It wasn't until I traveled to Thailand that I really became interested in Buddhism. We visited the golden reclining Buddha at Wat Pho on a hot, sticky Bangkok morning. I was awestruck by the sheer enormity of the Buddha, and the blissful expression on its face. Afterward, while waiting for my pad thai at a little street café, I read part of Karen Armstrong's book, *The History of God*. I learned that the Buddhists conceive of God as a feeling of transcendence.

I couldn't believe that the concept of God could be as simple as a feeling, a heightened awareness. I filled my notebooks with what seemed like incredibly pithy observations. I wrote: God is in me; God is in the trees; I am God. It was the one time in my life I wanted a T-shirt with Goddess emblazoned across the chest.

I had been completely turned off by the Jewish images of God as "Our Father," or as "the King who commands us." When I was younger, I didn't have the maturity, education, or insight to see beyond those metaphors. Besides, how could any young woman be enticed by such patriarchal images? Once I discovered the Buddhist conception of God, I couldn't imagine believing anything else.

I devoured the rest of Armstrong's work, and then read a variety of books about Buddhism. I learned that Buddhism describes God as The Natural Law. In Buddhism, God is the way the water flows, and the way the wind blows. God is the way things naturally occur. God is as God does. God is ultimately indescribable and unknowable.

It was liberating to discover a definition of God that was open to interpretation. I felt the real power, the real magic of not having to define God concretely. I was exhilarated by my new ability to conceive of, and relate to God. For the first time, I experienced complete awe.

Other travelers did not share my enthusiasm about *The History of God*. I expected the book to provoke stimulating discussions, but instead, it got a bad rap. Most people I spoke to couldn't get beyond their belief that the whole concept of God "just sucked." No one was even willing to engage in an intellectual conversation about Buddhism, even after I explained that the book was not about proselytizing. My travel buddy, Aileen, who usually provided stimulating debate, was unfortunately reading *The Hitch Hiker's Guide to the Galaxy*.

After reading about Buddhism, I wanted to experience it firsthand. I enrolled in a *Vipassanna* meditation course to study Buddhism more deeply. The ten-day course was held in a center in the countryside, outside of Kyoto. In my mind, I took the course because I wanted to reduce my stress. I didn't want to think of myself as a seeker, because I thought that if I was looking for something, that meant I was lost. I wouldn't admit that I was on a spiritual quest; that would be as embarrassing as belonging to a self-help group.

For ten days, I sat on the floor in the lotus position, trying to focus my awareness on my breath and body. I kept my vow of silence by pretending I was the only person in the course. Ten days is a long time to pretend that you're alone. As my brain charged around, hopping from thought to thought, I dredged up a lot of old, ugly feelings. I didn't like myself very much.

In the evenings, we listened to lectures about the theory of Vipassanna meditation. Vipassanna, or "insight," is a practice that was discovered two thousand years ago by Buddha. It is not an organized religion, though it is the core of what has become Buddhism. The goal of Vipassanna is to observe how your body feels, and not to become attached to those feelings. Since everything in life is in constant flux, there's no point in getting too attached or worked up about how you feel.

People of all faiths practice Vipassanna. I found the practice to be a natural and rational way to live with myself, and to get along with others. I agreed with most of the principles that were introduced in the course, especially the idea that attachment to material goods leads only to unhappiness. I left the course feeling that I had learned a valuable lesson in self-control. My mind had quieted down, and I was able to find a few brief moments of stillness in my brain. I believed that the sense of peacefulness I found in Buddhism was completely unrelated to my Jewish life.

After the meditation course, I traveled in India. By then, I knew I wasn't only interested in the intellectual aspects of Buddhism; I was also drawn to the spiritual practice. One of my first stops in India was Dharmsala. High up in the Indian Himalayas, it is home to the Dalai Lama in exile, and to a whole community of Tibetan refugees. Dharmsala has become a major spot for travelers lured by the majestic mountains and by the spiritual example of the Tibetans. If God resides anywhere, it's in the Himalayas. Maybe it's the high altitude or the magnificent scenery, but spiritual issues seemed first on many travelers' minds.

I felt the presence of something transcendent in Dharmsala, but I did not feel comfortable using the word God in that environment. The preferred spiritual term was *energy*. Like the much misused "karma" of previous years, "energy" was the catchall phrase for any and every spiritual experience. Energy was channeled in reiki sessions, manipulated in cranial readjustments, and analyzed in palm readings. It was witnessed during meditation and yoga classes. I wasn't used to having casual conversations about spirituality, or talking about energy. But I eventually realized that *energy* was just another word to describe the intense feeling of being connected to yourself, to the people around you, and to the environment. Essentially, talking about energy was another way to talk about God.

I was amused to think about the folks in the Bible Belt who also discuss "energy," but they call it "God" instead. In Jerusalem, energy is called *Hashem*, "the name." I realized that the difference is merely semantic. Energy, God, and *Hashem* are all concrete words to describe something we feel, but cannot really explain.

After meditating and hiking through India and Nepal, I felt confident about my relationship with God. I decided to find out more about my own religion, and I wanted to decide if Judaism could be a bigger part of my life. I was finally ready to go to a yeshiva, so I returned to Israel.

I enrolled in a full-time, intensive course of study at Pardes, a relatively liberal yeshiva in Jerusalem that is nondenominational and egalitarian. At first, I was hesitant to immerse myself in such an intensive program, but was reassured because the purpose of my studies and prayers was to celebrate *Hashem*.

The school turned out to be more traditional than I expected. I tried to remain open-minded: I took every class, attended special events, and took part in special prayer services. The logic of Judaism exhausted and often exasperated me, but I was also romanced by the bigger picture. I regularly participated in Shabbat, and I even kept my kitchen kosher. I began to learn the meaning of the Hebrew prayers, and for the first time, I prayed with all my heart and all my soul. I finally understood the purpose of prayer.

Walking to synagogue through the streets of Jerusalem on Shabbat, I stopped to gaze at the Old City. I was awed by the knowledge that I was celebrating Shabbat along with thousands of Jews all over Israel, and all over the world. I felt part of something much bigger than myself, and I liked the feeling. Living in Israel finally felt like being home.

My Israel experience was complicated by the fact that I had a non-Jewish boyfriend. I had dated non-Jewish men before, but Rob was different. In the past, I had kept my Jewish and secular lives separate, and moved easily back and forth between them. In Israel, things were different. There, everything about my life was Jewish. I studied, breathed, prayed, and lived Judaism, but I also pined for Rob.

We had met in India and had traveled together only for a short while, but I just *knew* that we were meant to be together.

During my time at the yeshiva, Rob was my sounding board. I e-mailed him about what I was learning, and relied on him for objective opinions. Rob kept me grounded. He was a constant reminder that at the end of my yeshiva experience, I would return home and be part of a diverse community again. I valued him as my anchor, but I also felt confused. I wanted Shabbat and a mezuzah, and I also wanted Rob.

I took comfort in *tefillah*. I prayed for guidance about how to negotiate being Jewish and being in love with someone who wasn't. But the very act of praying was complicated: the more I understood the meaning of the Hebrew prayers, the more problematic I found Judaism. Some prayers troubled me more than others.

For weeks, I had been reciting the set of prayers called the *Shmonah Esrei* three times a day, as dictated by the tradition. When I finally learned the translation, I discovered that some parts were beautiful, but that other sections were outdated and even cruel. I didn't want to pray about returning to the sacrificial practices of the temple era. I didn't want to smite, smash, or break down slanderers or sinners. And I felt uncomfortable with Judaism's exclusiveness; the prayers about the rebuilding of Jerusalem as a Jewish capital didn't jibe with my political sensibilities.

I didn't want to recite the *Aleinu* and proclaim that Jews are better than everyone else. I learned from my rabbi that Jews were chosen for higher obligations and higher moral behavior. But to me, Chosenness, no matter how you spin it, implies superiority. I decided not to say all of the eighteen prayers in the *Shmonah Esrei*. I chose the twelve that were meaningful to me: I prayed the *Shtem Esrei* instead.

Despite my growing uneasiness, I still wanted to sing the melodies that reminded me of my childhood. I liked going to shul and hearing the prayers, but everything felt different once I knew what I was praying about. For years I had been belting out lines like: "For they (the non-Jews) bow to vanity and emptiness and pray to a God who helps not." And I'd bowed while I said it. I couldn't believe that I had been singing those words with such gusto. I wanted to be blissfully ignorant again.

I felt conflicted, thinking, Who am I to change or ignore the liturgy of our honored rabbis? But I needed my prayers to be more personal. I didn't want to use the masculine language of the Bible and liturgy, which reinforced my childhood conception of God as Sky-Daddy. Instead, I decided to replace the word for King (*Melech*), with *Ruach*, which means "feeling" or "spirit." Since the names Father and King are just metaphors from a previous era, I didn't feel bad about dropping them. That helped a little, but I was really bothered by the fact that God just didn't seem very nice.

Jewish God was sometimes caring and beneficent; other times unkind and dictator-like. Jewish God was an unforgiving lawmaker who did not explain his rules with logic, and a demanding figure that expected praise. I didn't see the logic of extolling the glories of something as natural as flowing water. It was good to give thanks, but Judaism was excessive, repetitive. I started editing my prayers more. I was happy to give thanks, but I cut back on the praise. My prayers became much shorter.

I came back to that familiar question, What good is tradition for the sake of tradition? Some of my classmates at the yeshiva felt that keeping Jewish law would help bring the Messiah. That was too great a leap of faith for me. Since I wasn't finding what I needed in traditional Jewish prayer, I started to meditate more often.

The perilous balance between my obligation to myself and to my people led me back to my original feelings of guilt. It seemed selfish to ignore tradition and to light Shabbos candles only when I wanted to, but it also seemed silly to light them on time, according to *halacha*. I was beginning to regret my decision to learn about Judaism.

In Buddhism, I learned that I would be happy if I accepted life as it is. Jews seemed to be locked in a never-ending cycle of demand, supply, and thanks. *Kavannah*, inspired prayer, felt like an afterthought, something extra to add after fulfilling the required commandments.

I found *kavannah* in one prayer, in the last paragraph of the *Shmonah Esrei*. There, we pray, "my God, guard my tongue from evil and my lips from speaking deceitfully." Instead of focusing on external things like the prayers for the State of Israel, for the Jewish people, or for our collective God, I appreciated that one, because it is internally directed.

While I was in the yeshiva, I thought that I had to accept Judaism as a complete package; I had to buy into all of it, or give it up completely. To reap the benefits, I thought I had to participate in all aspects of religious life. But the more personal my Judaism became, the more I needed to change my prayers. And the more I changed the meanings and implications, the more alone I stood.

When I reflected on my earliest relationship with Judaism, I realized that my struggle was not new. My parents and the Conservative movement seemed to be caught in a similar dilemma. In the process of making Judaism more democratic, they had somehow removed God. At the yeshiva, we talked about God constantly, but where was *Hashem* all those years at my parents' Shabbos table?

Judaism for my parents was culture, history, and community. I can't imagine the people from my parents' congregation praying with their eyes closed or losing themselves in *tefillah* like we did at the Yakar synagogue in Jerusalem. Many Conservative Jews are embarrassed about spirituality. Many people don't go to shul to pray; they believe that the rabbi prays for them.

I recently wrote a letter to my father asking him about spirituality. I argued that in order to feel God's presence, children must be shown the connection between the prayers and rituals and God. In his response, he wrote that he felt like I had given him a report card with a failing grade on spiritual parenting. He explained that he had learned from his rabbi that whoever says *brachot* at the dinner table invites God to the table too.

My father eventually wrote to me, and described his relationship with Judaism in more detail. He explained that his spirituality had little to do with the synagogue. Like me, he felt that God had more to do with mountains. He described an experience he had when he was my age: he was skiing down a run at Lake Louise and took a wrong turn into some deep snow among the trees. As he turned to retrace his steps, he saw a magnificent view of the valley below, and the mountain on the opposite side. "What I saw in that instant," he wrote, "was the many layers of compressed sediment that had formed over many hundreds of millions of years to make up the mountain . . . in that instant, I understood the vastness of time, and realized that my time on earth was insignificant by comparison. That moment with God encouraged me to always have an optimistic outlook."

He didn't mention synagogues. He didn't mention following God's law as outlined in the Torah. Instead of teaching me Hebrew or reading me Bible stories, my father taught me to ski and bought me hiking boots so we could wander through the mountains of British Columbia.

Listening to my father speak about his intimate relationship with spirituality made me feel increasingly uncomfortable with how often God was publicly and casually mentioned in religious circles. At the yeshiva, I asked my teachers, "How are you?" and they'd reply, *Baruch*

Hashem, "Praised be God." I think that once God is a part of everyday language, some of the meaning is lost. I began to appreciate and value my family's silence. God was something personal, something my parents couldn't teach me. I had to experience it for myself.

Rob came to stay with me in Israel as part of his travels, and we decided to move back to Toronto together. It was not an easy decision, and we thought about it very carefully before committing to live together. It was not easy for my parents either; they have only recently gotten over the shock of my switch from studying at a yeshiva to cohabiting with a non-Jew.

When making that decision, I applied the valuable lessons I had learned about religious dating, but on my own terms. Unlike our Orthodox counterparts, Rob and I held hands before we moved in together. We also did a lot of soul-searching and intense talking about our goals, desires, and values. It was not easy, but we discussed how we would want to raise our children, which religious holidays we would keep, and how we wanted to live our lives. And we consciously decided to keep the conversation ongoing.

Rob's continual questions about the reasons behind my observance of the rituals can be frustrating, but he also challenges me to think more deeply about their meaning. Every time I light my Shabbos candles or sing *Modah Ani*, I am aware of the meaning of the words and my reasons for saying them.

Living with Rob has also helped me find balance in my religious life. I no longer feel as though I have to choose between an all-encompassing religious lifestyle and no participation at all. While I make an effort to keep Jewish elements in our life, meditation still brings me the most comfort. We have a mezuzah on our door, but we designed it and wrote our own scroll. And I am the only student in my Torah study class who can't come to the luncheon at the end of the semester because it's on Christmas. This year, I'll be spending the twenty-fifth with Rob's family.

My life with Rob is filled with loving compromises and *Hashem*. It is difficult to persuade Rob to participate in Shabbos on Friday nights, and I run the risk of finding myself without any Jewish community, but I know that my primary religious needs will always be met by my personal relationship with God. And I am more comfortable meditating by myself, than singing with a congregation at a synagogue. Ritualized group prayer just isn't the best way for me to contemplate the awesomeness of *Hashem*.

What is most important to me is how I manifest my personal relationship with God through my actions in the world. When volunteering at the Shaar Tzedek Hospital in Jerusalem, I was surprised when several patients wished me mazel tov for performing that mitzvah. I wasn't volunteering because I believed it was my obligation to follow God's commandment to visit the sick. I do humanitarian acts because I believe it's an important way to help people; I am not trying to bring about the Messiah.

My parents and community stressed humanitarian values that were not exclusive to the Jewish community. They expected me to have both Jewish and non-Jewish friends, and to be active and responsible to both the secular and religious communities. In that sense, I have to give my "godless" childhood a lot more credit.

My parents succeeded in teaching me the basic goals of Judaism without claiming that I had to do things because "God said so." They raised me without regulating my life with outdated *halachah*, and without excluding non-Jews from my life. They also taught me to love Jewish culture. By not emphasizing God, they gave me the space to explore Judaism's spirituality on my own.

References

Armstrong, Karen. *A History Of God: The 4000-Year Quest Of Judaism, Christianity, and Islam*. New York: A. A. Knopf (distributed by Random House): 1993.

Adams, Douglas. *The Hitchhiker's Guide To The Galaxy*. New York: Harmony Books, 1980.

6

Yom Kippur in Ecuador (Me and the Virgin)

ALEZA EVE KAUFMAN SUMMIT

Knowing *yizkor* candles flicker yellow
in a sink half a world away,
I watch wax pool onto the Virgin's bare toes.
Bathed in her sorrowful smile,
colored lights reflect her son's grimaces
onto our faces and the whitewashed walls.
Hands dance across the forehead, heart, span of shoulders,
tracing a cross to match his.
My hand follows, and I am scarred
where my fingertips have touched.
Burning, those spots must send out light
in the darkened church, announce to all
that I am a sister of Judas.

"Santa Mariá, Madre de Dios. . . ."
and I, a virgin, as Jewish as she is, and as white,
I turn my palms upward to match hers,
the two of us alone among these dark Catholics
laying their pains at her feet.
Dazed by the heat, I grope for October,
the clean geometry of black letters against white,
the shofar's wounded shriek.

56

I strain for the daveners' spiraling murmur,
but what echoes rises from
handworn strands of hailmarys and ourfathers,
and I try to catch her downcast eyes
as I pray, *Kol nidre, v'esurei.* . . .

7

Where the Mountain Touches the Sky

VERED HANKIN

I have always found solace in stories. For me, stories create a dream world: a place where everything is beautiful and anything is possible. As a performer and professional storyteller, I travel from city to city, listening and telling stories, living and searching for the beauty within them, within life. I especially love the wisdom of Jewish folktales, the stories of my heritage. Delving into these powerful tales enriches my own story, illuminating and binding together the bits and pieces of my journey.

I spent my childhood in Jerusalem, a city where every block, every crevice, holds centuries of stories in its midst. It is a city so full of history that it has been impossible to build an underground railroad, lest some of the most holy stories be disturbed. I grew up within this story-land, a whisper of breath in a whirlwind of history.

Since my parents are American, my first stories included *The Little Engine that Could* and Dr. Seuss's popular tales. My earliest childhood memory is of a dream: a Dr. Seuss character hung from the lamp in my room and introduced itself to me. In the morning I can remember standing in my crib, desperately attempting to describe my experience with my small child vocabulary. My mother, in her baby-loving voice, apparently tried to dissipate my revelation by saying, "It was just a dream." I stubbornly refused to accept her explanation. My dream felt just as real as waking life.

Songs were also an integral part of life in Jerusalem. Everywhere I went—at work, at play, at school, and at home—people sang. On holidays, everyone sang and danced. At school assemblies the audience participated with the performers. Rather than simply sitting quietly and nodding proudly, parents sang with their children. Sometimes when I walked alone, I sang to myself. I sang my thoughts, feelings, fantasies, and dreams. My stories unfolded through song.

At my Conservative elementary school, we prayed every morning. My favorite prayer was the blessing at the end of the *Amidah*, the "standing prayer": "Please let others not think badly about me. Help me follow the commandments for your sake, God. May you bring peace to us and to all of Israel. Amen."

At night, without anyone else knowing, I quietly chanted the *Sh'ma*. My brother and sister, who shared my room, were fast asleep. It was my time to look up toward God, to whisper my own prayer. Sometimes we spoke for a while before I nodded off to sleep. Other times I'd just check in. We became friends, God and I. Years later, when I yearned for this kind of connection again, a spiritual counselor suggested that I create a relationship with God. She told me: "It isn't just about the magic, the miracle. It's about the day to day." She was right, and I, too, had been right, once upon a time . . .

Once, a long time ago, a young shepherd lived in the hills of Jerusalem. Every morning she rose at the crack of dawn and led her sheep up and down the hills, until finally, she reached a spot where she could peer out onto the horizon. At that spot, it seemed as if the mountain touched the sky. There, she would look up to pray: "God, if you were lonely, I would be here for you. And if you were cold, I'd give you wool from my greatest sheep. God, we'll talk tomorrow, right?"

One particular day, a great scholar happened along. He saw the shepherd and stopped to watch. The shepherd walked until she could see the mountain touching the sky. When she reached that spot, she began to pray: "God, if you were sad, I would tell you the greatest joke. And if you were afraid of the dark, I would light a fire for you. And if I could, I would even hug you. It's sure nice talking to God. Bye."

The shepherd's prayer upset the scholar. He asked her: "What is it that you are doing?"

"Why," replied the shepherd, quietly, "I am praying."

"No, no, no!" insisted the scholar. "That is not the way to pray. Let me teach you the correct way to pray." The scholar covered his eyes and

chanted: "Sh'ma Yisrael Adonai Eloheinu Adonai Echad," *and invited the shepherd to repeat after him. The shepherd was eager to know the correct way to pray. She thanked the scholar, and they both went on their way.*

The next day, when the shepherd brought her sheep to the place where the mountain seemed to touch the sky, she hesitated. Then, slowly, she covered her eyes with her hands and began to pray, just as the scholar had taught her: "Sh'ma Yisrael Adonai Eloheinu Adonai." *The shepherd faltered. She could not remember the last word of the prayer. Try as she might, the word did not come.*

With each day, more of the words disappeared from her memory, until one day she could no longer remember the prayer at all. When she reached the place where the mountain touched the sky, she looked up but said nothing, and continued on her way.

That very night, the scholar had a dream. In his dream, an angel appeared, demanding: "God wants to know what happened to God's friend, the shepherd."

"The shepherd?" replied the scholar. "I taught her how to pray."

"I am afraid," whispered the angel, "that the shepherd already knew how to pray."

When the scholar awoke, he knew what he needed to do. He made his way back to the shepherd. When the shepherd saw him, she turned around and smiled. "Oh, it's you! Please remind me how to pray. I don't remember."

"No," said the scholar, shaking his head. "You knew how to pray all along. It was I who needed to learn."

Standing side by side, the two looked up toward God, finding the spot where the mountain seemed to touch the sky. They then covered their eyes to pray: "Sh'ma Yisrael Adonai Eloheinu. And God, if you are ever lonely, we'll send you all the prayers we can find."

When I was ten years old, I was whisked away from the magic of Jerusalem, my prayers unwinding into the land of suburbia. My parents divorced, and my mother brought my siblings and me to Kansas City, where both she and my father had grown up. Cousins and grandparents suddenly surrounded me. But my friends were faraway; songs were faraway; my father was faraway. And stories were far. At night, I continued to quietly chant the *Sh'ma*. When I started to speak to God, out flowed tears, wishes, dreams, and memories. I begged God to please give me back my *Aba*, to help me make friends, and to help me fit in. Sometimes, in the evenings, I would lock myself in the bathroom and sing and sing and sing.

But during the day, at school, my voice was silent. I knew myself to be loud and rambunctious and free, but others saw me as quiet, careful, and shy. My classmates were taller, more athletic, and seemed more "mature" than I was. (All the other girls wore bras!) I wanted so much to feel free and open like I had in Jerusalem: to be embraced by the community, to get out of my apartment and to run and play in the neighborhood. I wanted to laugh and sing aloud, but the words didn't come out. During the *Amidah*, I would pray: "Please let others not think bad about me. Help me follow the commandments, for your sake, God."

> *They say Moses was called by a burning bush: a bush that was not consumed. They say he tried to turn away from it and begged it not to call his name. But the bush entreated: "Moses, speak and ask for the thing you want most. Call it out; demand it." "What is this voice?" Moses asked and the bush replied: "Eheyeh asher eheyeh; I will be as I will be." Moses shuddered. His voice caught, his tongue skipped, and he begged to give the mission to someone else, anyone else. But the fire continued to burn; it burned inside him and he had no choice but to acknowledge it, to let it through, to let it speak. In this way, Moses changed the fate of many people, through the very thing that was most difficult for him—his voice.*
>
> *Many years later, after Moses had followed his heart and delivered its truth through his voice, the Holy One presented him with another mission. Moses was to speak to a rock and ask it for a life-preserving mineral—water. Moses' fears returned and his throat caught. But the lives of so many were depending on him, on his voice. So he lifted the staff, banging hard on the rock with all of his might. Water burst forth from the rock.*
>
> *By deferring to his fear, by keeping his voice silent, Moses found himself stuck in the same desert that he had wandered in for forty years. "You are not yet ready to go to the Holy Land," the Voice announced. Moses' power to bring forth life, as well as to progress in his own life, was in his voice, in the one part of himself that he perceived as his weakness. Had Moses let his voice roam, its rhythm would have led him to the next step of his journey. Only then would he have been worthy to dance into the gates of the Holy Land.*

It took years before my own gates crept open. Words began to slowly tumble out of me. They weren't always my words, but they were words nevertheless. At first, they seemed unfamiliar, like those stuttering from Moses' tongue. But soon, I began to let the words flow out. I learned by listening to the stories of others. I noticed how my classmates spoke and what they said: how girls spoke to boys, how boys spoke to girls. I imitated them. I noticed that boys seemed to like it when girls laughed and giggled, so I began to laugh and giggle. I would laugh. I would smile. Nothing ever bothered me.

I observed how to be a nice midwestern American. I learned not to stand out too much, to be polite and friendly. For the most part, it worked. I made friends. I joined the fringes of the "popular" crowd, went to the "right" parties, and sat with the "right" people at lunch. Underneath, I felt alone.

Growing up, many of my friends believed that I would eventually end up in hell, "on account of not believing in Jesus, and all." My difference was insinuated with comments from my classmates like, "Where are you from?" or "Your hair is so *black*," or "Your personality seems so *prominent*." Most of the time, if I suppressed myself enough, it would be okay. I would be okay, as long as I smiled.

Years later, in college, everyone told me how happy I seemed. "You're always happy," my roommate once insisted. At that moment, I realized that everyone was fooled: even me. I had become my smile. In my first women's studies course, I learned that women smile much more than men. I came to understand how socially, politically, and personally important it is for women to feel what we really feel and to express our authentic feelings.

> A long long time ago, in a faraway kingdom lived a king, queen and prince. Each evening, the three would sit down at their long elegant table: the king at one end, the queen at the other, and the prince in the middle. The three would discuss affairs of the palace, eating slowly and politely, making sure to dab the corners of their mouths with a royal napkin between courses.
>
> On one particular evening, between their second and third courses, the prince did something he had never done before. Just as the king and queen began to dab the corners of their mouths, the prince stood up, ripped off his clothes, crawled under the table, and refused to eat anything but kernels of corn. This he did while flapping his arms, singing: "I am a rooster, no matter what I do. I am what I am, Cock-a-doodle-doo!"
>
> The king and the queen both squinted, to make sure they were seeing and hearing their son correctly. The royal couple decided to give the prince some time; reasoning that he would surely outgrow his rooster phase by dessert. But when dessert finally arrived, the prince was too busy singing and crowing to even notice.
>
> After a week of this behavior, the queen summoned her royal advisors. The prince's behavior left the advisors baffled. The prince, who was very polite, made sure to bid each of them farewell with a flap of his arms and his "Cock-a-doodle-doo!" song.

One day, an old man carrying a large stack of books wandered into the palace. "I understand," said the man, "that the prince thinks he is a rooster. I believe I can cure him." The queen raised one brow skeptically, but agreed to give the man one week.

The old man walked over to the table under which the prince sat crowing. With everyone watching, the man slowly set down his books, ripped off his clothes, crawled underneath the table, and crowed. "Psst," whispered the prince, "What are you doing?" "I'm a rooster," replied the old man, "just like you." "Cock-a-doodle-doo!" the prince crowed, and the two of them flapped their arms and sang.

Later, the old man grabbed his clothes, put them on, and crawled back underneath the table. "Psst," whispered the prince. "What are you doing? Roosters do not wear clothes." "I was a bit chilly," said the old man. "And besides, I'm a rooster and I'm wearing clothes, so I guess it's okay for a rooster to wear clothes." Since the prince, too, was a bit chilly, he also ran out from underneath the table, put on his clothes, and crawled back underneath. The two then flapped their arms and sang.

That evening, the old man asked for a platter of royal food. "I'm hungry," said the old man. "And besides, roosters can eat whatever they want to." "Really?" asked the prince, and ordered a platter of royal food for himself.

Later, the old man crept out from underneath the table and sat on a chair. The prince slowly followed. Soon, the two were discussing the weather, the affairs of the palace, and their favorite games. When the queen and king walked in, they were thrilled. Their prince was cured!

The prince grew to be a fine king. Sometimes, when no one was looking, he would wander to a corner in the palace, flap his arms, and sing, "I am what I am, no matter what I do! Cock-a-doodle-doo!" It was important to make sure he was indeed still a rooster.

Like the prince, I did what everybody else did, but deep down, I was still a rooster. I always knew I was different, especially when I was with my non-Jewish peers at school. I had Jewish friends from my youth group, but they were in a different world from my school friends. As Jews in the Midwest, we were different. For many of us, our sense of difference led us to identify with our Jewish heritage: to fight for it, to believe in it, and to be it. In Kansas City, we struggled to keep time with images and stories of other places, where the joy of being Jewish could be shared by all.

By the time I went to college at the University of Kansas, my Jewish identity was an active political decision. I was Jewish because it was important to be Jewish. I was proud, because it was important to be proud. I announced it, because it was crucial to represent my true identity.

But a part of me still wanted to be like everyone else. I joined the blondest, perkiest sorority I could find. It was nonsectarian, except that a passage from the New Testament was read at every chapter meeting. I was the only Jew. During the winter holidays, I suggested that the sorority sisters place a menorah next to their Christmas tree. Eager to do the "right" thing, they complied. That year, the Hanukkah menorah stood next to the Christmas tree and the Christmas formal was called the "Winter Formal." I was convinced that I had truly made a difference.

During my second year a Jewish friend of mine was running for a student government office. Though elections were on Yom Kippur eve and Yom Kippur day, she felt she had no choice but to stay and campaign. I was outraged. I contacted the student government office and immediately informed them about this act of religious discrimination. By holding elections on those two days, the university would virtually eliminate the entire Jewish vote. The woman in the student government office shrugged her shoulders and apologized, but insisted that there was nothing she could do.

I wrote a letter to the editor of the school paper, *The University Daily Kansan*. I urged people to speak out, to stand up for what they believe in, and not to let acts of discrimination go unnoticed. I used my sorority as an example of a place of tolerance, a place where people listened when I spoke out.

The response to my article was overwhelming. My writing was reprinted in the university alumni newspaper and I was interviewed for a college orientation video. I even received a commendation from the vice chancellor. Jewish women from other sororities approached me, telling me that my courage inspired them to speak out, to act, to change. I felt wonderful.

That is, until I stepped foot into the sorority house. Around me, the sorority sisters whispered to one another, turning the other way and leaving the room. I did not know what I had done wrong; I though that my article glorified the sorority. They called me in to their "Standards Committee," where I was chastised for using the sorority's name without permission. "We are to remain quiet," they urged me. "We don't want people to know what goes on here. Think of your sisters. We are your sisters."

The following year, the Christmas tree stood alone. The novelty of my "difference" had dissipated, and the menorah was nowhere to be found. Before winter break, they wished me "Merry Christmas!"

and during meetings, they continued to read from the New Testament. It wasn't malicious, just unperceptive, but it hurt nevertheless.

In the spring semester of my sophomore year, I enrolled in my first women's studies course. A friend told me that it was easy, and it fulfilled a requirement, so I enrolled. "You sit there and talk about rape," my friend explained. I didn't know that the course would change my entire worldview. We read essays that made me think differently about my place in the world. I became angry: at Men (with a capital M), at history, at women who chose to ignore their own cages, and at myself for living in mine.

I noticed systems, people, and couples. Again, I witnessed my social world, just as I had when I was ten. But this time, I watched to analyze, to understand, to break down—not to imitate. I watched the women in my sorority and I leaped out, fleeing like a bird breaking through its cage. I watched the prayers in the synagogue and I couldn't say them; I couldn't feel them. Judaism didn't seem like my place anymore. During that time, I wrote:

> G-d (?)
> You've been fed to me
> In deep voice
> And male pronouns
> As I gobbled and swallowed
> Your white-bearded face.
>
> You entered me
> In suit and tie
> And I engulfed you
> Breasts and thighs
> Resting on the pulpit as I tore
> Through my siddur.
>
> You transcended me
> In masculine
> As I tried to pray
> Base in soprano,
> Struggling to keep time
> With the community below.
>
> And as I mouthed
> Your kingly image
> I trembled

Through white lace
Squinting hurriedly between the holes
Searching
For my reflection.

Soon after, I read *The Tribe of Dinah: A Jewish Women's Anthology*. In that anthology, I found Jewish feminism. I discovered a new way of thinking that combined the two inextricably connected yet seemingly disjointed parts of myself. With my former women's studies instructor and a couple of friends, I created an informal community of Jewish women. Encouraged by the new Hillel director, we decided to organize a university-based Jewish women's group.

Deciding what to call the group was a difficult process. We were afraid we might offend people by using the term *feminist*. After animated discussion, we realized that we needed our name to accurately reflect our intentions. If we tried not to offend anyone, our name would be meaningless. We became the Jewish Feminists of Kansas University, or J-FOKU (a not too oft-mentioned acronym of which we were quite proud).

Our first event was a panel discussion with Jewish feminist faculty members, called "Judaism and Feminism: Exploring the Connection." The program drew nearly a hundred students. Our feminist Seder attracted seventy participants. Inspired by our success, we decided to plan the first annual Midwest Jewish Feminist Conference, a tradition that is continued by the students every year.

I double majored in women's studies and religious studies, with a Judaic studies concentration, and wrote an honors thesis called "The Evolution of Lilith." Upon graduation, I intended to work for a Jewish women's organization. My plan was to work in the nonprofit world for a couple of years and then to head back to graduate school for a Ph.D. (in something).

But plans sometimes change. I fully intended to continue on my academic track, but each time I saw a live performance, I felt a rush of sadness wash over me, urging me to get up there, out there, in there, in here. I felt a squeaky voice within me silently waiting for its turn to speak, to sing as freely as it once had, when I was a child in Jerusalem. The voice would inch out for a second, but I dismissed it, laughing it off. There were more important things to do. Smarter things. More acceptable things, like graduate school.

But one day, I was on my way to a fellowship interview, when a spot of oiled gravel on the road changed my path, and my life. With its slippery strength, it grabbed hold of my car wheels, swinging them to the opposite direction. I fought it, trying desperately to straighten the tires. My car slipped and slid, hitting the highway guardrail three times. I escaped without a visible scratch, but the accident lingered in my body, unearthing a host of other painful memories.

The squeaky voice I had tried to ignore continued to hover. It crept in to my back, my jaw, my neck. I searched in vain for something in the medical field to relieve what was slowly becoming chronic pain. I had no choice but to seek alternative forms of healing. I wanted the pain out of my body. I wanted my body out of me. I looked up to pray, but there were no words. I looked in to pray, but there were only ideas, decisions, thoughts. My body was aching, and the voice was crying out: *Why is this pain haunting me? What is it trying to say?*

> Once, there were two friends who were beggars: one was Jewish, the other was not. Every Passover, the rich Jews of the town invited the poor Jews to their homes for a great festive meal. Passover was approaching, and the Jewish beggar had an idea: he would teach his non-Jewish friend about the Seder so that he could pretend to be a Jew. That way, he too could partake in the feast.
>
> The Jewish beggar taught his friend all about the Seder: the prayers, the songs, when to dip, when not to dip, how to lean, and so on. With lavish detail, he described the delicious meal that would follow the rituals.
>
> The two parted on Passover eve, each to a different home. The Gentile beggar performed the rituals of the Seder successfully: dipping, blessing, and doing all the right things. Nobody knew the difference. Finally, it was time for the bountiful meal.
>
> But, alas, his friend had forgotten to tell him about the maror, the bitter herbs. The beggar took one bite of the bitter herbs and spit it out. "Is this what they eat?" he thought. "This is awful!" He threw down his napkin and ran out the door, gasping for some water.
>
> The next day the two friends met up, one hungry, the other full. "What a meal," sighed the Jew. "How'd you like it?" The Gentile beggar angrily related the story of his "meal."
>
> "Oy," said the Jew. "I forgot to tell you about the bitter herbs. You see, it's just like life: sometimes you have to dip into bitterness before you can experience the pleasure."

I, too, needed to experience bitterness in my life before I could feel pleasure. During a visit to Jerusalem, I wandered into the reflexology office of the most beautiful holy woman in the world. Shulamith took one look at my feet and was somehow able to see my pain, loneliness, and yearning. She dug into the crevices of my body, the corners, and the knots. She urged me to feel, because feelings are Truth. "The peace is within you," she said, "you just need to listen." Out leaped memories, breath, tears, anger, love, and *my voice*.

Later that night, laughter sputtered out from deep within me. It had been there all along, hidden among my tears, waiting to leap out and be exposed. It yanked me into life as fully and forcefully as a baby uttering her first cry. Laughter destroyed my veil of numbness. I laughed and then I danced, sang, played, and acted. I decided to go to New York. And nothing was going to keep me quiet.

As the cars honked loudly below my New York apartment, I looked upward, begging for strength, for direction. My weary voice begged for a new name, a name befitting my new path. I thought about Jacob, who was given the name *Israel*, because he struggled with God and survived. I, too, was ready to uncover my true identity, one that proudly displayed my battle wounds, as well as the magic that accompanied them.

That night, in a dream, a large winding slide appeared before me and I knew I had to descend. A young girl approached me. Sensing my terror, she challenged me: "Why are you scared? Haven't you read 2 Proverbs?" When I woke, I reached for my Bible, and opened it to the previously untouched pages of 2 Proverbs I read:

> My child, take my words, and my commandments will direct you. Incline your ears to wisdom and your heart to understanding. For if you call out to wisdom, you will give voice to understanding. Then, you will comprehend the fear of the Holy One and find knowledge of God. (2 Proverbs II: verses 1-5)

I listened, this time letting my heart lead the way. It led me to a synagogue, where I began teaching Torah through stories. The children and I came alive as we acted out the holy passages. Soon, we expanded our repertoire to include Midrash and Jewish folklore. I researched new material, and out poured a mountain of folktales. Ancient and beautiful Jewish stories settled within me, touching a space in my heart, and resting in my soul.

As my storytelling expanded, I found places where stories wove into my life and into the lives of children, teens, college students, and adults. As I told my stories, we traveled together to another place, another world. It was a world of magic, a moment suspended in time. My life was transformed by stories, and my stories are shaped by my life.

> *Once, a rabbi gathered three of his students, and asked: "If you had one hour left in your life, what would you do?" The first student picked up his book and answered: "If I had one hour, I'd spend it studying Torah." The second student looked up: "If I had one hour, I'd spend it deep in prayer." The third student looked at the rabbi and said, "If I had one hour, I'd spend it with my family."*
>
> *"You have all given wise answers to my question," assured the rabbi, smiling.*
>
> *"But Rabbi," asked the students, "what would you do with your last hour?"*
>
> *Smiling even wider, the rabbi replied, "If I had but one hour, I'd do what I was doing. I'd do what I was doing because all of life is sacred."*

I no longer designate time during my hectic day to sift through the *Amidah*, but sometimes I tap into the silence through yoga, dance, meditation, or stories. At night, when I am alone, I still sometimes speak to God. I recite the *Sh'ma*, and my cat, Yalla, runs across the room, following the vibrations of sound to join in prayer. Then God and I talk. Sometimes, in the stillness, I sense the waves of the Divine hovering in the dark, crawling into the crevices of my body, shifting memories into stories, and stories into new beginnings.

References by Topic

PRINCE

Maasiyot U'Meshalim in *Kachavay Or* (Jerusalem, 1896) (a tale of Rabbi Nachman of Bretslav).

SHEPHERD

Danoff, Susan. "The Shepherd's Prayer." *Chosen Tales: Stories Told by Jewish Storytellers*. Ed. Peninah Schram. Northvale, NJ: Jason Aronson Inc. 76-80.

Gurion Bin, and Joseph Micha. *Mimekor Yisrael: Classic Jewish Folktales*. Vol. 3. Bloomington: Indiana University Press, 1976. 1259.

Rumi, Jelaluddin. "Moses and the Shepherd." *This Longing: Poetry, Teaching Stories, and Selected Letters*. Trans. Coleman Barks and John Moyne. Putney, VT: Threshold Books, 1988.

Tolstoy, Leo. "The Three Hermits". In *What Men Live By: Russian Stories and Legends*. Trans. Louise Maude and Aylmer Maude. New York: Pantheon, 1943. 69-76.

ABRAHAM

Frankel, Ellen. *The Classic Tales: 4,000 Years of Jewish Lore*. Northvale, NJ: Jason Aronson, Inc., 1989.
Gaster, Moses. *The Maaseh Book: Book of Jewish Tales and Legends*. Philadelphia: Jewish Publication Society, 1981.

SACREDNESS OF LIFE

This old *Hasidic* story follows a long string of storytellers, including Arthur Strimmling, Elizabeth Dunham, Doug Lipman, and Judith Black. Its original source is unknown.

JEWISH FEMINISM

Kaye/Kantrowitz, Melanie, and Irena Klepfisz, *The Tribe of Dina: A Jewish Women's Anthology*. Boston: Beacon Press, 1989.

CHILDREN'S LITERATURE

Piper, Watty, Mabel Caroline Bragg. *The Little Engine That Could*. New York: Platt & Munk, 1961.

8

Sister

ALANA SUSKIN

This is about the bones hidden in the river
Eddies in the water that are thick and grasping,
The placid surface, the current that catches.

These are the things we all fear:
    Blood, desire, hope, no hope, sleeping,
Speaking these words out loud and being ridiculed
Or understood.

What would your Ruth say to my Naomi?
"Don't follow me. Go back to your people.
Only the silence of earth is companionable to me."
Even a river speaks too loudly, and often.

You are sitting, looking up at the pink sky,
I can see the smoke from your cigarette as it rises up
Diffusing, joining into the wide, whole, holy night sky
While I sit there, and you here, burning,
Each of us full of our flames and our ashes.

9

Mazel: The Luck of the Irish

CHARLOTTE GREEN HONIGMAN-SMITH

According to decades of predictions, statistical research, and inspired sermons, I am not supposed to exist. I am the Jewish and Jewishly committed daughter of an intermarriage. My Ashkenazi mother and Irish Catholic father raised me in a Jewish home. I grew up lighting Shabbos candles and observing the Jewish holidays, major and minor. I attended a Reform religious school and was called to the Torah as a bat mitzvah. As an adult, I attended rabbinic school, was employed by the Jewish National Fund, worked for a couple of synagogues, and I sit on the board of a Jewish human rights nonprofit organization.

On the Internet, I saw a photograph of an attractive middle-aged woman with dark, curly hair and an identifiably Jewish face. She's neatly and conservatively dressed, and sits smiling into the camera before a blackboard on which some classroom notes have been scribbled in chalk. Superimposed over the photograph is a vivid green slash in the style of a no-smoking sign. This woman, whoever she is, has been banned.

I found this banned woman on the web site of the on-line magazine of the Jewish Theological Seminary (JTS). It accompanied a responsa issued by the Conservative rabbinate, answering a question about whether it is acceptable to hire a Jew who has married out of the faith to teach in a school run by the Conservative movement. The answer was no. A Jew married to a Gentile is inherently a bad role model for Jewish children. The photograph of the banned woman (who both physically and metaphorically could have been my mother) illustrated the decision.

For as long as I can remember, there has been general agreement that intermarriage is a fundamental threat to American Judaism. That idea has become so axiomatic that it's almost impossible to find words to challenge it. Intermarriage, it's said (and truly believed), is an irrevocably broken link in an ancient chain, a deadly weakening of the Jewish people. Jewish continuity—the most often evoked Jewish buzzword of the '90s—depends on the successful stemming of the dreadful tide of exogamy. My local federation's young adult newsletter carried an article from the new president of the group that discussed how "interdating" leads to intermarriage (so come to the next event and meet some Jewish singles!). *Lilith* magazine ran a cover story on the "new minority": Jews who choose Jews. A new study, announcing the same dismal news, appears in the Jewish press every six months or so. Still, the intermarriage rate has not dropped.

In casual conversation, in the Jewish press, and in High Holiday sermons, interfaith marriage is denounced. No one imagines that anyone listening might take this personally. After all, says common knowledge, the intermarried are also the "unaffiliated." They don't participate in the life of the community. And their children are lost to us forever. As I said, I'm not supposed to be here. But, as it happens, here I am.

The fundamental theological split of the Western world was presented to me as a mild family disagreement when I was five or six. I asked my parents who Jesus was, having heard the name from the little girls up the block. I was told (as I remember it), that Jesus was a great teacher who lived a long time ago, and that Daddy thought that he was the son of God, and Mommy thought that he was just a wise man. It satisfied me entirely at the time. In fact, it still works for me.

I was raised with a strong Jewish identity and a father who was not merely Gentile, but a practicing Catholic. Some believe that a child can be raised Jewishly in an interfaith marriage, but only if the Gentile parent has no real religious identity. If, however, someone in the house is actually a believer in some other religion (a branch of Christianity in particular), the child will grow up so fundamentally confused that she will never turn out "really" Jewish.

For the record, my father has been a Catholic all his life. He has been in active communion with the church for as long as I can remember. This was never hidden from me. I grew up with icons pinned to the corkboard and rosary beads on my father's dresser. I was taken to Mass as a child, and I still attend with my family on holidays and on special occasions. For several years, we even had a Christmas tree and I hunted for Easter eggs with my cousins a number of times.

I, however, was raised Jewish. I was raised in a Jewish home, with a mezuzah on the door and Hebrew books on the bookshelves. I was brought up knowing that I was a Jew because my mother was Jewish and because I was being taught to live a Jewish life. Judaism was an integral part of my childhood: sometimes loved, sometimes boring, but constant. As a child, I insisted on lighting Shabbos candles when staying over at my Catholic grandparents on Friday nights. My Jewish identity, while perhaps no greater than that of many women with two Jewish parents, is surely no less.

It was not always easy. To this day, I can't look at a copy of *Are You There God? It's Me, Margaret* without shuddering. That book (a much-loved young adult novel by Judy Blume about religious identity and puberty) caused me trouble well before puberty was anything except a word in the dictionary for me. I got at least three copies as gifts. People told me that it was about a girl "like you," that is, from a family with one Jewish parent. Margaret was nothing like me. And since I was a voracious reader, and had been tackling "young adult" material from a very young age, I was about seven or eight when I got a hold of Margaret. Margaret lives in her nonreligious home and has a father who roars "Margaret is nothing!" at his mother-in-law when the question of his child's religious identity is raised. I didn't relate, but I thought that maybe I should. I was at the age when the line between reality and stories in books or on TV is easily confused, the age when kids sometimes think they can run away from home to be like Tom Sawyer.

From Blume's book, and from the tone of the people who suggested that I read it, I learned that I was supposed to be conflicted. I think that this is why, when I was eight years old, and was interviewed by a nice lady with a camera-toting partner at the Jewish community daycare center, I told her that my mom was Jewish, and that my dad was Catholic, and that they were "always asking me which one I wanted to be." That was not true. Unfortunately it was aired on a local TV station as part of a special interest piece. My parents were troubled. I was mortified. I realized that what I'd said wasn't true, but couldn't explain, even to myself, why I said it. I felt rotten. Without quite making the connection, I shoved my copy of *Are You There God?* to the back of a small cabinet in the living room where we kept pet food. I stashed it behind the birdseed and tried to forget that it was there.

By that age, I had figured out what my role as the child of an interfaith marriage was supposed to be. In fiction, my only model was a character with no religious upbringing and no religious identity. That didn't reflect my life, but it very accurately reflected what people believe about children like me.

The official line from my religious-school teachers and Jewish day camp counselors was that my having a Gentile parent "didn't matter." They considered me undeniably Jewish. But it was clear to me that it *did* matter, since the primary focus of a Reform religious school education in the 1980s was to inoculate its pupils against assimilation. Christmas trees and intermarriage, both of which were a part of my life, represented assimilation. It was sometimes hard to figure out just what I was being told.

The truth is, I was raised in a more observant and consciously Jewish home than most of my classmates. I was the kid who always knew things like the meanings of Hebrew words, or the difference between Orthodox and Conservative Jews. Some of my knowledge resulted from my reading habits, but a lot of what I knew was due to my family's community involvement and my parents' interest in Jewish learning. I felt pretty authentic as a Jewish kid. But then there was the December Dilemma, a phrase that should never have been coined.

My beloved fifth-grade religious-school teacher told my class that Christmas wreaths represented the Crown of Thorns and that Christmas greenery in the home was a betrayal of centuries of Jewish torment under Christian oppressors. We were told an inspirational story about a little boy in a previous class of hers who, when his parents put up a Christmas tree, sat out on the porch and refused to enter their home until they threw out the tree. We were told that all of us should be prepared to do the same.

I raised my hand. (I have never been very good at being invisible.) "We have a tree, because my dad is Catholic," I said. "That's different," my teacher said. "You just have that tree for your father." I felt uneasy. It was clear from the story that having a tree in a Jewish home was a sin terrible enough to warrant defiance against one's parents. How could a tree be justified simply by the presence of my Gentile father?

I have taught religious school classes myself since then. I'm familiar with the desire to tell the kids, in no uncertain terms, that a "Hanukkah bush" is not a Jewish custom. To let them know, in language they will understand, that their defection over the wavering line of assimilation will cost their people dearly. I understand what my teacher was trying to tell us. But it's cold and lonely being ten years old and beginning to realize that one of the main points of your religious education is to prevent you from going and doing as your mother has already done—marrying out of the tribe.

The story about the little boy who refused to enter his parents' home was familiar. The story was a watered-down version of one of the core myths on which I was raised. The little boy represents the archetypal figure of Jewish survival. He is the prophet who raises an angry voice and cries out for obedience to God: Moses destroying the golden calf; Eliahu defying the prophets of Ba'al; Hannah sacrificing her children, rather than losing them to idolatry. These figures refused assimilation at all costs. To do so, of course, is a great mitzvah.

My teacher conveniently excused me from my generation's mild-mannered version of this mitzvah. At the age of ten, I was let off the hook: due to my family background, I didn't have to save the Jewish people. As any Jewish feminist can tell you, being exempted from a mitzvah is never a compliment. Jewish tradition gives respect and power to those who are obligated, not to those who are excused.

Times have changed, at least in some congregations. Once, when I taught a Hebrew class at a Reform synagogue, a lesson drifted into a discussion about the differences between Christianity and Judaism. "My grandparents, my dad's parents, are Episcopalians," one of my sixth-graders announced casually. "My dad converted, but they're still Christians, and so are my uncle and my cousins."

"Yeah, my mom is a Unitarian," said another kid. "Uh huh," someone else said. "My dad is Catholic." "Mine too!" I said, delighted. The kids nodded wisely: it happens a lot, it's all cool.

This would never have happened when I was that age. If there were other children from interfaith families in my religious school classes, it wasn't discussed. It sounds extreme to say that I was made to feel shame about my family, but I was encouraged to keep my mouth shut. The generation coming up now (at least in San Francisco), is matter-of-fact about their Gentile relations. It's not such a big deal for them. It can't be. There are too many of them.

Their numbers, and their cultural diversity, became apparent to me when I worked for the Jewish National Fund. My job included typing certificates for trees planted in Israel in honor of b'nei mitzvah by their congregations. Synagogues all over northern California sent me lists of the kids who were turning thirteen. I read the names with increasing interest and joy. There were, of course, lots of Cohns, Abulafias, and Rosenthals. There were also a good number of

McCarthys, Yamamotos, Rossinis, and Changs. Some of these were probably the children of converts, of course, but I laughed to myself as I read those lists. These were my tribe.

Like me, those kids have both Jewish and Gentile parents. And, like me, they are being raised as Jews. Their parents are members of congregations. They will, as I was, be called to the Torah as *b'nei mitzvah*. They might become religious-school teachers, rabbis, cantors, synagogue presidents, Jewish writers and artists, and Hadassah volunteers.

Dozens of times, I have been told that the children of interfaith marriages aren't raised as Jews. I reply, "I was." To which the answer is: "Most aren't like you." As time goes by, we are going to see many like me, more than anyone believed.

It's time to examine what we believe and why. Preventing inter-marriage has been a preoccupation of the American Jewish commu-nity for over forty years. The non-Orthodox community has primarily focused their argument against intermarriage on their fear of losing people, rather than in terms of *halachah*. I can't dismiss the fear of losing Jews. But despite all the fervor that goes into opposing inter-marriage, it has not declined. In addition, interfaith couples are often willing to go to great lengths to raise their children as Jews. If we're so worried about losing Jews, what are we doing to make things easier for interfaith couples who want to bring up Jewish children? Don't we have a responsibility to challenge Jews (no matter who they marry) to raise Jewish children and to continue their own Jewish education?

There is a common assumption that a Jew who marries out is already "unaffiliated." Sometimes this is a self-fulfilling prophecy. Pro-grams for interfaith parents universally assume a very low level of Jewish knowledge and practice. Having taught a course that included a number of interfaith partners, I know that this is not always the case. Jews who marry Gentiles are often both knowledgeable and committed Jews.

Any interfaith couple who is raising a Jewish child does so against the popular belief that it is impossible. Often, they face condescen-sion and obnoxious behavior from people who should know better. When I began religious school, my parents were bombarded with questions about their Christmas tree. I doubt that all-Jewish families were being quizzed about their home practices. Ironic, since the con-gregation was such an old-fashioned Reform temple that learning Hebrew was optional.

Despite the lack of institutional support, a surprisingly large number of interfaith couples have successfully raised Jewish kids. Rather than treat this population of Jewish children as an anomaly, we should accept them and consider how they will impact the future of American Judaism. The facts are clear: a very large number of American Jews are marrying non-Jews; and synagogues now have a remarkable number of Jewish children with Gentile family members who are part of their Jewish communities.

The American Jewish community must begin to think in new ways about intermarriage and the families that intermarriage creates. We must be willing to reexamine common assumptions and come up with new ideas about what constitutes a Jewish family. We are going to have to articulate and define more clearly the responsibilities of a Jewish parent. And also, we need to clarify the responsibility of the congregation or community to that Jewish parent.

I could claim that I'm an activist for human rights today because of my Jewish heritage and my feminist principles. It would be easy to credit the legacy of Emma Goldman and Abraham Joshua Heschel and the concept of *tzedek*. Jews are called upon to stand with the oppressed and do justice.

But there are other aspects of my identity that contribute to my commitment to social justice. I do not have to renounce my father's heritage in order to be a Jew. My Irish Catholic dad borrowed a *tallis*, and made up a song in honor of having been arrested with a bunch of rabbis in front of the Soviet Consulate. My father has given more than twenty years of devoted activism to the movement for Soviet and post-Soviet Jews. I believe that his sense of responsibility to the oppressed is at least partly due to his Catholic education.

Irish history, literature, culture, and music: all these, I claim as my own. I was taught, as a child, that the Irish are crazy poets and tough fighters who never back down from doing what's right. I still believe this. I am Irish-American and proud of it. My Catholic and Celtic inheritances are also intrinsically part of me. And I believe that what I take from my Irish heritage makes me a better Jew.

I am tired of regularly having to educate people not to insult my family to my face. I get angry at the casual remarks people make when they don't realize that my father is not Jewish. I once listened to a coworker talk for fifteen minutes about how Jews who married Gentiles were "granting Hitler a posthumous victory." He tried to include me in his diatribe, asking, "Would you marry a man who wasn't Jewish?" I was glad to be given the opportunity to shut him up. I replied, "It was good enough for my mother, and it's good enough for me." And I have to admit, I grinned a little while he spluttered.

I get angry when I'm told that I'm an exception, that all other interfaith families are ignorant, and raise their children with "nothing." Now, when I realize I'm about to hear another sermon about "preventing your children from marrying out," I leave the sanctuary. I wonder if it ever occurs to the rabbis who deliver those sermons that inevitably, sitting in the sanctuary are Jews married to Gentiles, Jews whose children are married to Gentiles, and Jews with a Gentile parent.

My father's dedication to working on behalf of Jews in the former Soviet Union inspired me to serve on the board of a Jewish nonprofit agency that does advocacy and community support for that population. At one meeting, I complained when the local federation cut our funding for yet another year. A fellow board member spoke up in defense of the budget cut, saying: "We have to think about Jewish continuity."

"What about Jewish continuity in Russia?" I demanded. "They're in worse shape than Jews in the San Francisco Bay Area."

"We have to think about the children," she chided. "People with children understand how important that is, especially with all the intermarriage and everything that's happening today."

I put my hands flat on the table in front of me and practiced deep breathing. I know that she knows. If my presence—as a synagogue member, an employee of a Jewish agency, and a member of the board of this organization—does not interfere with her fantasy of what intermarriage produces, probably nothing will. And hitting her with the coffeepot would be violent and counterproductive. I let it go.

But when I found that photograph of the banned woman on the web, I wasn't willing to let it go. I wrote to JTS and demanded that they remove the graphic from their web site. My anger was visceral and unexpected. Perhaps it was because the woman in the picture had black curly hair like my mother's. Perhaps it was the intense hostility represented by the placement of such a powerful symbol over a human face.

My mother has worked in Jewish community agencies for most of her adult life. She taught me to light Shabbos candles, and listened for hours as I practiced chanting the *Fir Kashes* before the Pesach seder. She raised a Jewish child. To see the banned woman infuriated me. They had marked my mother *treif*. I wanted that picture down, and I wanted it down immediately.

It was a small victory. JTS responded to my e-mail and removed the graphic. It remains cataloged in their archive, but it has been removed from that particular web page. Of course, the responsa that accompanied the photo is still there. The official position of the Jewish Theological Seminary remains the same: a Jew married to a non-Jew is an unfit role model for Jewish children. I realize that while I won the battle over the graphic, the debate over who is, and who is not a good Jew, is a much larger issue.

My own status as a role model is also tenuous when judged by those standards. I recently watched a debate on a Jewish feminist e-mail list with mounting frustration: I discovered that no rabbinic college in the United States will accept a student with a non-Jewish partner. Some time ago, I did a year of rabbinic school, and left because the time wasn't right for me. Ever since, I vaguely planned to go back and finish someday. I've since learned that if I stay with the non-Jewish man I am currently dating, I won't be accepted anywhere as a candidate for *smicha*.

I don't plan to leave the man I am in love with to seek ordination. I will have to make plans without considering the rabbinate for now. Times do change, and so do policies. And I have limits—very clear ones—about how far I will allow the changing whims of the Reform and Conservative movements of America to dictate my Jewish life.

Still, it's the Reform movement's nontraditional approach to interfaith marriages that angers me the most. In the 1980s, the Reform rabbinate passed a resolution on the status of patrilineal Jews. Essentially, this document states that a child of one Jewish parent is considered Jewish if she demonstrates, through her involvement with Jewish religious life, a commitment to Jewish identity.

I find this approach problematic. I was raised to believe that I'm Jewish, because my mother is Jewish. Under current doctrine, if my parents had raised me without Jewish identity or community, the Reform movement, in theory, might not acknowledge me as a Jew. This makes me crazy: why should my Jewish status as the daughter of a Jewish woman (unchallenged since Rabbi Yehuda ha-Nasi compiled the Mishnah), be suddenly up for grabs? And what about my future children? I intend to raise my children in a Jewish home, and give them a Jewish education. I plan to bring up proud, conscious, educated Jews. I am outraged to think that anyone would say that my children have more to prove than other Jewish children. Does the

Reform movement plan to have them jump through even more hoops to prove that they're Jews?

This issue also raises a challenge for me as a Jewish feminist: am I valuable to my people only as the wife of a Jewish man? Is my worth to my community solely defined by whom I marry and whose children I give birth to? I don't believe so. We must find a better way to adapt to the realities of intermarriage without resorting to the creation of a group of probationary Jews.

I now define myself as a nondenominational Jew. I may eventually feel at home in a contemporary Reform synagogue, but as long as the movement's leadership threatens my status as a member of the tribe, however slightly, I will not feel comfortable calling myself a "Reform Jew." I currently define myself as a quasi-*halachic* feminist, who is deeply committed to both secular and spiritual Jewish culture.

My beliefs are closer to the *halachah* and philosophy of the Conservative movement, except for the fact that the United Synagogue of Conservative Judaism is not willing to accept intermarriage at this time. That means that I'm not considered acceptable. I'm a package deal with my family. I live and work in the Jewish community as the Irish-Ashkenazi activist, writer, and loudmouth that I am. I won't be made ashamed of any part of myself.

People are quick to offer biblical examples of intermarriages that reflect their feelings about modern-day intermarriage. They project their negative feelings onto Moses for choosing his non-Jewish wife, Tzipporah, and on the foreign wives that Ezra railed against. I rarely hear about Hiram, an obscure character from the First Book of Kings. He too, was a child of an interfaith marriage. Hiram was the son of a craftsman from Tyre and a woman from the tribe of Dan. He was the metalworker responsible for the brass and copper work for Solomon's Temple. Presumably, he learned his skills from his Gentile father, and he brought those talents to his work on the First Temple. Hiram is my role model. He is proof that for the past three thousand years, the children of interfaith marriages have been making rich contributions to the Jewish world.

I have confidence in the McCarthy and Yamamoto kids at Sherith Israel. They, too, are growing up to be fabulous Jews who will bring the strength of their multifaceted identities to the Jewish people. I have confidence that together, as American Jews, we can find the right answers. With a little mazel, and the luck of the Irish, perhaps someday we will.

References

Lilith: The Independent Jewish Women's Magazine. New York, NY: Lilith Publications, 1976.

Blume, Judy. *Are You There God? It's Me, Margaret*. Englewood Cliffs, NJ: Bradbury Press, 1970.

II
Nefesh

Ourselves in Relation to Our Bodies

10

Blessings in Boxes

GABRIELLE KAPLAN-MAYER

As a child, I never saw anyone lay *tefillin*. I never touched their leather straps in my hand. At our small Reform temple in Altoona, Pennsylvania, I learned the *aleph-bet*. I learned about Abraham, Isaac, and Jacob, and sometimes about their wives and children. I collected canned food for hungry people because, I learned, that is a valuable and necessary part of being a Jew. Once, I was so excited to be called to the *bimah* to light a candle for Hanukkah that I accidentally set my prayer pamphlet on fire.

The Judaism I knew was comfortable and pleasant, almost Protestant. Most of the service was in English, and the hymns were accompanied by organ music. When I brought my Christian friends to Friday night services, they said it was really just like church, except for the strange standing up and sitting down.

I sometimes felt God in the purple flame of the Shabbat candles that my mother sometimes lit. But I grew up hungry to find the God I knew in my bones, in my dreams, in the ocean, and in the sunset. This hunger, this desire, has led me to places I never expected.

In my early twenties, while pursuing a career as a playwright and performer, I felt drawn to Jewish text study. I explored how ancient Jewish rituals fit into my own ultracontemporary, urban life. I became so enamored with Judaism that I began to imagine myself as a Jewish teacher: a rabbi. I applied and was accepted to two rabbinic schools. I chose to attend the Reconstructionist Rabbinical College, and I eagerly prepared for my move to Philadelphia.

Inspired by my packing, my mother went looking through one of my grandma's boxes. A few years before, my grandma had moved to a nursing home, so she could be closer to our house in Altoona. My mom and I had maniacally packed her things, wrapping cups, and saucers in newspaper and throwing clothes into heaps. No longer in fashion, but too good to give away, we hung her suits and skirts in plastic bags. We packed in a daze, in a dream. I am the dutiful daughter of a dutiful daughter.

We have not yet sorted through all of those boxes. I spend my days exploring the strange, dusty boxes of my family's journeys. I will pack and unpack these boxes as long as I live.

The night before I left for school, my mother (the insomniac) knocked on my bedroom door every fifteen minutes or so, showing me some lost treasure. Just as I was going to sleep, she came to my room one last time. She held a brown velvet bag with Hebrew letters embroidered with orange and green stitches. "Do you want these?" she asked, "They belonged to my Zayde, Jake." I opened the bag and pulled out the brown cracking *tefillin*. I unwrapped the long leather straps and let them fall through my fingers. I didn't know what to do with them.

I packed them with my things, in a special bag that I wouldn't let the movers touch. They sat on the passenger seat of my car, on the short trip from my parents' home. It was a trip that I would take forward and backward, time and again.

That night, like so many others, I spoke quietly as I lay in bed after I said the *Sh'ma*. My ritual is to I ask things of my dreams. This is the way I communicate with the Divine. I ask for pictures and sometimes I make the pictures into words, and then into poems. They break through my thoughts into my heart. They live in the place that I mean when I say the *Modah ani*. It is my *neshamah*, my "life force," and my creative power. I go there in dreams.

That night, I asked for a teacher to show me how to lay *tefillin*. I asked if I needed to lay *tefillin*. I asked about my great-grandfather Jake and about why I had been given that gift. I cried softly with exhaustion and fear and confusion as the questions bubbled in my brain. I fell asleep and woke up again around three in the morning to pee. On the toilet I was overcome by a feeling of peace. An angel whispered: "Relax, a teacher will show you about the *tefillin*. Keep them with you. That's all. Go back to your dreams."

In my preparatory year at rabbinical school, I studied Hebrew, so that (God willing), I could read directly from our ancient texts the following year. I also took a class called "Jewish Traditions," a survey course for students like me who did not grow up in a "traditional" Jewish home.

On the syllabus for the course, the professor listed a requirement: we were to take on a traditional Jewish practice that we have never done before. I thought of the *tefillin*. The professor was a rabbi named Shai Gluskin. He shared his journey of coming back to Jewish practice with the class. He is a patient and kind man, and I asked him to teach me how to lay *tefillin*.

On a brilliant October morning, I went to Shai's house and helped him measure wood for his sukkah. We set up the basic structure of the booth that would be covered with just enough *schach* to let stars shine through in the dark. Shai showed me the basics of laying *tefillin*, how to wind them, the *brachas*, which box goes where. It wasn't so difficult, so mysterious. They fit well on my head. I had a book at home that helped me with directions.

Putting on the *tefillin* by myself for the first time was a nightmare. I knew I was winding them the wrong way—the goddamned pictures in the book didn't help me at all. I forgot to say the right *brachah*. It took twenty minutes just to get them on. I thought: *Forget it; who needs this; what the hell does this have to do with God? Maybe I'll talk to Shai about doing something else.*

I went home for Thanksgiving vacation, and talked to a member of the congregation about my new practice of laying *tefillin*. I mentioned that I had never seen a pair of *tefillin* when I was growing up. She told me that I was being ridiculous, and pointed toward a pair that lay in the glass case across from the secretary's office, by the social hall. In disbelief, I sprinted to the case and the *tefillin* were there, exactly as she had said. They were displayed with some other very old Judaica, and some certificates awarded to the now defunct brotherhood, for money they raised to benefit the Society for the Blind. I had walked past that case at least three times a week during the formative years of my life, but I had never seen them. At our temple, *tefillin* live in a remote case that no one looks at, on a top shelf where no child can see them. They are like second-rate museum relics: not worth much, but not easy to throw away.

With new resolve, I decided to try wrapping *tefillin* again. My pride and arrogance saved me: I'm not a quitter. I read the book again, studying the pictures intently. I set my alarm so that I had thirty extra minutes to practice. It got easier. I looked in the mirror and I even kind of liked my reflection. It made me smile, made me laugh, this huge wooden box resting on my head. It began to feel comfortable. I wondered: *what does my great-grandfather Jake think?*

I decided to wear them in public, at the Tuesday morning *minyan* at school. Lots of people wear them, lots of women, I reassured myself. But when I got there, I panicked: *I'll do it wrong, and someone will see me. They won't believe my ignorance. It will offend them. But that's crazy,* I convinced myself, *if I can't remember what to do, I'd just ask someone. I'm a new student; who would be upset?* I reminded myself that I'm a perfectionist and that it's only me who is embarrassed when I can't do something well. I remembered that I had been given my great-grandfather's *tefillin* and given a teacher. My self-doubt subsided: *I know how to lay them. I will do it in public. That's that.*

The first time I wrapped my *tefillin* in a room with other rabbinic students and faculty, I hoped that none of them noticed the shaking in my hands. I closed my eyes and breathed deeply as I said the *brachas.* I sat down with my siddur and I noticed people looking at me, smiling. Jake's *tefillin* are not the kind most people use today. They are big wooden boxes with straps that fold and unfold automatically, as they did in my great-grandfather's hands six days a week. I closed my eyes as I *davened.* I felt hands resting above my head, strong sweet ancient male hands. The were not touching me exactly, just sort of hovering above, blessing me. A thick field of energy was coming from his hands to my head. It was my great-grandfather. I thought: *Hello, Jakie. It's good to know you.* I began to cry, really cry as I prayed, and I thought of Hannah, who was the first to cry as she prayed. I didn't care who saw.

I don't know much about my great-grandfather Jake. He came to this country just after the turn of the century. He was a young man from Russia, a peddler. He worked hard enough so he could open a grocery store in Phillipsburg, New Jersey. My grandma said much more about her mother, Sarah: how modern she was, how intelligent. She encouraged my grandma to go to college, which was unheard-of in those days. And even though she had five children herself, she talked about Margaret Sanger and birth control.

Grandma said that her father was a pious man, and that he spent most of his time working in the store. This much I know about him: during the Great Depression, he gave food away. He marked people down for credit in a book, but he never bothered if he got paid. He fed his wife and children, and even sent them off to college, but he never bothered if he got paid.

I also know that like me, he had diabetes. He developed the illness late in life, and was probably among the first to get insulin shots. I have had juvenile diabetes since I was ten years old. As a kid, it was painful to stick myself with needles and to worry about what I was eating; to get low blood sugar at school and to be afraid of passing out. I had dark thoughts about the future, about all the complications that could happen. I imagined my life if I would lose a leg or go blind. People were always telling me stories about their aunt or someone, whose kidneys had failed or whose fingers got gangrene, as if that would help.

My diabetes has been a blessing and a curse in the truest sense, and I'm just starting to come to terms with that, in a deep way, in a peace-making way. The blessing part is this: every day I think about my choice to live. Without the insulin, it would be over. A tiny needle gives me the stuff to keep going. I want to be as healthy as I can be. I want to live a long time. I am full of love for people and animals, love for colors and smells and books. I think I have a lot to do here on earth.

Every few months, I take a blood test called the "Hemoglobin AIC" that measures an average of my blood glucose level during that time-span. For as long as I can remember, the results have shown my average sugar level outside of the normal range. When blood glucose levels are too high over extended periods of time, complications like blindness, kidney disease, nerve damage, digestive disorders, and heart problems can occur.

During the first months that I saw my new endocrinologist, Dr. Weiss, I made some serious changes to my insulin, exercise, and diet. But still, my blood sugars were averaging way too high. He talked to me about getting an insulin pump, a small machine that filters doses of insulin to me throughout the day, just like a real working pancreas would. The machine is attached to a tube that is attached to a needle that would go in my belly. It is worn like a beeper on a belt, he explained.

Before I met Dr. Weiss, I had never even been willing to hear about the pump, because I am vain. I reasoned that as a single woman, I couldn't possibly wear the pump. I didn't want to wear it, because I could not imagine an external thing sticking out of my body, a man-made thing attached to me, twenty-four hours a day. How could I ever be seen as attractive again? I wouldn't hear of it. I would rather suffer.

I had gone through my adolescence feeling like damaged goods because of the illness in my body. Because my pancreas didn't function like other people's, I didn't feel like a whole person. I imagined rejection; that no one could ever really love me if I were to become very sick one day.

To cope with the schism of holding that belief, while at the same time longing to love and to be loved, I entered a deep state of denial. I tried to look as healthy as I possibly could. I had diabetes, but no one had to see it. No one needed to witness my blood sugar swings. Not even a lover needed to know that my body could deteriorate if I didn't take care of myself.

My attitude allowed me to stay at an arm's length from my illness, and from the fear of sickness and death that it represented to me. I could make myself look pretty and vital, and pretend nothing was wrong. Once, on a first date, dinner was delayed for half an hour because of a Saturday night rush in a trendy restaurant. My blood sugar dropped, because I needed food. I felt so dizzy that I excused myself to go to the ladies' room, where I sat on a toilet and shoved a Hershey bar down my throat to avoid passing out.

I invented every excuse I could think of not to get the pump. I explained to the doctor that I was in the middle of my second semester of rabbinical school, and that I didn't have the time I needed for the drastic adjustment. Dr. Weiss pointed out that there might never be an ideal time.

I thought about my *tefillin*, of the way those ancient brown boxes connect to my body, how they fit, and what richness they bring me. I thought of their beauty, of how the external symbol penetrates right through my flesh, right into my heart. The pump is even similar in dimension to the boxes of Jakie's *tefillin*. So why not an insulin pump that could help to lengthen my life? Inventions help us sustain and improve our quality of life, I reasoned. These too, are part of creation, of our divine unfolding plan.

I knew that once I said yes to the pump, there was no going back. My beliefs and behavior would have to shift. I was terrified, but I could no longer sit in a toilet stall bordering on unconsciousness, just to avoid looking weak.

Something was opening in me. The months of laying those *tefillin* across my heart, over my hand, and on my mind were shifting my psyche. The *tefillin* I choose to wrap, are straps of honesty and integrity: mine and Jake's. I am not in this game of life only for myself. I need to be healthy to carry out important work, to live out the important teachings of my ancestors. I now know that I would rather live with fear showing on my face, than to continue trying to hide it. The universe holds great forces of injustice and mercy, and I have the choice to live in fear or in strength. As I committed to living each day with honor, the universe returned the commitment, and promised to take care of me.

I told Dr. Weiss I would get the pump right after Pesach. I wanted the experience of again leaving Egypt, and crossing the Red Sea, and that way, I had two weeks off from school to prepare myself. Dr. Weiss felt it would be best to monitor my blood sugars as we tried to find the correct insulin dosage. So I arranged to take off two days of school to spend in the hospital. My body would be going through adjustments as I moved from using long-acting insulin, to the more efficient pump that would give me continual insulin in small amounts.

I was a little freaked out about telling my professors that I'd be missing classes for a few days. Despite my worries, none of them were concerned that I'd fall behind. They encouraged me to do whatever I needed to take care of my health. They sent good wishes and prayers. I was the only one who held superhuman expectations for myself. No one thought that I was too sick or weak or not perfect enough to become a rabbi.

The day of my first pump insertion was a brilliant Wednesday morning in April. My friend Melissa picked me up in the morning and drove me to the hospital. I felt excited about my decision, and surprisingly was not scared at all. Since I'd been diagnosed with diabetes at age ten, I had not felt so in control of my health.

A representative from the Diesetronic Company came by first thing in the morning and showed me how to insert the pump. It wasn't hard. I played around in the bathroom mirror, figuring out different ways to wear it on my clothes.

The first day in the hospital was wonderful. My friends called and came by all day. Shai, the rabbi who taught me to lay tefillin, phoned to make sure I was okay. I paid for cable TV, but didn't have time to watch it, because I was having so much fun. It felt like a celebration of my health and of my life.

Dr. Weiss was supportive as we worked to find the right insulin dose. Within hours, my blood sugars stayed in the normal range, which hadn't happened to me in a sustained way for quite some time. I was filled with hope. Hope was a giant bubble of love percolating in my heart and rising in my throat. Hope was in each visit and phone call; it was in the flowers my sister, brother-in-law, and nephew sent me; and in the red lipstick and trashy magazine my friend Rachel brought. I wanted to dance and scream and shout: life! Life! LIFE! I didn't care that the nurses had to wake me up every two hours all night to measure my blood sugar. I wanted to be there to experience all of the love that the universe could hold. I knew, for the first time, that I had some power in making that reality come to be.

The second morning I woke up exhausted and scared. My blood sugar had gone up the last few hours of the night (an occurrence common in diabetics called the "dawn phenomenon"). I realized that the pump wasn't a cure, just a way to make taking the insulin adjustments a lot easier. It would still take a lot of work to keep my blood sugars within the normal range.

I looked out my hospital window and felt incredibly small and insignificant. I saw people walking quickly back and forth; doctors, nurses, and technicians rushed through the courtyard on their way to save and lose lives. I saw people smoking cigarettes and drinking coffee, others sitting on benches, holding their heads with grief. I wondered what was going on at school, and what antics my beautiful cats were up to in my apartment. I got scared that the pump wouldn't work for me, that my two or three days in the hospital would turn into infinite days or weeks.

I remembered being in the hospital when I was first diagnosed as a little girl. My mother stayed with me at night, because I was too scared to sleep. I remembered how the doctors poked me and how I hated them, how people came by to say how sorry they were to hear that I was diabetic.

I took a deep breath and put on my *tallit* and my *tefillin*. As I wrapped the leather strap around my middle finger, I said the traditional *kavannah* from the Book of Hosea: "And I betroth you to me forever, I betroth you to me with righteousness and justice, I betroth you to me with loving kindness and compassion, and you shall know *Adonai*." As I said these words, I began to breathe and weep and my tears held all of those memories. As I *davened* the morning blessings, I felt my tears watering my strength. It was truly a wedding ceremony for me. I vowed to lead the most hopeful life I could, and to not be hindered by pain of my past experiences as a diabetic.

After I had finished my prayers and rewound my *tefillin* straps, Dr. Weiss came by and we worked on changes in my dose to counter the dawn phenomenon. I went for a short walk, and chatted with a man in the hospital lobby who worked at the coffee cart. He asked about my insulin pump and I explained. He said, "God bless you" and I said, "Thanks." I went back to my room and worked on my biblical Hebrew assignment from the Book of Ruth.

I was allowed to leave the hospital by Friday afternoon. Dr. Weiss made sure I'd have plenty of time to get home and prepare for Shabbat. A friend came over and brought dinner, and I managed to figure how much insulin to dial into the pump without much trouble. I felt tired, but good.

On Sunday, I went on a second date with a man who is now my boyfriend. He has been incredibly supportive. My fears about not being attractive because of the little catheter tube have been completely disproved. If anything, my positive feelings about my health and my body have increased our romantic and spiritual connection.

Since getting the pump, I've talked to other women with pumps, who share similar experiences. Even Miss America 1998, Nicole Johnson, is a pump wearer. Obviously, a deep commitment to one's health is a very attractive quality. I was sort of a bonehead not to get that.

The next few weeks of pump wearing resembled my first attempts at wearing *tefillin*, only worse, because life and death were at stake. Almost everything I did was wrong. I forgot how to change the batteries and how to deal with air bubbles in the tube. I misjudged my carbohydrate counting. I gave myself too little or too much insulin when I did yoga or went running. I sat in classes barely paying attention, taking my blood sugar with my little blood glucose monitor every forty minutes or so because I couldn't get my adjustments right. There were times when I just wanted to rip it off. I spoke with Dr. Weiss every night on the phone.

I stayed home from school one day because I'd been up throughout the night having low blood sugars. In the morning, with little sleep and still feeling dizzy, I cried when I opened my closet and looked at my clothes. I couldn't figure out where to attach the pump when wearing my favorite dresses. I went to the mall and broke down while talking to a saleswoman. She told me about her diabetic father and assured me that I'd made the right move. We found some cute pants and skirts that made it easy to wear the pump. I charged way too much on my credit card, but I didn't care.

I was letting the world watch me go through this transition—my friends, professors, salespeople, you name it. I was sometimes bold and sometimes exhausted, sometimes strong and sometimes scared. But I wasn't hiding my diabetes, my struggles, or my choices. I was letting the universe witness my process and getting love love love in return.

The first Shabbat morning that I felt up to it, I went to my synagogue and asked for an *aliyah*. I asked that my *Misheberach* blessing be in honor of my new insulin pump, and in appreciation of the great care my doctor had given me. I felt elated as I chanted the blessings before and after the Torah reading: *Bless Adonai, the blessed one! Blessed is Adonai, now and forever.*

There is no logical way to explain the power I feel as I hear the words of Torah. What lies in the scroll is pure mystery to me. Sometimes the words inspire me, and at other moments they enrage me. The process of connecting to those words, which have been transmitted from one generation to the next, is a power that I can't begin to understand. That morning, I moved very close to the Torah reader, and I was shaking as I held the Torah scroll.

As I stood before my congregation, I felt the marriage between my health and me moving from the betrothal state to *yichud*, our sacred, private time of joining together. A sacred union was born and sanctified inside me as I stood before my community.

My friend Jason hugged me hard after I was blessed. He sensed that something out of the ordinary was happening. That hug is what Torah represents to me: there are letters in the white spaces between the black words. We don't logically know them, but they dance with the black letters of our reality. It takes faith, devotion, and intuition to look at all of the words in the Torah, and to let ourselves see what we can't see.

I am getting used to wearing my insulin pump. "Wear" is a funny word for it: the pump is not something you throw on, like a sweater. It is not like a pair of earrings that you absolutely need to hang from your ears to make an outfit look just right. But what is the correct phrase to describe this relationship? I am attached to my insulin pump. I am one with my insulin pump. My pump is in me, is part of me. It is as delicate as any other part of the complex systems of cells, veins, arteries, and organs that allow me to think, move, feel, and breathe.

But unlike my other vital organs, I am extremely intimate with this new part of my body. Every time I eat something, I dial the correct amount of insulin needed on its tiny computer, to cover the carbohydrate in the food. I decrease or increase my level of insulin through the dial, depending on my activity. I change the vials of insulin in the pump once a week. Every two or three days, I change the small catheter tube that carries insulin from the body of the pump to my own body. And I can detach from the pump for finite periods of time by choice, by removing the tubing from my body.

On my twenty-eighth birthday, I learned that the numbers for two and eight in Hebrew spell *koach*, "strength." That was the year of my strength. For much of my life, I had feared and pushed away my strength. Now, with each choice I make, my strength breathes through me, demanding to be free. I can no longer keep my strength down, and I don't want to.

Mostly, I don't feel my pump: it doesn't hurt me in any way and I don't think about it being there. It simply is. It is a miracle for me. Each day, life is miraculous and also mundane. It goes on. It gets sweeter, deeper, and richer. I marvel at my body, at the house of my soul. I marvel that the disease I once thought of as my body's failing has turned out to be my greatest teacher.

Now, on some mornings I lay *tefillin* and on other mornings I do yoga. I see how I feel that day. I like yoga: how my chest opens up when I breathe deeply, how my shoulders relax. I like to stretch every part of my body, to relax into the stretches from my eyebrows to my little toes. On the days I do yoga, I say the *Modah Ani* and *Sh'ma* and try to be sort of Jewish about the whole thing. Then I jump in the shower, get dressed, test my blood sugar, make coffee, put on makeup, feed my cats, pack my lunch, and grab my books for school. As I walk out the door I inevitably forget something. When I return to my bedroom, I see the *tefillin* bag sitting there. I pick it up and kiss it. I need help every day, to be reminded with visceral physical objects, of how precious, sweet, sad, and wonderful the gift of life is. My great-grandfather's *tefillin* really help me, and so does my pump.

I have become an advocate. Now, I'm happy to talk about my diabetes, and to explain about my pump when people ask me. Usually, someone mentions an aunt or friend or father who is diabetic. Instead of focusing on complications, I give them information about the pump. I have had a lot of e-mail dialogues and phone calls with other diabetics. Before getting the pump, I wouldn't have done this; I preferred to stew in the privacy of my self-destructive juices.

This fall, I'm planning to do a walk for juvenile diabetes. I intend to raise a lot of money for research. If enough money is raised, a cure could happen in my lifetime. I now allow myself to believe that a cure can happen; I can imagine the freedom of my life without diabetes, a life of sweetness and strength and balance. I will do all that I can to make that day a reality: it is part of my work here, my contract with the Divine, and my individual contribution to healing the earth.

I've been wearing my *tefillin* for almost a year now. When I daven with them, I kiss the boxes as I say the words of the commandment to "bind them as a sign upon my hand, and let them be symbols before my eyes." I want to kiss my insulin pump, too. I want to add my own prayer, something like: "Be aware of the miracle of existence and don't be an asshole." I don't know. I'll keep working on it.

I told my parents that I wanted my own set of *tefillin* for my twenty-eighth birthday. Jake's are quite delicate, and the *shlepping* my life requires are causing them some damage. They are precious to me and I want to protect them. I'd like my own children to see them one day. The *tefillin* hold a story inside them that they must survive to tell.

Maybe someone will find my *tefillin* someday and say, "These were my great-grandmother Gabrielle's *tefillin*." What stories will they carry? What will my leather straps say? My *tefillin* will say that I didn't let my illness stop me from opening up to love, and that I faced my life with strength. And I know with certainty that they will be filled with my love of Judaism.

My new *tefillin* arrived in the mail a week after my birthday, but I haven't opened them yet. I'm not ready. I love my great-grandfather Jake's so much, and I am a little scared to start with my own. But I will break in the new ones soon; I can feel it. I will ask the universe to let me know when I should begin.

11

At Home in My Own Skin

CLARA THALER

My mother draped me in pink from the moment I left the womb. I was born thirteen years after my parents were married, and they knew I was going to be their last child. After two boys, my mother had hoped fervently for a girl. There are photos of me as a newborn with a delicate pink bow Scotch-taped to my few strands of hair. My mother dressed me in frilly, ruffled outfits, and surrounded me with dolls and tea sets. When I was older, she painted my nails and pierced my ears.

She believed that being female was about ornamentation and appearance. Her own womanhood involved meticulous attention to her hair, makeup, nails, and clothing. She was proud of her appearance, and wanted her daughter to feel a similar pride, to celebrate herself in a similar fashion. In her eyes, my girlhood allowed me access to a special, exalted place filled with makeup and shopping excursions, gossip, and trips to the beauty parlor. I was a part of a magic circle from which my brothers were excluded.

Despite her efforts, I am not a graceful woman today. I took ballet lessons for years, but I always felt fat in my leotard. I don't remember how to stand in third position, but I can still recall the cruel remarks from the other girls. My mother had to remind me to sit with my knees together when I wore a skirt, because I had a hard time remembering.

I was in seventh grade when I got my first period. I left computer class to pee and saw a blotch of blood in my pink underwear. I stuffed some toilet paper in my underpants and walked home that afternoon with my brother, as usual. When I got home, I nonchalantly asked my mother to take me to get some sanitary napkins. She responded with complete enthusiasm. The look on her face told me that I had passed over a threshold; I had entered the inner sanctum.

Around that time, my mother bought me my first bra. The plain white bra strap broke on the first day I wore it to school. I tugged on it all day; the boys in choir class leaned over, pointing at me and snickering.

As my friends began to prepare for their bat and bar mitzvahs, I resisted. The thought of public scrutiny terrified me. I informed my parents that I wasn't interested. My mother tried to persuade me to consider, but I was convinced. I'd see my brother go through the ordeal, and I knew it wasn't for me.

I was five when my oldest brother had his bar mitzvah. I remember him standing on the *bimah* with a *tallis* draped around his shoulders and a white, faux-satin yarmulke perched on his head. He had a terrible haircut and angry-looking acne. I don't remember the ceremony at all, but I can't forget how much he complained about being forced to memorize line after line of Hebrew. After the party, he whined that the meager amount of presents hadn't made his suffering worth it. Then I had to witness the misery all over again, when my other brother went through it.

Their experience persuaded me; I echoed my brothers' objections loudly and insistently. My parents' desire to raise independent and confident children was stronger than their wavering commitment to Jewish rituals, so they allowed me to have my way. At the time, I felt relieved and grateful. But years later, when I felt uncertain about my Jewish identity, I regretted my decision. I think the memory of a bat mitzvah might have grounded me. Maybe I wouldn't have felt so lost.

My brothers and I received the same Jewish education that my parents had—formally weak, but culturally rich. Our parents both grew up in New York, and were raised in Jewish neighborhoods by Russian parents. My parents' conversation was peppered with the Yiddish they learned as children. Like me, they grew up with parents who felt more loyalty to their cultural heritage than to the tenets of their religion.

As a child, my mother went to shul once a year, on Yom Kippur. But even then, she rarely went inside the sanctuary. When her family arrived at the synagogue, her father instructed his wife and daughters to wait outside. When my mother first told me this story, I asked if she ever wondered what was going on inside; whether she could hear the singing or understood any of the prayers. She told me that she remembered feeling bored. "I just wanted to go home," she explained, "being Jewish had nothing to do with shul."

Unlike their own parents, my parents made a conscious effort to educate their children about Judaism. They encouraged us to go to temple and attend Hebrew school. But I was the third of three children: by the time I was six or seven, my parents had run out of steam. Eventually, we began to follow our family's tradition of going to temple only on the High Holidays.

The only thing I remember about those mornings at temple each year is the colors: the stained glass window behind the rabbi, and the Torah scrolls covered with deep blue and red velvet. I have no memories of the rabbi's voice, or of the words he said. The eternal flame mesmerized me; my mother had once whispered that its light never died. I contemplated this puzzle endlessly: it had to be a lightbulb, I reasoned. *But how could they be sure it wouldn't go out in the middle of services? That would be so embarrassing.*

By the time I was twelve or thirteen we stopped going to temple, even on the High Holidays. Instead, my Jewish education continued in the form of bagels and lox, chopped liver and brisket, and blintzes and latkes (the frozen kind). I was also fed a steady diet of Jewish humor. I even adopted patterns of speech that I only later discovered were particularly Jewish.

My parents' lax commitment to temple paralleled the sporadic way they celebrated the other Jewish holidays. Our menorah was a tiny row of stone people with upturned hands. I remember pressing the Hanukkah candles into their hard palms. My oldest brother was the only one of us who could recite all the words to the blessing. We remembered to light the candles for the first and second nights, some years even the third. *When did we start forgetting to light all the candles?*

I have very strong memories of our Christmas celebrations. I grew up believing in Santa Claus, a fact that in later years made me wonder whether I was really Jewish. When I was in first grade, I told my friends that I was half-Christian and half-Jewish, to explain why I celebrated both Christmas and Hanukkah. Years later, I learned to justify our celebration by crediting my mother's love of the secular side of Christmas.

My family was better about Passover than Hanukkah. My aunt and uncle usually held the seders, complete with good linen tablecloths, Manischevitz wine, haggadahs with orange and brown covers, and an obscene-looking shank bone. My aunt and uncle's house smelled like delicious food and polished wood. From their deck, I could see the sun set over their sprawling land, and I watched the darkening green mountains in the distance. I loved every part of the seder, especially when it was my turn to read.

When we read about the four children, the implication was always: which child are you? When I was young, the wicked child fascinated me. Later, I felt a kinship with the child who did not know how to ask; I too felt muted by my own ignorance.

The Passovers at our own house were shorter, less magical. We complained about every ritual, and rushed through the haggadah to get to the meal. Looking back, I feel sorry about how much I complained. Now, I relish each moment, each syllable, and ponder my place in the chain that connects me to my history. I remember that the words I recite are the same prayers that my great-great-grandparents said in the shtetl. Only recently have I come to understand that a person without a history is not whole.

Two years after my bat mitzvah didn't happen, I announced to my family that I didn't believe in God, and that I no longer considered myself Jewish. My mother was shocked—less by my renunciation of God than by my rejection of Judaism. "You were born a Jew," she pleaded, "it's who you are." I told her that I didn't feel Jewish and that I knew next to nothing about the religion.

A year before that, I had stopped eating. I felt fat, and I decided that the simplest way to bring down the numbers on the scale was to stop eating altogether. At home, my deception was precise: every morning, I left a bowl in the sink with a puddle of milk and a few flakes around the brim, to make it look as though I had eaten breakfast. At school I didn't need to be covert; I tossed the lunch my mother packed in the wastebasket with a flourish. I wrote the word CONTROL in black letters across the back of my hand, to dissuade me, in case I reached for food. I felt happy and smart.

Then my mother found out. She confronted me and forced me to eat. For weeks after that, she monitored my breakfasts and dinners. I dutifully resumed eating, secretly relieved to be caught. I watched the numbers grow higher on the scale with a feeling of horror muted by calm inevitability. I fantasized about college, where I would be free to make my own rules, and to keep food out of my mouth.

My mother's anger was fueled mostly by surprise: she could not believe that I hated my own flesh strongly enough to starve myself. Several months after she found out about my starvation, she invited me to attend Weight Watchers. There, I learned what she had known for years: how to meticulously monitor and record every meal in a little notebook. My mother was never able (or willing) to draw a connection between the body-hatred that motivated my eating disorder, and the endless dissatisfaction that had led her to count calories and fat grams for decades.

She was appalled at my free-form starvation, but encouraged me to seek happiness in structured, sanctioned food deprivation. I wasted hours at meetings in a crowded church basement. What I needed was therapy and love. What I got was weekly weigh-ins and a little beige card to keep track of my progress. Instead of emotional guidance, I got recipes for low-cal desserts.

I worried about being attractive, and I compared myself incessantly to the unattainable ideal that I saw in television shows, movies, ads, and billboards. I spent so much time worrying about being attractive, that I neglected to notice who I was attracted to myself.

During my senior year of high school, I tentatively began to acknowledge my attraction to women. I remained quiet in class, hugged the edges of the hallways, and cultivated crushes: on a lovely sophomore with green eyes and on a friend's younger sister. I searched magazines and newspapers for images of women loving women, but found nothing. I wrote poetry with transparent metaphors about love and truth and women's breasts, and submitted them to the school literary magazine, half-hoping that people would understand what I was trying to communicate. By the end of the year, I was wearing a pink triangle pin on my denim jacket. When my mother asked me about the symbol, I stammered, and said something about supporting a persecuted minority. Two weeks after graduation, I kissed a girl for the first time.

I came out as bisexual as soon as I arrived at college, but dated boys exclusively for two more years. I had not dated at all in high school, and was amazed when the guys I met at college seemed to be interested in me. I dated one for a few months, another for a few weeks, and saw several for only a night or two. I learned how to drink, and I learned how to fake orgasms.

At the beginning of my sophomore year I met Edward. I promised myself that I would be the perfect girlfriend, so the relationship could last. I baked him cakes, bought him flowers, cleaned his apartment, and wondered why I didn't feel happy. When Edward broke up with me after five months, I felt defeated, empty, lost, and relieved.

After the breakup, I embraced celibacy, gave up meat, and cut my hair short. In my journal, I expressed my anger toward the boys I dated. I stopped trying to find a boyfriend, and began to eat the foods I craved, listen to music I enjoyed, and take long walks without direction. I learned to be patient with myself: forgiving and indulgent. I realized pleasure in my own body, and unearthed a love of women that was deeper and stronger than I ever anticipated. I began to value my thoughts and the products of my mind. A lasting, vibrant self-esteem was born out of the fire that was my writing.

Learning to love my body helped me come out as gay, and coming out helped me learn to love my body: the two evolutions happened simultaneously. Looking in the mirror and seeing my body as beautiful was akin to finding beauty in another woman's body. When I allowed myself to stop looking for a boyfriend, I discovered a love for myself that merged and melded with my love for women.

My persistent and unignorable attraction to women was a catalyst that led to my discovery of feminism and eventually to my return to Judaism. Acknowledging my queerness allowed me to recognize that I deserve love. Loving myself motivated me to engage with my cultural and religious heritage, to ask questions about these aspects of myself, rather than ignoring them.

I began to uncover the possibility of creativity within Judaism when I enrolled in an introductory course on religion and studied the significance of rituals. I took more classes, and found authors whose writing stirred and excited me, who helped me to draw new connections. I learned from Gerda Lerner that patriarchy is not natural or inevitable, but is a cultural construction that can be dismantled. I learned from Nelle Morton the importance of describing my personal journey, of weaving my own stories into every narrative. I read *Standing Again at Sinai*, and took Judith Plaskow's words to heart: "What is new about Jewish feminism," Plaskow writes, "is that women are claiming the right to define and assess our differences, that we are revaluing and renaming what has been used to oppress us." As I studied feminist spirituality, my mind stretched like flesh in childbirth, like muscles that hadn't moved in decades.

During my junior year, I began dating a Jewish woman. She too had learned a few Yiddish words from her parents. We quizzed each other: "Do you know the word for head?" one of us would ask. "Do you know the word for potatoes? For kitten? For face?" *Keppe. Bulbes. Ketzeleh. Punim.*

On Friday nights, we recited the blessing over the Shabbat candles together. We sat in temple, holding hands. For the first time, I began to feel Jewish. Not just in isolated moments, but all the time: a Jew moving through the world, a Jew in every motion I made.

In my religion courses, I learned that God could mean an infinite number of things. The God I had pictured as a child—the one I disowned—was a blend of illustrations of Merlin the Wizard and Michelangelo's painting on the ceiling of the Sistine Chapel. He was an old white man with a long beard and a serious expression, whose fingertips could shoot lightning bolts and end lives. Renouncing a belief in God felt like the ultimate rebellion: I said fuck you to the being who created me and cast off all sense of obligation to a greater power. I called myself an atheist because no one could give me a reason to believe in Him. Because I thought religion was long, boring hours in temple and words I didn't understand. God seemed like nothing more than a cartoon other people needed. God was extraneous.

I found out later that this God was once a Goddess, that matriarchal cultures had once flourished, and that religion can be as individual as a fingerprint. I learned that some people find God/dess in a blade of grass and in the smell of wet earth. God can be the quiet but unshakable whisper in my gut that tells me that my grandmother's spirit was not simply erased by her death.

I have grown to believe in a profound heartbeat under the soil, and in everything that lives. I believe that I am praying any time I recognize or respect this power. Every time I bow my head in deference to the beauty of a full moon, a tree branch, or my lover's body, I carry into that motion a sense of myself as a Jew. I am no longer an atheist, because I admit that I need to walk through my days knowing that there are arms around me, and that I am part of a tradition of love and faith. This is my Judaism.

I learned about Rosh Chodesh from the rabbi at college. She explained that it was a ritual celebration of the new moon, a time for Jewish women to come together to sing, pray, and be creative. A small group of women and I began to plan monthly Rosh Chodesh meetings. We met in the Jewish Center, a building whose stark white walls and heavily varnished floors felt imposing. Moving the heavy coffee table, we spread a tapestry on the floor and lit white candles. In that atmosphere, our voices sounded hushed and holy. We began by singing a wordless melody, and reciting the blessing over the new moon.

Miriam's cup was always in the center of our circle. At first, we used a plain glass, until someone's aunt (a potter) donated a ceramic goblet adorned with a dancing woman. We passed the cup around the circle, taking small sips of water. Each woman recited her own name, her mother's name, and the names of as many female ancestors as she knew. Eventually we became familiar with the names of our friends' mothers and grandmothers, and the countries they came from: Australia, Ireland, Austria, Japan.

Every month, we encouraged each other to tell stories about our lives. One woman told us that she had spent twenty-four hours alone in the desert with no other company than her journal. I talked about my great-grandparents' old house on the Connecticut shoreline, and confessed my dream of buying it back one day and reclaiming the site of my grandmother's childhood. We also told the story of Miriam, Moses' sister and a prophetess in her own right. And we sang Debbie Friedman's "Miriam's Song." Alone in the building at night, with the room illuminated by candlelight, we could hear no sound but our own singing.

At one of our most powerful and memorable meetings, each woman wrote a blessing on a scrap of construction paper. We put the folded papers into a hat, and took turns reading aloud the prayer we chose. The blessings ranged from the mundane (May you remain peaceful and sane during your exams), to the transcendent (May you find a path that leads you to the Goddess, whether you find her in the moon, in a prayer book, or within). I drew a blessing from the hat that was simple and beautiful: "Remember, when you are feeling alone, that others care about you and that your friends love you." I read and reread that scrap of paper, reciting those words to myself at night before falling asleep.

We ended our Rosh Chodesh celebration with food: grapes, oranges, challah, and cookies. The roundness of the bread and fruit echoed the moon and the curves of women's bodies. We filled our bellies with eagerness and without hesitation. Our women-only sacred space was an escape from body-consciousness and self-doubt; it was an oasis for me, and I suspect for the other women as well. We made time every month—no matter how crowded our schedules were—to come together, to make a circle, and to sing.

Rosh Chodesh helped me to trust myself. I learned that I could be a strong leader, and that Judaism and feminism weren't mutually exclusive. Through our Rosh Chodesh group, I met a lesbian rabbi, a remarkable woman who helped me to map the intersection of my two worlds. I discovered an on-line community of Jewish lesbians, found *Bridges: A Journal for Jewish Feminists and Our Friends*, and *Lilith: The Independent Jewish Women's Magazine*. I realized that there is a vibrant and strong community of queer Jewish women, writing and thinking and meeting and talking. I learned that women who came before me had created new traditions without relinquishing the old.

Finding that space made it possible for my Judaism and lesbianism to harmonize. Both lesbianism and Judaism require bravery to make light amid the darkness of prejudice. Both identities call for the willingness to claim a history of hiding, fear, and persecution. And both are pregnant with the opportunity to create new stories.

My life is blossoming in ways my parents never expected. When I came out to my mother, she was devastated. She told me that I had broken her heart. In the years since then, she has repeatedly urged me to "become" heterosexual. Our conversations are often strained and tenuous, as if we are picking our way among land mines. In spite of this, I love my parents deeply, and continue to try to work with them toward mutual understanding.

My pride in myself as a lesbian, a feminist, and a Jew continues to grow. Each thread of myself draws strength from the others. In these identities, I have found a place where my self-love is thorough enough to hold every inch of my flesh and expansive enough to embrace the rituals that my ancestors passed down to me. It is a place of strength, a place where I feel utterly at home.

References

Lerner, Gerda. *The Creation of Patriarchy*. New York: Oxford University Press, 1986.

Morton, Nelle. *The Journey is Home*. Boston: Beacon Press, 1985.

Plaskow, Judith. *Standing Again at Sinai: Judaism from A Feminist Perspective*. San Francisco: HarperCollins, 1990.

12

Boiled Beet

ANNA SWANSON

Each seder is a retelling.
We come together and taste our way
through the story: Matzo,
unleavened because fleeing women
can't wait for bread to rise;
Charoset, the mortar used
to bind stone together;
Bitter herbs, the taste of slavery.

She passes me the haggadah
and I read out loud about the shank bone,
the blood which marked the doors
of Jewish houses with a message
to the angel of death
saying, *spare this home*.

This year we use a cooked beet
instead, smear beet juice on doorposts
and white picket fences.

I want to run around the city
with a boiled beet, mark the skin
of women everywhere, screaming
may this body
this body
this body
be spared.

Even for a night, a week,
I would like to know we all
were safe. Give a new meaning
to *Passover*.

13

Who is a Jew?

LOOLWA KHAZZOOM

I was sixteen when Israel began the "who is a Jew" debate, about the legitimacy of non-Orthodox conversions. I was a born, bred, and practicing Orthodox Jew, but it suddenly became questionable whether I would be recognized as one of the tribe. My mother had a perfectly kosher conversion by Orthodox standards, but the Conservative movement had ordained her rabbi. Since her conversion certificate said "Conservative," my mother, sister, and I were all branded "questionable" Jews.

My head spun with the possibility that I might not be considered Jewish. I was a child prodigy in music, but since every competition was on *Shebbath*, I could not pursue that path. I was a talented speaker, yet was unable to participate in any high school debates, which were also on Saturday. Though I was strong and coordinated, I could not consider a career in dance or athletics.

From age eleven on, I struggled to make it through school. I missed more days than the sickest kid around, so that I could observe Jewish holy days. When teachers learned of my religious restrictions, I was kicked out of the orchestra, demoted from first to last chair flute in band, and prevented from participating in school musicals. There was no place for Orthodox Jews in those worlds.

After being denied access because of my religious observance for so many years, I could not believe that rabbis in Israel might not believe that I was a Jew. I was angry and confused, but also relieved. If I wasn't Jewish, I could do whatever I wanted. I could pursue my dreams without a zillion limitations, eat whatever I wanted, and live a life free of Jew-hatred. I knew that if I had the choice, I would choose not to be a Jew. Support Jews: yes, be one: no. But I really didn't have a choice. What the State of Israel believed about my status as a Jew didn't actually make that much difference in my life. G-d knew that my mother had a kosher conversion, so I was stuck being a Jew.

I'd obviously internalized a lot of Jewish self-hatred. Everyone knows the stereotypes: Jews are pushy, loud, obnoxious, stingy, and backstabbing. I was embarrassed that we did not celebrate Christmas. And I felt inferior because I did not have blond hair or blue eyes like my mom, or a ski-slope nose like her cousin Patsy. My mother grew up half WASP, a quarter Irish Catholic, and a quarter Danish Protestant. On the WASP side, her family has been in the United States since the ship after the Mayflower. On the Irish and Danish sides, she's a second-generation American. She never liked Christianity and since she was nine years old, she made it her business to study other religions. When she was twenty-six, she converted to Judaism. In the process of her conversion, she met my father: an Iraqi-Israeli Jew. Through her marriage to my father, my mother wholeheartedly and enthusiastically embraced Middle Eastern Jewish identity as her own. Nonetheless, she was left with traces of her Middle American, Anglo-Saxon upbringing.

My mother's understanding of beauty was rooted in the Anglicized ideal. According to her upbringing, anything falling outside of that framework was not technically pretty. So I grew up not only saturated with these images from the media, but also having them reinforced at home. As a biracial girl, these images were especially complicated and painful for me. I grew up learning that my features—my long, dark, curly hair; my big, brown eyes; and my Mediterranean nose—were inferior at best, and ugly at worst.

When I was six, I asked my mom if I was pretty. She said no; I was cute, but not pretty. Confusing matters for me, my mother told me that my sister (who is darker than I am) had classic beauty. It seemed I was too dark to be beautiful for a light girl, and too light to be beautiful for a dark girl. At the time, I didn't understand that those messages were socially rooted in sexism, racism, and Jew-hatred.

In Iraq, my kind of hair was coveted as being "blond." Soft and light by Iraqi standards, it was as "good" as you could get. My sister envied my hair and hated her own, despite the fact that I had always loved her hair: it was black and thick, bouncy and intense. She tried to grow it long for years with no luck; it only grew out. Her hair could only be brushed with an Afro comb. I learned that her hair was "bad" and mine was "good." But still, I never felt that my hair was truly beautiful, because it was not really blond.

My sister inherited other physical traits from our Iraqi side and she frequently compared her body to mine in ways that devalued and denigrated her own features. As a result, I had a sense that I "lucked out" by inheriting some of my maternal grandmother's Scandinavian (i.e., non-Jewish) traits. That kind of racially based comparison was a regular part of my life when I was growing up.

Yet my father also instilled in my sister and me tremendous pride in our Iraqi heritage and indignation about the prejudices against us. My father's family lived in Iraq since the Babylonians conquered ancient Israel and exiled the Israelites to the land of present-day Iraq. His family stayed put for twenty-five hundred years, until Iraq forced them to flee for their lives. Iraqi masses tried to wipe out the entire Jewish ghetto and almost reached my father's house. Iraqi government officials hung my great-uncle by his thumbs and left him there for seven days until his thumbs broke. He had been a gifted surgeon but was never able to practice medicine again. The Iraqi government confiscated my family's property and personal belongings; my family arrived as refugees in the modern State of Israel with close to nothing. My father grew up under British imperialism in Iraq, and then faced Ashkenazi contempt and discrimination for being Mizrahi in Israel. Yet all my life, he was headstrong about being an Iraqi Jew. This made it difficult to recognize the more subtle indications of his internalized self-hatred and racism.

The first thing my father ever said to my mother was a compliment about her beautiful blue-green eyes. I'm sure he was attracted to her light skin and blond hair as well. Consciously or not, I believe my father felt a sense of accomplishment when they married. That became clear to me when my father remarried a few years ago. His second wife was also a blond-haired, blue-eyed convert.

I suspect my father was delighted to see me, a light-skinned child, pop out of his wife's belly. I think he felt an additional sense of having "made it" because his daughter did not look Iraqi. As I grew up, my father was obsessed with my hair. "Golden hair," he called it. He would pet my hair in an erotic, almost desperate way that made me cringe and squeeze shut every particle of my body.

My father used to call me "Loolwa the Beautiful." When he wanted to find me in the house, he called out "Loolwa the Beautiful," like it was this great thing. He wrote it on my checks too: "Pay to the order of Loolwa the Beautiful Khazzoom." I hated it. It certainly didn't make me feel beautiful.

The irony of my biracial reality is that I grew up with a single identity: Iraqi Jew. My father's identity subsumed my mother's. Pictures of my father's family hung on our walls, while pictures of my mother's family were stuffed in a box. My mother was concerned that my sister and I would become Christian if we knew our Christian family. Aside from the fact that we have Jesus freaks in our family, my mother worried that we would simply relate to the Christian side of ourselves more. She knew that it was easier to be Christian than Jewish in America, and believed that exposure to her relatives—who, unlike our Jewish family, spoke English and lived in America—would make us want to be Christian. So my sister and I never met our family on our mom's side, and the photos were hidden on the top shelf.

When I discovered the box of my mother's pictures, I was ecstatic. There was a portrait of my mom and her little brother. They looked like those kids in the 1950s TV show reruns that I'd watched a million times. It was like a bona fide scene out of *Leave It to Beaver!* I was overjoyed that I was related to them. I felt valid for the first time in my life. For years after my discovery, I spent every *Shebbath* sitting and staring at those pictures. *I'm related to them, so I'm a real American!* I would think to myself. *I'm related to people who celebrate Christmas!*

In the pictures, my mother's blond hair grew darker in her adult years. I felt hopeful: if my mom's hair could change from blond to brown, maybe my hair would change from brown to blond. I prayed that my children would look like my mother's family, so they wouldn't be plagued with my curse: my blood was mixed with that despicable dark Jewish blood, so I was doomed. I wondered where I could find a Jewish man who looked like a WASP. I knew that I would have to marry someone blond to wipe out my dark lineage. I wanted to give my children a chance to feel good about themselves.

When my mom found me looking at the pictures, she chastised me. She seemed ashamed of her side of the family. She reminded me that I am an Iraqi Jew, and said that the people in the pictures were not my family. My Jewish relatives, the family I knew—they were my family. It was very confusing: I learned that her family was superior, but I was supposed to be ashamed of identifying with them.

My mother made anti-Jewish comments throughout my childhood. She didn't want to be associated with Jewish stereotypes: she practically hid when "improperly behaved" Jews entered a restaurant where we were eating. To compensate for the Jews in our midst, she bent over backwards to accommodate non-Jews. I learned that being Jewish meant being disgusting. My mother didn't realize that her pointed comments about Jews were, by extension, comments about my family and about me.

I inherited my nose complex from my mother. Her Irish nose wasn't good enough, she explained, because it came down straight, rather than curving up at the end like a "proper" nose should. "I used to sit like this all the time," she said, showing me how she pushed up the end of her nose with her finger. I always felt that my nose was too "Jewish." My nose complex started with my mom's, but since the Jewish nose is the subject of disdain throughout the world, there was enough material in mainstream culture to fuel my hatred.

This type of internalized racism has been a historical source of conflict for the Jewish people. For centuries, Ashkenazim faced hostility, discrimination, and even death because of their Middle Eastern and North African roots. For the sake of survival or status (depending on the time period), Ashkenazim tried to assimilate into Christian Europe by appearing as un-"Semitic" as possible. Ashkenazi detachment from the Middle Eastern and North African roots of the Jewish people is simultaneously a form of self-hatred and self-preservation.

But like it or not, our people originated as a tribe indigenous to the Middle East. And as with all Middle Easterners, we possessed the features of a desert people: dark skin, thick dark curly hair, dark eyes, and a nose especially designed to moisten the hot desert air as it traveled toward our lungs.

Mizrahim are the Jews who never left the Middle East and North Africa. Consequently, we generally still have these physical features. Over time, however, Ashkenazi features became increasingly Germanic and Slavic. These changes resulted from miscegenation with Germanic and Slavic people: through marriage, rape, or conversion. Even as their coloring lightened, Ashkenazim frequently retained certain Semitic traits, like the "Jewish" nose and frizzy "Jewish" hair. And they were punished for it. Anti-Semitism is a term that specifically describes the anti-Jewish experience faced by Ashkenazim. Persecution of German, Polish, and Russian Jews was, in part, based on the premise that they were not "real" Europeans; they were Semites. Because of European racism, Semites were seen as undesirable foreigners.

Ashkenazim continue to shun the Middle Eastern and North African roots of Jewish heritage, in favor of an identification with central and eastern European culture. The Middle Eastern and North African origins of numerous aspects of Jewish culture are rarely acknowledged or honored: Hebrew originated in the Middle East; the first yeshivas were in ancient Iraq; Purim celebrates the story of Iranian Jews; and Pesach tells the story of Egyptian Jews. Abraham and Sarah came from Mesopotamia (ancient Iraq), and Moses and Miriam came from Egypt. Jews lived in the Middle East and North Africa for 4,000 years, in contrast to the 1,000 or so years that Ashkenazim lived in Europe.

Despite these facts, Ashkenazim have all but completely dissociated from their Middle Eastern and North African roots. Jewish education throughout the Western world (and in Israel) includes little or nothing about Jewish people or heritage from the Middle East, Africa, Central or South America, Central or East Asia, or the Mediterranean. As a result, there now exists a crisis of Jewish identity, manifest in the invisibility of non-Ashkenazi culture, language, and traditions in the mainstream Jewish lexicon. The desperation to qualify as European has led to both widespread ignorance of Jewish multiculturalism, and also to overt hostility, racism, and discriminatory practices toward all non-Ashkenazi Jews.

This inequity is most visible in Israel, where the majority of the population is Mizrahi, yet Jewish education continues to reflect Ashkenazi culture and tradition almost exclusively. Ashkenazi Jews in the United States and Israel propagate a European hegemony that parallels the European hegemony of the larger world: Ashkenazim enjoy a power, privilege, and status not afforded to non-Ashkenazim. Mizrahim are perceived as backward, dirty, and violent.

Anything Jewish actually reflects Ashkenazi identity, while all other Jewish realities are devalued. Jewish history books always include the modern history of Jews from Poland, Russia, and Germany but rarely mention the modern-day existence of Jews from other lands. Education about Mizrahim is either exoticized or absent. Jewish schools always teach Ashkenazi prayers, but never teach Indian, Ethiopian, or Tunisian Jewish prayers. Purim parties sponsored by the Jewish community always include *hamantashen*, but many Jews have never even tasted a *sambousak*, a "Middle Eastern Jewish pastry" for this holiday. International Jewish assistance groups pride themselves on aid provided to Russian Jews, whereas Ethiopian Jews were left waiting for years in Ethiopia while Israel decided whether to accept them as real Jews.

I have experienced numerous incidents of Ashkenazi racism and arrogance in my own life. In college, an Orthodox peer challenged my practice of certain traditions, which are contrary to Ashkenazi *halachah*. Always eager to educate, I explained that my practice reflects the traditions of the Iraqi Jewish community. "Well the entire Iraqi community does it wrong," he replied.

More than once, Ashkenazim have felt the need to explain to me that my "backward" Mizrahi ways originate from the Arab influence on our community. They claim that we "lost the Jewishness" of our practice, due to our assimilation. It is as if they believe that Moses and Miriam crossed the Rhine River, instead of the Red Sea. Outrageous as it may sound, experiences like these have been common, not only for me, but for every conscious non-Ashkenazi Jew I know.

In Hebrew school, we learned only the Ashkenazi traditions, so my father had to reeducate my sister and me every day after school. "What did you learn?" he asked. "We learned about eating latkes and playing with dreidels on Hannukkah," we replied. "We say *H'nikkah*, not Hanukkah," he advised us. He taught us how to pronounce the guttural *h*, and explained that Iraqi Jews do not play with dreidels or eat latkes. He pointed out that Ashkenazi menorahs looked very different from the Iraqi *hanukkiah* hanging from our wall.

I loved learning our traditions and wanted to share my ancestral customs with my teachers and peers at my Jewish day school. In the second grade, I was met with virulent hostility. "Why do you pray in that book?" one teacher loudly asked, when she noticed I was reading silently from my Iraqi prayer book. I lowered my eyes, feeling both afraid and ashamed as I answered: "Because it's my tradition." My teacher looked disgusted. Teachers made nasty comments about my culture and embarrassed me in front of the class.

Even the rabbi misused his authority, masquerading his own prejudices as Jewish law. In Bible study class, our rabbi read to us from the Bible in Hebrew and then translated each verse into English. One day, as if he were reading from the Bible, he said: "It is against Jewish law to pray from a Sephardic prayer book, and it is against Jewish law to pray by yourself." The students in my class turned to me and said: "Shame, shame, shame on you Loolwa!" My parents took me out of the school that day, and I transferred to public school for the rest of my education.

Instead of internalizing this racism, I learned to hate Ashkenazim. From an early age, I planned to somehow, someday resurrect my heritage. I realized, firsthand, the importance of carrying on my tradition.

My father, sister, and I attended the only Mizrahi and Sephardi synagogue in San Francisco. With determined dedication, we walked three miles there and three miles back on Friday night, Saturday morning, and Saturday afternoon. With rare exception, my sister and I were the only children, and two of the very few females that ever showed up.

I loved singing the prayers. By the time I was eight years old, I could sing the entire *Shebbath* and weekday evening services in the traditional Iraqi tunes. I knew dozens of Iraqi *Shebbath* and holy day songs, and I could sing a good portion of the haggadah in both Hebrew and Judeo-Arabic, with Iraqi melodies.

It was rare for a child my age to know all these prayers. I sang with the distinctly Iraqi pronunciation of every word, which was unusual for Iraqi adults to maintain, much less for their children to preserve. I felt so proud, so accomplished, that I was able to lead my family in prayer, and I longed to lead our congregation as well.

If I were a boy, I believe that my entire synagogue would have been ecstatic about my commitment to maintaining my Jewish heritage. They might have encouraged me to continue in my Jewish pursuits in every possible way. But since I was "only" a girl, I did not count, and I did not receive the attention I deserved.

I was not allowed to lead any part of the main prayers. But after considerable fuss, I was allowed to lead parts of the supplementary prayers (since those did not "really count"). Still, I was only allowed that privilege if there were no boys around.

When a boy would walk in, I would be shoved aside. Any boy would do. Even if he were dressed more for a street fight than for the synagogue, and could barely read Hebrew. It didn't matter that he would stumble and sputter through the prayers, and didn't know his own tradition from Christianity. He would be privileged to lead the prayers instead of me.

Once, just as I was climbing the steps of the *bimah* to do my thing, a boy walked in. There was a communal sigh of relief as several men went clamoring after the kid, shoving a prayer book in his hand. One of the men from the synagogue literally pulled me off the *bimah*, so that the boy could read, instead of me. I tried to say something, but the man only grunted, as if I did not exist. I sat there and watched the boy bumble his way through the prayers. Several men stood around him, encouraging him, helping him along, and giving him all the attention. I was relegated to nothingness on the side, knowing that

maybe next week, if no boys showed up, my prayers might be tolerated again.

Each time they relegated me to the sidelines in favor of a boy,
they strengthened the message that I was undesirable, that my intelligence was meaninglessness, and that my abilities were worthless. It
was a degrading and humiliating experience. I was like a starving
child denied permission to eat from the rich food on the table and
forced to grasp for scraps of food from off the floor.

The Mizrahi and Sephardi culture was disappearing, yet my community chose to ignore the potential of a child who was eager to learn
and carry on the traditions. I had dedicated my life to my religion and
heritage, but it meant nothing. It didn't matter that I who woke up
early every Saturday morning to walk across town to the synagogue, or
that I spent every *Shebbath* learning about Mizrahi/Sephardi Jewish tradition. It made no difference that I knew more than many others in my
generation. My unique knowledge and passion for Iraqi Jewish heritage
was irrelevant. My unusual commitment to Judaism was superfluous.
The fact that I was bursting with the energy to lead, and that I was
planning to resurrect my heritage was meaningless to them. Had I been
a boy, they would have rejoiced in the prospect of ethnic continuity
and the potential of renewed leadership for the community.

That was how I learned about the role of women in our society.
My father comforted me, agreeing that the way I was treated was
unfair. But we kept going to the synagogue. We did not revolt against
the system, and we did not reject it. I learned that although the
treatment was unjust, it was acceptable. I had no meaningful outlet
for my pain, no context to understand it, and no power to fight it. So
I internalized the powerlessness and worthlessness I was taught. I
learned to fear my intelligence, creativity, and new ideas, knowing
there was danger in expressing myself. At best, my contributions would
fall on deaf ears; at worst, they would be scorned. I began to live from
a place just behind my potential.

I knew that the men in my community were waiting for the day
when I would reach *bath mouswa* age, and technically become a woman.
Then they could officially banish me to the back of the synagogue
forever. Indeed, being cast off to the women's section was a devastating and degrading experience for me. With just one day of my life,
one birthday, I was separated from active participation in the synagogue and stripped of what little Jewish freedom I had enjoyed up to
that point. In a boy's life, his *bar mouswa* is a rite of passage where he

claims his full place in the Jewish community. My *bath mouswa* marked the ritual of my shrinking place in the community. Being confined to the women's section taught me that coming of age for girls is not an honor, but a punishment.

After my *bath mouswa*, I sat in the front row of the women's section. I hung over the top of the *mechitzah* as much as I could get away with, and heartily sang along. Vocally joining in the prayers was my last shred of connection to the congregation. I felt a deep sense of despair in the gap between my passion for my heritage and what the community tolerated. It was humiliating to give so much of myself to the synagogue and then to be stuck in the back of the room, behind a wall. I felt tremendous sadness, anger, and hurt from being shut out. But apparently, out of sight was not enough. I had to be muted, as well.

Once my sister went away to college, I was almost always the only female at services. So mine was usually the only female voice that could be heard. Instead of being delighted that there was a female congregant attending services, instead of being thrilled that she whole-heartedly participated in the prayers, and instead of encouraging her attendance and participation, the rabbi decided that I was not to sing audibly. He purported to be upholding the law of *Kol isha*, in which a woman may not sing if she is in audible distance from men. It did not seem to matter that the practice was not a custom in Mizrahi or Sephardi communities from which synagogue members came. It was an authoritative means to silence me.

That was my first of many experiences in which Mizrahi and Sephardi communities bent over backward to ensure that women could not participate in praying, learning, and leading. While it is in fact permissible in our tradition for women to be involved in these activities, the communities adopted Orthodox and ultra-Orthodox Ashkenazi practices, which guarantee women's exclusion. Again and again, I ran toward the Mizrahi community with my arms open wide, and the men of the community repeatedly shut the door in my face.

My family eventually left the community. I spent the next couple of years attending Ashkenazi synagogues, but those traditions meant nothing to me. When I was fifteen, I stopped attending services altogether.

Nobody has the right or the power to shut me out from who I am: not the Orthodox Israelis who question my mother's conversion; not the Eurocentric society that attempts to turn me against my own body; not the Ashkenazim who try to undermine my heritage; and not the Mizrahi men who want to silence me. I don't hate my people, my heritage, or my body; I simply detest what has been done to them, and with them.

I'm now a Jewish multicultural educator, a Jewish musician, and a Jewish writer. I organized the first egalitarian Mizrahi services in the United States and co-organized the first in Israel. And I edited the first anthology about Mizrahi women. I stand here today—a proud, young, Iraqi-American Jewish feminist. I have taken my identity into my own hands. I demand to be seen and heard as I am.

14

The Kibbutz (1989)

DEBORAH PREG

We work in silence, only occasionally
breaking into song. So physical is
the continuous strain of shoulders
and the straightening, shifting, squatting.
I stand and look behind me. How far
have I come? How many weeds have I
tossed aside? Lifting my shirt
I wipe the sweat from my face and neck,
gathering particles of grit. I can smell
the musky dirt-sweat paste that clings to me
and taste the salty water from above my
lip. The cries of bombers over head
remind me that I am in the Holy Land, furrowing
the desert sand. Did I once shape and paint
my nails, spend hours curling my hair
just so, and sleep til noon? Now my sleeves
are rolled and tucked under the straps
of my bra, my hair sporadically shoveled
into a ragged cap. Blood and pus ooze
from my palms and I can't remember the color
of my shoes. We've been hacking since
before six, when the morning mist
still smothered the fields. I hear the
truck's horn, signaling lunch and the end
of our morning task, and we, the
volunteers, clamber onto the bed of the truck.
I watch the green rows of tomato plants,

119

separated by dry, cracked sand, merge
into a thick, luscious strip of vegetation.
I have come so far.

First published in *Bridges: A Journal for Jewish Feminists and Our Friends*, vol. 6, no. 2, 1997.

15

When You're Looking for G-d, Go Home

JESSIE HELLER-FRANK

When people ask me how I became a *baalas teshuvah*, I tell them G-d conned me into it. My discovery of religious Judaism unfolded as a series of chance encounters, coincidences, and accidents, which I now see as part of a Divine plan.

I was the only Jewish child at my school in Vallejo, California. I was known as "the Jewish girl," even though my entire understanding of Judaism started and ended with the knowledge of three things: (1) our Messiah hadn't come; (2) we celebrate Hanukkah, not Christmas; and (3) for one week a year, we eat matzo. I attended Sunday school, but as soon as I was old enough to make my own choices, I quit. No more Sunday school, and no bat mitzvah either. I knew there was beauty in Judaism, but I didn't find it at my Reconstructionist Sunday school. I was yearning to find meaning; I just didn't know where to look.

A few years ago, I asked a friend who was Jewishly connected how to find G-d. She told me, "If you're looking for G-d, go home." At first, I had no idea what she meant. Now, after returning from my sixth trip to Israel, I am starting to understand. My journey back to Judaism began seven years ago, while packing my suitcase for the first of these trips. Unlike many people making this journey, I was not going to the Promised Land in search of G-d. I was going with my mom to visit my Hasidic uncle. Even more importantly, I hoped to meet a handsome Israeli man, and have a summer filled with romance. The last thing I expected was to fall in love with the land, find G-d, and discover a whole new side of myself.

Before we arrived, my uncle reminded us that he lived in a very religious area, and asked us to dress modestly: skirts below the knee, shirts with high necks, and sleeves that covered our elbows. He also asked that we keep the Sabbath and observe the dietary laws of kashrut while living at his house. My mom and I agreed, without really knowing what we'd gotten ourselves into.

I packed two skirts and two long-sleeve t-shirts in my carry-on bag, but I filled my suitcase with shorts and tank tops—more reasonable attire in a country where the average summer day is over a hundred degrees. I didn't finish packing until 2:00 A.M. At 6:00 A.M., when my mom's best friend picked us up, I sleepily grabbed my carry-on bag, and away we went.

At the El Al counter, when the woman asked how many bags I would be checking, I glanced down, and realized I had left my suitcase at home. I quickly realized that I would be going to Israel with only the clothes in my carry-on bag. I changed my clothes before I got off the plane, and greeted my religious family looking like one of them.

When I told my relatives what happened, my Hasidic aunt offered to share her wardrobe with me for the summer. I was fifteen years old, and dressed like a middle-aged Hasidic woman. As soon as I could, I went to buy a pair of Levi's but discovered that the same jeans hanging in my closet at home cost a hundred and fifty dollars in Israel. I decided that I'd rather dress like a religious woman than pay those prices. What seemed like an arbitrary decision about my wardrobe turned out to have a profound effect on my identity as a woman and as a Jew.

The first time my mom and I visited my uncle's family, they lived in a very religious section of Chicago. Once, during our stay with them, I watched my aunt frantically searching for a scarf to cover her hair before she would open the drapes. It seemed absurd. I thought that my aunt was crazy for allowing her husband to talk her into his repressive Hasidic lifestyle. I believed that Orthodox Judaism repressed women's sexuality. I told her that I would never dress like that. Instead, I intended to wear sexy clothes. I was only a girl, but I already thought that I understood what made women valuable.

After a week in Israel, I was disappointed when not a single Israeli man had glanced my way. At home, I was used to getting men's attention, and I heard that Israeli men were especially attracted to women with blond hair and blue eyes like mine. I thought about the tank tops I'd intended to wear. I felt insecure, and asked my aunt why

I wasn't getting any attention from men. I was shocked when she told me that people assumed from looking at my clothes that I was religious. It upset me to think that I was being judged by my appearance.

Then I met Gil. He was not at all the tall, dark, and handsome soldier I'd been hoping to meet, but I went out with him anyway. He was skinny, short, and quiet: an eighteen-year-old Israeli man who was worried about his branch assignment in the army. After a few dates, he invited me to his apartment.

It was Friday night, but I thought little of it. I was going to meet him at 9:00 P.M., after dinner at my uncle's. Since Shabbos dinner was barely beginning, I excused myself from the table and told my family I'd be back in a few minutes. Since it was Shabbos, it was forbidden to use the phone at my uncle's house, so I ran over to Gil's apartment a few blocks away. I took in the scene at Gil's: two Israeli men, sitting on the floor with beer bottles and a guitar.

The atmosphere at my uncle's house was still fresh in my mind: children singing around the table waiting anxiously for an extra slice of challah; my grandmother enjoying her matzah ball soup; and everyone dressed in their finest to greet the Sabbath bride. And there I was, sitting on the floor of a dirty apartment with two guys who didn't even care that it was Shabbos.

I stayed about fifteen minutes before explaining to Gil and his friend that I had to leave. Since that moment, I have never again been conflicted about honoring Shabbos. It's simple: any other night of the week is for mundane activities, but the Sabbath is reserved for *kedushah* for "holiness."

One night, my uncle got me a ticket to a concert being given by his spiritual teacher, Rabbi Shlomo Carlebach. He was an hour late for his own concert, and he sang only in Hebrew. He seemed as distant from me as the moon. I was completely bored.

After the concert, the rabbi came back to my uncle's house to tell stories. A large group of us sat on the floor of the courtyard: women on one side, men on the other. Reb Shlomo began by saying, "Friends, get a little closer." We moved in, forming a tight circle around him. Sitting a few feet away, the rabbi seemed warm and approachable; he was different from the man I'd seen on stage. I listened to his stories, absorbing every word. Sitting on the cold, stone floor, I thought: this is the Judaism I have been looking for.

Reb Shlomo seemed to embody the Russian folk tales I'd grown up hearing from my mother. It was as if the Old World shtetl lived inside of him; the pain and wonder of Judaism came forth with his every word. In one of his stories, the life of a child was saved when the boy's father opened an icebox to feed a poor man on Shabbos. The child, half frozen, was found by accident: his father was performing a mitzvah and was given a miracle. That simple story showed me that our actions have repercussions far beyond our human knowledge.

When my uncle introduced me to Reb Shlomo at the end of the evening, I was so in awe that I just stood there and smiled. I had no words in his presence. After that, I knew that the Judaism I longed for did exist, and I had finally found it.

My mother was also moved by our experience in Israel. Like me, she felt committed to becoming more religious once we got home, and even dreamed of someday moving to Tsfat.

On the way to the airport, we unexpectedly shared our cab with an older couple and their severely handicapped son. They were obviously religious: the men were both wearing black hats and the woman wore a wig, a long-sleeved blouse, and a long skirt. I realized, in an instant, that this coincidence was really an act of Divine providence.

We normally wouldn't have initiated a conversation with strangers, but as we drove, my mom and I began talking to the woman. She told us that she was from Brooklyn, and called herself a Hasid of the Lubavitcher Rebbe. She passionately described the Chabad Lubavitch movement, which I learned was engaged in a worldwide effort to educate Jews about traditional Judaism. When my mother asked for advice about keeping kosher, she even told us about a rabbi near us, in Berkeley.

After a few days of jet-lag and culture shock in California, we contacted Chabad of the East Bay. Rabbi Ferris wanted to meet with us before agreeing to *kasher* our kitchen, to determine whether we were serious about this dramatic lifestyle change. At the time, I was unsure of how serious about it I was myself. Before we met the rabbi, I told my mom that I was willing to keep kosher at home, but outside of the house, she could forget it.

Even though the rabbi was clearly religious, he didn't seem as religious as my uncle in Israel. He had no long *payes* and his wife didn't cover her hair. The rabbi's thirteen-year-old son played Monopoly on the floor with a neighbor, his tzitzit hanging from beneath the untucked shirt of his Boy Scout uniform.

Once the rabbi agreed to *kasher* our kitchen, I started to interview him about his level of observance. If he was going to be our rabbi, I needed to ask him a few questions too: Do you keep Shabbos? Kashrut? I noticed your wife doesn't have her hair covered . . . Rabbi Ferris interrupted, explaining that his wife always covers her hair with a wig. I felt foolish and embarrassed.

Rabbi Ferris was unfazed. He said that he wanted us to experience Shabbos with his family, and invited my mom and me to stay. The Ferris' had seven children, and were hosting a family from New York who had seven children of their own. Still, he welcomed us.

After Shabbos dinner, I stayed up talking with the older kids. I felt especially connected to a girl my age, named Miriam. She listened to every question I had about Judaism, and patiently answered even my most remedial concerns. She had grown up in an exclusively religious neighborhood: Crown Heights, Brooklyn. I'd grown up in Vallejo, California. She had six siblings; I had none. I was her first nonreligious friend and she was my first religious one.

The holiday of Sukkot began right after Shabbos. My mom and I felt so welcome in the atmosphere of warmth and joy, we stayed at the rabbi's house for four additional days. Neither of us felt like we ever wanted to leave. By the end of the holiday, I was questioning everything I thought I wanted out of life. Before, my plan was to grow up, get married, have one child, and get divorced like everyone else I knew. When I envisioned my future, I thought only to replicate my own experience: I never imagined myself having more than one child or marrying for life. For the first time, I understood that something was missing.

When my mom and I finally returned home, the quiet of our house felt empty. The silence in our home awoke something new in my consciousness. I decided to make Judaism my own. I realized that I had to forge my own connection with G-d, and I felt compelled to figure out how to pray.

In Israel, I had gone through the motions of Jewish observance, but had not connected to the rituals in a personal way. I was no longer sheltered by my Hasidic uncle's home. The clothes in my closet were no longer my aunt's, and I was not in a community where kosher food was easily available, I knew that in order to build a traditional Jewish life for myself in California, I had to find the inner meaning of the prayers, holidays, and observances. The process would not be easy, but I knew I was ready to begin.

Back at college that fall, I had a difficult time balancing a life of observance with the demands of academia. As the High Holidays approached, I asked a professor for an extension on a paper that was due on Yom Kippur. I tried to explain my obligation to obey G-d's law, but he insisted it was not an obligation, but a choice. He argued that it was my choice to observe the holiday or not. He refused to grant the extension. After a long internal struggle, I decided to follow the law as commanded.

The professor's arguments compelled me to begin sorting out the difference between choices and obligations for myself. I needed to distinguish my own will from the word of G-d. I remembered my friend's advice, and finally understood that to find G-d, I needed to search within myself.

I remembered the powerful effects that dressing modestly had on me in Israel, and decided to try this practice at home. To fulfill the mitzvah, I needed to expand my wardrobe, so I went to the mall. I stood outside Contempo Casuals clothing store watching a few teen-age boys leer at the girls passing by. To those boys, the young women were prizes to be acquired. I was disgusted. It was shocking to watch them interact with the kind of girl I once was. Just three months earlier, I had hung around the mall, waiting to be noticed by boys like them. I had mistakenly interpreted their looks and yells as compli-ments. It made me sad to realize how reliant I had become on men's advances to help me feel valuable as a woman.

In the shelter of the dressing room, I looked at my former self: I remembered wearing low-cut shirts and tight jeans. I put on a long brown dress with small pink roses. I looked different. I felt different. I bought the dress and went home subtly changed.

My *rebitzen* told me that every Jewish child has an angel living with her in her mother's womb who teaches her the entire Torah. When the child is ready to be born, the angel touches her in the space above her top lip, and the child forgets everything. When she begins to learn Torah, she is, in fact, relearning something she already intrinsically knows.

This story speaks to me. The longer I live in this world of G-dly consciousness, the more I realize that it is intrinsically within me. The term *baalas teshuvah* is used to describe people like me, who have returned to Judaism. This does not feel like the correct term for me: once I returned, it felt as though I had never left. I now understand that my behavior is not a choice. My actions reflect a Divine system of obligations.

I once believed that women were second-class citizens in tradi-tional Judaism, chained by domestic responsibilities and powerless to control their lives. I was appalled by the *mechitzah* separating women from men during prayer, because I assumed it signified that women were less worthy. I now understand that the *mechitzah* is meant to allow privacy in prayer.

When I pray, I am begging the One Above to bless me with good. It is my time to work on my connection with the Divine. I am only comfortable showing other women the sense of vulnerability that I feel during prayer. The *mechitzah* gives me a sense of security. In a mixed setting, I would not be comfortable letting down my emotional walls.

I know that in some shuls, the women's spaces are small. I believe this is the mistake of people, not G-d. Women are not inferior to men in Judaism. The laws of Torah, when followed correctly, do not permit gender discrimination.

Many women are not taught that women's mitzvot are fundamental to the core of Judaism. In fact, three essential mitzvot are entrusted to women: family purity, kashrut, and lighting Shabbos candles.

The practice of lighting Shabbos candles has profoundly affected my life. The moment I bring in Shabbos with their light, everything around me dissipates into calm. The world is at peace, my home is at peace, and I am at peace. After lighting the candles I lie on the couch looking at their light, watching how my special mitzvah illuminates the world. Through this tiny physical action, I have the power to bring light into my life. This light brings heaven down to earth.

This ritual inspired me to learn more about women's mitzvot. Now, I stringently observe the laws of modesty, covering my collarbones, knees, and elbows. Instead of a systematic way to repress women, I have come to understand modesty as a way for women to separate the sacred from the mundane. This practice has helped me realize that my body is sacred: precious to G-d, and to me. When I allow my body to be seen, it is for sacred purposes and with conscious awareness.

The more Judaism permeates my life and my soul, the more I am challenged by tests to my faith. I particularly struggle with the laws related to intimate relationships. Initially, I had trouble finding meaning in the practice of *shomer negia*. At first, it sounded insane to think that I could be forbidden from touching any man who isn't my relative or my husband. But then I remembered the awkward obligation of hugging acquaintances and strangers. I have always felt a little uncomfortable with that type of superficial intimacy. When the instant gratification of touch isn't there, a more authentic connection must be made through words.

I started being *shomer negia* because I realized that I wanted my relationships with men to have the same kind of emotional intimacy and holiness that I felt in other parts of my life as a religious woman. I decided to try to elevate my consciousness about the importance of touch.

I first felt the power of this practice when I agreed to a *shidduch*, a date arranged for the purpose of marriage. We walked together, side by side, without ever touching. For two months, we shared our lives with each other, but he never kissed me; I never held his hand. Our relationship was elevated through our interactions with one another, and we developed mutual respect and appreciation based on more than physical attraction. I felt closer to him than I'd ever felt with my secular boyfriends.

I was extremely physically attracted to him. If we had been secular, I know that our physical relationship would have obscured our intellectual connection. Instead, the Torah provided us with clear boundaries about acceptable and unacceptable behavior during our time together. The laws allowed me to listen closely to what my inner voice was telling me, and enabled me to decide what would be right and true for me.

It was a transformative experience for me. Now, I get to know someone before we have a relationship, which helps me avoid creating intimacy through physicality. I now understand the intrinsic logic and spiritual meaning in *shomer negia*. In fact, this practice is one of the most powerful I observe. It has been a crucial aspect of my *teshuvah*, my "return," because it challenged my ideas about the essence of my identity.

Conducting myself as a spiritual person is not always easy. I have been tested by G-d on this issue and have failed miserably more then once. Each time I am challenged by an experience connected to sexuality and dating, I try to use these difficult situations as opportunities: spiritual barometers with which to determine my current relationship to Judaism, and to G-d.

Sometimes, I find that I am able to face obstacles with a self-assurance that I didn't know I had. Other times, I feel myself slipping into a familiar, but uncomfortable pattern. In those situations, I find it difficult not to judge my own behavior. Even though I have made dramatic changes in my life, I sometimes feel guilty about my past behavior. My rabbi's advice helped me to accept my *teshuvah* as an ongoing process. He told me that growth comes from the experience of changing my behavior, of breaking old patterns. I try to remember that each day brings opportunities and challenges for my increased spiritual self-awareness.

In learning to value my journey and myself, I have come to know that I am part of a long history of women who also struggled to find their place in Judaism. In the process, I have discovered a rich community of strong women role models across history. Jewish women's voices are valued in the Torah, for being bearers of truth and wisdom.

From my *rebitzen*, I learned about the important ways that Sarah, Rebecca, Rachel, and Leah influenced the lives of their husbands, their children, and the Jewish people. Miriam foresaw the Jewish people's redemption from their exile in Egypt and led the women in celebration after their exodus. Devorah served as a general of war and as a symbol of justice for the entire people.

I learned that our female ancestors had a special gift called *binah*, or "feminine wisdom." *Binah* is the understanding of human nature and of universal truth. My *rebitzen* told me that in American culture, *binah* is called "women's intuition."

During my first semester at the University of California, Davis, I found the words to express my understanding of *binah*. It was not explained by a teacher or by an inner feeling, but by a painting on a wall at school. Everyday on my way to my British literature class, I passed a wall where someone had painted the words of Rebecca West: "I have yet to determine what a feminist is: I only know that's what people call me when I differentiate myself from a doormat." These words express my understanding of myself as a strong woman. This quote has become the slogan that epitomized my connection with feminism and Orthodoxy.

I no longer see religious woman as weak and repressed. Today, some of the most empowered feminists I know are Orthodox women who are living their lives according to Jewish law. I cannot think of a more radical Jewish feminist than a religious friend of mine who has eight children, runs a summer camp, is the codirector of an adult learning project, and serves Shabbos dinner to forty people at her house every week. I know Orthodox women who, in addition to their roles as wives and mothers, are lawyers, psychologists, midwives, teachers, doctors, artists, and writers. Their common bond is Torah. All of them work toward the goal of drawing G-dliness into the world.

They are not bound to the stove by chains, or restricted to the role of baby factory, as I once believed. Religious women are rising above social norms. They make conscious choices to honor themselves and each other as women. They respect one another and because of that, I respect them too.

I have a friend who lives in a very religious part of Israel. She changed almost every element of her life to come back to Judaism. I asked her whether she ever feels that the changes she made are too much. I wanted to understand why she chose an ultra-Orthodox path, when there are so many other ways to live a religious Jewish life. I will always keep her response close to me. She said, "I would do anything for truth; I believe the lifestyle I have chosen is truth, and nothing is more important to me than that."

Her words express my feelings about my own path toward religious Judaism. As I live a life according to the laws of Torah, I am constantly amazed by life's truth and beauty. The longer I am involved in my community and the more I practice the *mitzvot*, the more truth I find. When a person finds her truth, all of the gates of heaven open to her. In my journey back to Judaism, one gate after another has opened before me. My job is to walk through those gates with an open mind and an open heart.

I am now aware of the many ways in which G-d acts in my life. I now understand that what seemed to be a series of accidents, is really Divine providence. Every day, I thank G-d for showing me this path.

Reference

West, Rebecca. *Penguin Dictionary of Twentieth-Century Quotations*. Ed. J. M. Cohen and M. J. Cohen. London: Penguin Publications 1993.

16

Orange

❈

ANDREA GOTTLIEB

My eyes change color
sometimes they're green or brown
and sometimes they're orange
bright and big
and mad
I think anti-establishment
is actions
not hair color
I believe in embracing thoughts
completely
and honestly
I don't think love is dead
though sometimes I think I hear
it crying in the corner
I think apathy
is sin
I think my toenails twist
in weird ways
when I am angry
I love staring at distant galaxies
and realizing how small
and yet incredibly important
I am
I am a teacher
and a fighter
and a sinner
(and a Jew)

I don't want to change the world
when I grow up
I want to do it now
And sometimes when I'm mad
my eyes change color

17

A Woman of Valor, Who Can Find?

JULIE PELC

On Tuesday nights, I go dancing with God. It's a cathartic work-out for my body and soul. I sweat my prayers as I dance through the room, and the rhythm of the music moves through me. My mind is clear, my body is stretched and receptive, and my heart is open. The chatter of the world is distant; I live in the moment and in the music. I dwell in the heartbeat of my connection with the Divine.

My dance class is a practice of movement meditation. It was created by a theater director and healer, Gabrielle Roth, and has since developed into an international phenomenon with workshops and classes offered in cities throughout the world. Every week, a group of women assemble to dance in the studio of our all-women's gym in Boston. Our guide is Gabriella. She has studied extensively with Gabrielle Roth and also brings her background as an expressive thera-pist to her understanding of the practice called "5 Rhythms." She inspires and challenges us, week after week, to dance the stories of our souls with honesty and faith.

The journey begins when Gabriella dims the lights of the dance studio. We begin by walking. She invites us to move freely through the room, looking for open places and using the three hundred sixty degrees of space around us. I feel my bare feet touching the wood floor. I try to sense whether I am physically and emotionally grounded. As we move in circles around the room, I sometimes make eye con-tact with the other women, noticing and reacting to their mood and energy. The spirit in the room is palpable, as the cool air begins to warm, and our bodies begin to move.

I take inventory of my limbs and muscles, stretching and shaking the parts of myself where I hold the most stress. I become acutely aware of the tension in my shoulders, neck, and back; I notice the aches in my arms and hands. These are the places where my body has built protective walls to store my anger and sadness. In class, I must consciously and gently allow an emotional release. I close my eyes and strive to enter a sacred space: where the essence of my soul, the spark of the Divine, dwells. I allow the music to communicate directly with my spine. There are no steps, no choreography, and no teachers to follow. My dance on Tuesday nights comes from within.

We move through the five different rhythms of music: Flowing, Staccato, Chaos, Lyrical, and Stillness. Each rhythm possesses its own beat and its own personality. Flowing is the rhythm of fluidity: of curved, continuous motions. My arms float around my body and my hips sway smoothly and steadily to the music. The music changes, and Staccato punctuates the room with abrupt, linear movements. I punch and kick to the steady beat of the music, slicing the air with abrupt hand and arm motions. There, I express the anger usually locked inside my tense, controlled muscles. Chaos is where the curves of Flowing and the lines of Staccato meet and are pushed to the edge. The anarchy of the music urges me to surrender my body to the beat. During Chaos, sweat drips from my black curls onto my face and I reach a point of exhaustion. Then the music shifts again. With Lyrical, the energy of the room lightens. The indwelling, feminine presence of God, Shechinah, enters the room.

By the time we reach Stillness, I am ready to slow the pace of my movements. Stillness embraces and holds the previous four rhythms. I take inventory of my body and mind again. This time, looking inward: eyes closed, heart open. Sometimes, my body stands motionless during the slow music of Stillness. Other times, my back and arms sway steadily to the melody of a song only my feet can hear.

This dance is the steady, grounded dance of a woman who lives fully in her spirit, honors all of her emotions, listens with love to her body, and frees her mind. I encounter new parts of myself each Tuesday night as I allow myself to enter and learn from each rhythm. Every week, the dance is an attempt to release the thoughts that clutter my mind and to soar with Shechinah into the transcendent.

The 5 Rhythms dance class is an answer to my prayers for healing. After years of overextending myself, my body forced me to pay attention to a dull ache in my arms and hands. Until then, I had managed to squeeze one last task into every waking hour of the day. I scribbled notes in class, chopped vegetables for a Shabbat dinner, snapped countless photographs of my friends, clutched the telephone receiver in one hand, and lugged a heavy backpack with the other. I rushed from one meeting to the next and checked my answering machine and my e-mail account obsessively.

Late one evening as I pushed myself to type one last e-mail, the pain finally pierced my fingers to a halt. When I turned off the computer, I could not hold a pen, turn a key, grasp the steering wheel of a car, or open the childproof cap on the Advil bottle. It hurt to wear a wristwatch. I was unable to take notes in class or complete my assignments. I could not prepare a Sabbath meal. Doctors told me that I had developed a repetitive strain injury. They prescribed physical therapy, strong pain medication, and rest.

At the time, I was a full-time graduate student and was also in the process of applying to rabbinic school. After nearly ten years of struggling, searching, and thinking about what it would mean to become a rabbi, I wanted my essays to reflect that journey. I bought voice-activated software for the computer so that I could finish my application somewhat independently. Unfortunately, talking into a microphone did not give me the private moments of release I experienced when I wrote with my hands.

Since the age of eleven, I had kept a daily journal. I wrote life as I lived it, filtering experiences through my pen. Writing felt as natural and necessary as breathing. It was how I defined myself and how I made sense of the world around me. My journals, poems, and stories were handwritten letters to God: asking, searching, analyzing, and struggling to understand what was written between the lines of my life's story. The words, like prayer, came from a soul-place that felt beyond reason and logic. But now my ability to communicate with God, to spiritually come alive, had become painfully difficult.

My physical therapist instructed me to do a regiment of exercises five times a day. I wore braces to keep my hands immobile for the first weeks after the injury. Mundane tasks took much longer to complete than they had before. My hands now dictate the rhythms of my life. My hands were crying out for a Shabbat of their own.

Because of my injury, I stopped wrapping the leather straps of *tefillin* around my hands and arms when I prayed in the morning. Traditionally, one strap of tefillin is wrapped around the head and one around the hand and arm, signifying the union of thought and action in service to God. I wore the head tefillin, but decided to keep the braces on my arms, instead. I wanted to unite my thoughts with the inaction of my hands.

During the week of Hanukkah, I was called to the Torah for an *aliyah*. I recited the blessings before and after the reading, and the *gabbai* standing beside me chanted the traditional *Misheberach* prayer to honor my coming up to the Torah. I listened carefully as he recited the blessing, "May the Holy One bless her and her family, and prosper the works of his hands." My hands had inadvertently received the wrong blessing. With one tiny slip in the Hebrew, the blessing for my female hands had been accidentally taken away.

During the *Amidah*, I silently read a passage that is added to the prayer on the holiday: "You delivered the strong into the hands of the weak, the many into the hands of the few, the corrupt into the hands of the pure in heart, the guilty into the hands of the inno- cent. You delivered the arrogant into the hands of those who were faithful to Your Torah." I wondered: Which hands were mine? The strong or the weak? The guilty or the innocent? The arrogant or the faithful to Torah?

I went home and tried to work on my rabbinic school applications by talking into the microphone attached to my computer. The endless flow of thoughts and emotions that used to tumble one by one onto the page were caught in my body, in my throat, and in my mouth. I yearned to release the anger, the fear that my hands would not get better, and the worry that I would never again be able to juggle all of life's responsibilities.

Even after the acute pain dissipated, I could not shake the stiff- ness in my arms, back, or hands. I realized that I needed to get back in touch with my body's messages. I showed up at the gym one Tues- day night, hoping that a dance class would give me the opportunity to loosen my muscle tension, and help me to release the tight control I still struggled to hold over my own life.

At first, I was most comfortable with the music of Staccato, with its strong backbeat and repetitive rhythm. It was the rhythm of my daily life. I had internalized and mastered the modern skill of multitasking. I had learned to achieve, accomplish, and attain. I con- stantly felt like I was running out of time: always in a hurry to go somewhere or do something. I pushed the gas pedal progressively closer to the floor and drove well past the healthy speed limit. I tried to be the perfect student, the perfect daughter, the perfect girlfriend, and the perfect sister.

During services one morning, I flipped to the back of the prayer book and found the section in Proverbs about the Woman of Valor— the extolled model of traditional Jewish womanhood. It is traditional for Jewish men to sing this song to their wives each Friday night at the Shabbat table. For a few moments each week, her countless actions in the world are noticed and appreciated. The celebrated Woman of Valor does it all: she works, helps, supports, stretches, and extends. Once a week, she is honored, valued, and even glorified because of what she does.

> A woman of valor, who can find?
> Far beyond pearls is her value.
> . . . her hands work willingly
> She arises while it is still nighttime,
> and gives food to her household and a ration to her maidens.
> She discerns that her enterprise is good—
> so her lamp is not snuffed out by night.
> Her hands she stretches out to the distaff,
> and her palms support the spindle.
> She spreads out her palm to the poor,
> and extends her hands to the destitute.
> . . . Give her the fruits of her hand,
> and let her be praised in the gates by her very own deeds.

I thought about the Jewish women I knew. They all seemed to excel at the crazy balancing act of modern life: they had successful careers, meaningful relationships, and made beautiful homes. By watching them, I had learned how to take care of others, how to give, and how to do. I remembered learning in religious school that deeds were more important than beliefs and intentions.

When I was twelve, I longed to participate in the service: to have my own role, to sing from the deepest part of my soul, and to discover the words of Torah dancing within me. At our synagogue, women did not count in a minyan and were not allowed to lead services. At the time, every Conservative synagogue in Milwaukee was nonegalitarian. At my bat mitzvah, as I stood before the congregation, I knew I wanted to be a rabbi.

In high school, I developed a close relationship with the new assistant rabbi at our synagogue. Rabbi Buckman and I studied

Talmud each week. He lent me *The Ordination of Women as Rabbis*, a book with complicated halachic arguments both in favor of, and against, the ordination of women. Though he encouraged my interest in the rabbinate, he did not personally believe that women should be ordained. My dream to become a rabbi defied the convictions of my mentor.

I faithfully attended Shabbat services every Saturday morning. Each time a boy ascended the *bimah* to lead the *musaf* service on Shabbat, anger mounted within me. I sat restlessly in my seat with my jaw clenched, my hands tensed, and my heart aching. How could I become a Conservative rabbi if my ordination meant nothing in the sanctuary of my own synagogue?

I had never met a woman rabbi. The male rabbis I knew worked long hours. Their work demanded most of their time and emotional energy. They lived every moment in the public eye, serving as role models and community figures even when they were at home or away from their official places of work.

Rabbis' wives were also expected to be all things to all people: they were expected to come regularly to synagogue, be perfect mothers, have perfect children, and look perfectly put together. Each week, I spent several hours helping my rabbi's wife with her kids. It was she who taught me about the juggling act required of a homemaker who was raising a young family.

On Shabbat evenings, the rabbi sang the Woman of Valor song to his wife, Rachel, as their four sons listened and watched with intent. Rachel seemed pleased, almost embarrassed by the song that praised her long week of giving, loving, and doing for her family. Listening to him sing the Woman of Valor, I wondered whether the rabbi really knew how much Rachel did each day to make their beautiful, traditional, loving home run smoothly. I realized that I wanted to be both the Woman of Valor and the rabbi.

In college, I took both Jewish studies and women's studies courses and learned that my issues were part of a larger Jewish feminist discourse. I sought out other Jewish women to help me negotiate my identities as both a Jew and a feminist. I became a leader in the Jewish Student Council at Washington University and thrived at Hillel. And I found a community where I counted as a woman, where my contributions mattered and my actions made a difference.

I felt driven to dedicate all of my spiritual and personal energy to my work. After college, I took a job as an intern in Boston's Jewish community. When I was not working, I was volunteering. I was constantly busy. I didn't have time to think about my own connection to God or about my own spiritual needs.

I envisioned a twenty-first century Young Woman of Valor: squeezing every moment of silence from her daily existence. I lived for the moments when I could see the impact of my work on the community and on the Jewish people. The adrenaline rush I experienced from my constant action was like a drug that seemed to replace my need for God. I wasn't sure if I was happy, but I knew I was making a difference. My lifestyle exhausted all of my personal and professional resources. I started to believe that I didn't need or even deserve rest.

I learned to squeeze my palms shut for a few seconds when my fingers became tense, after a full day at work. I tried not to clutch the steering wheel of my car when my arms felt tired during the short drive to buy challah in Brookline. I ignored the dull ache in my fingers as they hammered each letter onto the keyboard of my computer. The external world had dictated my rhythm for years. Yet it somehow seemed abrupt when I developed the repetitive strain injury.

Even after the injury, I continued to live my life in the rhythm of Staccato. But the pain in my hands established the new pace of my life. My days were filled with physical therapy appointments and stretching exercises: it was merely a different endless list of tasks to complete. I struggled to maintain a sense of control in my life, but it was pointless to dictate orders to myself that my body could not deliver.

I knew that in order to heal, I needed to radically change everything about my life. I could no longer control my hands, my health, or my destiny with the plans, schedules, or the activities of Staccato. My health required me to relinquish control. My rhythm changed to Chaos in my frustrated moments of desperation.

On Tuesday nights, God was there in the dance studio, asking me to let go, urging me to trust, helping me to heal. My arms hung limply at my sides, and I twisted my spine to the rhythm of the music, allowing myself to lose control. I felt God interacting with me in the space outside my head, outside my hands, outside my body, and all around. God was teaching me that I needed to let go.

When we danced Chaos in class, I untied the rubber band that kept the hair away from my face and allowed my curls to shake free. With intricate combinations of gel and hairspray, I had been restraining my hair for years: coaxing it to stay bound in a barrette, begging it to stay flat against my head. When I danced Chaos, I shook my head fervently, as if to unhinge the remnants of control still that still clung to my mind. Dancing in Chaos was about admitting that I could not maintain control. I had no choice but to give in to the disorderliness of reality, to acknowledge that I could not be everything. I began to understand that only God can be everything, and that surrendering to Chaos was a true act of faith.

My submission to the strong, sweet Chaos of my life filled me with a sense of exultation that I had only previously experienced in the joyous release of writing. As I danced, I began to listen to the wisdom of my body's Torah. Taking care of my body, my teacher, the house of my soul, was a religious obligation. The exercises prescribed by my physical therapist became chances to repeatedly remind myself to stay in relationship with my hands and with God. They were my *Shacharit, Mincha,* and *Maariv* prayer offerings.

My dance grew increasingly playful. I danced Lyrical: the rhythm of joy, growing maturity, and celebration. At Passover, I imagined myself crossing the Red Sea from slavery to freedom, dancing with a timbrel in hand as I watched the raging sea on either side. I counted the omer, marking each day from Passover to the holiday of Shavuot. With each day, I found myself a little farther away from Egypt.

I celebrated my rabbinic school interviews and acceptances with the flying motions of my shoulders, spine, hips, and feet. I imagined myself drinking fully from the overflowing wine glass on Shabbat evening. I danced my rabbi dance, feeling the exhilaration of a wedding ceremony between my body and soul.

The image of the Woman of Valor who was praised in Proverbs never left my mind. I had grown up watching my mentors emulate her. They, too, arose while it was still nighttime, and their lamps were not snuffed out by night. These women strove to meet the needs of others, even when it meant working without replenishing their inner resources or resting their own hands. I had been raised, nurtured, mentored, and loved by many such women. I thought that it was my responsibility to follow their example. I wanted to show them that they had wisely invested their time, love, and energy in another future Woman of Valor.

I continued to dance on the edge, dangerously close to my old, dizzying routine. Everywhere I looked, I saw that the world needed repair: I received e-mails each week, asking for volunteers to help in women's shelters or to serve food at soup kitchens. There were

Hebrew schools in need of qualified teachers. My small egalitarian minyan needed Torah readers on Shabbat. I wanted to comfort every friend experiencing a crisis and rejoice in every celebration.

As my hands began to improve, I inched closer and closer back to the aching days of endless to-do lists and phone calls. I never allowed myself to completely rest my body or mind. I knew that a Woman of Valor would never take a luxurious bubble bath or curl up on the couch with her favorite book, when mounds of laundry went undone and dinner remained uncooked.

Even in the dance studio, I managed to carefully sidestep any real, lasting change. I delighted in the dynamic energy of Staccato, Chaos, and Lyrical, but could not settle into the softer, slower rhythms of either Flowing or Stillness. When we began class with the rhythm of Flowing, I squirmed, searching for a steady, reliable backbeat. My arms felt too tense to sway, my back was too stiff to bend, and my shoulders remained locked. I struggled to relax into the slow, melodic rhythm of Flowing. Movement and change felt laborious. My life felt laborious. My weariness, fatigue, and painstaking journey through the dance studio mirrored my body's slow journey toward genuine healing. It was as though my body was protecting me from real release, keeping me from making the life-altering shift that I so desperately needed for true, whole healing.

As I stood on the brink of my career as a rabbi, I realized that I needed to find a healthier model for my career and my life. I was wearing out my body—my hands—my tools for action in the world. I looked into the abyss and saw the impossible challenge of trying to be any type of Woman of Valor. The life of such a woman seemed antithetical to Judaism. In the Torah, God provided a continual cycle of work and rest, action and renewal. Every week, we are commanded to rest on Shabbat, refraining from all acts of creation. Yet Women of Valor can never rest or refrain from creating, even on Shabbat: they are the ones busily making Shabbat possible for everyone else.

I believe that to truly live a Jewish life means affirming and sanctifying polarities: work and rest, celebration and mourning, noise and silence. The Jewish life is a circle that honors the steady passage of time: days rolling into nights, childhood into old age. It is dipping sweet apples into thick honey on Rosh Hashanah, listening to the youngest child sing the Four Questions on Passover, and standing to hear the last shofar blast on Yom Kippur. I discovered new meaning in the Hebrew word *kedushah*—usually translated as "holiness"—which also implies creating clear boundaries of separation.

Jewish living sanctifies the rhythms of a life. By listening to the rhythms of Staccato, Chaos, Lyrical, Flowing, and Stillness, I found another system that allows for a full cycle of labor, rest, and renewal. In many ways, Jewish law epitomizes the holy wisdom of Staccato. The dance of Staccato is a dance of separation: between sacred and mundane, permitted and forbidden, life and death. I began to connect this wisdom to the *kedushah* of my hands. Every day, it was my decision to wake up and conscientiously choose life: to make distinctions and boundaries in my daily activities that honored and respected healthy living.

I started to notice the ways in which Staccato permeated my commitments: the rules I followed that provided ritual, ethical, and emotional boundaries in my life. I felt Staccato as I rocked forward and back to the rhythm of the *davening* at the traditional weekday services. As I prayed, I planted my feet firmly on the floor. The fringes of my *tallit* tickled my legs as they danced back and forth to the repetitive rhythm of the service.

I realized that I needed to create a physical, private, sacred space in which to communicate regularly with God: a place to collect my thoughts, to feel God's embrace around me. I needed to reconnect with Shechinah in my daily life by experiencing the rhythm of Flowing outside of the dance studio. Flowing is about connecting to the Divine spark. It is about nourishing internal resources.

I looked around me for models of Flowing as inspiration. I felt the rhythm in the bodies of Jewish women, who for generations have waved their hands in three smooth circles over the flames of flickering Shabbat candles. Flowing is evoked as they pull the light toward their bodies and gently bring their hands to their faces to recite the ancient blessing.

I began to *daven* every morning. When I chanted the blessing as I wrapped my *tallit* around my body, I was telling God that I was committed to the covenant of our relationship and would be present and focused each time I draped this fabric of light over my shoulders. When I said the Sh'ma, I wound the four corners of the *tzitzit* together around my fingers. For those few moments, I felt as though I was untangling the complexities and confusions of my life, and unifying the corners of my soul.

A month before I began rabbinical school, I went to a beauty salon to cut off five inches of my hair. I had it cropped closer to my face: crazy black curls now flew in all directions. It no longer felt important to control them, pull them into a tight ponytail, or coax them to stay flat against my head. When I danced later that night, my dark, Jewish mane flung through the air—free and alive. Curls bounced from my scalp in all directions—even when my body stopped dancing. I was learning to nurture, honor, and love my whole self, naturally.

The first four rhythms led me back to the place where life starts: Stillness. Stillness taught me to dwell in the spaces between full and empty, open and closed. Stillness is Shabbat, Jewish time. It is the silent *Amidah*, the hum of moving waters in the submersion of the *mikvah*, and the hush of quiet before a groom stomps on the glass at his wedding. Stillness is the white parchment upon which the letters of Torah are carefully printed.

As I started to earnestly explore the rhythm of Stillness in dance class, Gabriella suggested that I allow my mouth to drop open slightly, to relax my jaw. Stillness came to me when I allowed my tension to dissipate, when I invited God back inside my mind, body, and soul. Only when my human hands failed, could the hand of God guide me. God's hand taught me to listen: to move my body, quiet my mind, and bring my soul back to life. I learned what it means to truly daven when I learned to dance Stillness.

In dancing these five rhythms, I rediscovered my Divine partner. I know that I am dancing in harmony with a life rhythm older and larger than anything I can imagine. I feel in my soul that God is the rhythm that shapes our lives and gives them meaning. God's rhythm is the union of heaven and earth, firm land and moving waters, action and inaction.

My hands are my greatest teachers. I am learning that my value is not measured in deeds or pearls—I am infinitely priceless, because I exist. I don't have to create, help, or do in order to be a Woman of Valor. These are valuable lessons for my future as a teacher, a rabbi, and a Woman of Valor who knows that even God's hands rested on the seventh day of creation.

Every morning during *Shacharit*, it is traditional to count the passing days of the week according to the rhythm of Jewish time. Each morning, when I recite the Psalm of the Day, I remember and count aloud the number of days until the Shabbat for my soul, which happens each Friday evening as daylight rolls slowly into night.

Each morning, I also silently count the number of days according to the holy Shabbat for my body and mind, which happens each

Tuesday evening as Gabriella dims the fluorescent lights of the dance studio, when mundane space and time are transformed into the sacred.

Reference

Greenburg, Simon, ed. *The Ordination Of Women As Rabbis: Studies and Responsa.* New York: The Jewish Theological Seminary of America, 1988.

III
Neshamah

Our Emotional and Intellectual Selves

18

Chutzpah and Menschlekeit: Negotiating Identity in Jerusalem

CARYN AVIV

I came to Israel on a dissertation fellowship, and to understand why my marriage fell apart. Or more precisely, why I chose to leave my marriage, get divorced, come out of the closet, and then wind up writing about American immigration. (Such drama in so short a life!) My ostensibly "objective and detached" research agenda grew out of my convoluted, painful struggle to understand what it means to be an American Jewish woman, a sociologist, a self-defined queer, and a human being in the last-gasp moments of the twentieth century. In the process, I discovered the paradoxes of belonging and not belonging, of wrestling with what it means to be simultaneously American and Jewish in an Israeli immigrant context, and what it means to be queer in an overwhelmingly patriarchal, heterosexual society.

I married Ilan (a pseudonym), when I was twenty-four. Twice in the previous years I had called off wedding plans. I later recognized these decisions as stunning moments of clarity, quickly drowned out by the din of my own internal chorus urging me to be a nice Jewish girl and just to get married.

Ilan wanted to visit Israel for our honeymoon to see his extended family. (He is an American child of Israeli parents.) I willingly obliged, having only been to Israel once, on a Camp Ramah summer trip, almost ten years earlier. For me, the trip was a bewildering and fascinating reacquaintance with Israel, where I realized my own vast ignorance: of Hebrew

147

as a linguistic reinvention, of Israeli and Palestinian cultures, and of the weighty burden of the region's history.

We then spent the next summer in Jerusalem, attending courses at Hebrew University and traveling around the country. Ilan and I heatedly discussed militarism, the Israeli-Palestinian peace process, the merits and pitfalls of American immigration to Israel, and the linguistic and cultural challenges of an increasingly heterogeneous, multicultural Israeli society. I grew more interested in learning about Israeli and Arab feminism, interpretations of Palestinian-Israeli conflict, and feminist critiques of nationalism. Aliyah became a common topic of debate, anxiety, and fantasy between us.

Ilan was convinced that Jewish life in the United States was headed for existential disaster. I disagreed with his claim of the inevitable de-mise of organized Judaism in America. "Look at all the sociological evidence," I countered, pointing to the seeds of innovation, revival, and of course, the explosion of creativity in Jewish feminist ritual, publishing, thinking, and activism. These frustrating conversations in-evitably led us to the intellectual impasse of whether aliyah would "res-cue" American Jews from the alleged vagaries of assimilation. In retrospect, I realized that our conversations (almost rote arguments after a while), represented an emotional impasse we had reached over whether aliyah would save us, and our marriage, from ourselves.

Meanwhile, I began graduate school in sociology at a Catholic university. Although eclectic and erratic in our Jewish observance at the time, Ilan and I were living in an Orthodox Jewish neighborhood in Chicago. I felt like an outsider to the extremely right-wing and gender-segregated religious culture surrounding me. To alleviate my alienation from the Catholic environment of graduate school and to learn about Jews very different than myself, I studied the Orthodox community around me. I wrote an ethnography of Orthodox Jewish women's practices of Yiddishkeit, based on fieldwork with my neighbors and in neighborhood religious institutions. I read everything I could find on Jewish feminism, Jewish women, and the sociology of Ameri-can Jews. Then, I began to dabble in the literature on immigration, ethnographies of Israel, and theories about the meanings of "home." I didn't realize that I was also laying the groundwork for what would eventually become my dissertation topic.

I continued to visit Israel at least once a year, to see my extended family. My sister was now living in Jerusalem and debating the notion of aliyah for herself. In a tentative step to see if I could imagine myself making a life in Israel, I joined an e-mail list in 1995, devoted to practical and ideological discussions about aliyah. Through this network, I met several Americans in Israel, talked with them about their experiences, weighed my own feelings, and gathered information about the practical and bureaucratic processes of becoming a citizen. At the same time, I became more and more dubious about the viability of my marriage for a whole host of other reasons that had nothing to do with the simmering conflict over immigration.

I knew that I could no longer define myself as strictly heterosexual, and felt repressed by the confines of monogamous marriage to a man I loved dearly, but wasn't in love with anymore. I began secretly planning how I could leave without totally destroying my relationship, my sense of self that I had built with this person for most of my adult life, and my precarious, marginal financial situation as a graduate student. In short, I wanted out—out of my marriage, out of the roller-coaster conflict over whether to make *aliyah*, and out of the dank stuffiness of the closet. After a long period of searching and struggling, I finally decided I could neither agree to make *aliyah* with Ilan, nor could I continue being married to him.

Over a tumultuous and emotional Thanksgiving weekend in 1996, I came out as an unapologetic American Diasporic Jewish queer. Gently, but with conviction, I told Ilan that dissolving our marriage would allow him to realize his dream of making *aliyah*, and would allow us both to do what we wanted: to find a nice Jewish girl. He sat, immobile and ashen, on the living room couch, and then asked that we obtain an Orthodox *get* (divorce) so he could remarry without any problems. A few days later, Ilan announced his imminent departure to Israel, and finally moved there by August of the next year.

If this sounds like a relatively straightforward account of how I got from point a to point b, let me assure you that it wasn't. I woke up at 4:00 in the morning every night for weeks after leaving Ilan, my body wracked with grieving sobs and a terrible dread that I was making the worst mistake of my life. At times I wondered in anguish why I chose to endure such a torturous, painful process of transformation. Yet, leaving freed me from feeling trapped in a life trajectory not entirely of my own making.

Alone, I had time to explore different communities and relationships in Chicago through the feminist bookstore where I worked. I blossomed into an independent and more confident self. For the first time, a clear, silent space opened up in my life, which allowed me to reflect upon things I still don't entirely understand, and to nurse the wounds and scars of a life in transition.

During the four desolate winter months immediately following the rupture of leaving, I hibernated in the lonely solace of my own tiny apartment by Lake Michigan. I knew something useful could come from this cluttered debris in my personal life. The boundaries between my research interests and personal relationships always seemed blurred and messy. I thought long and hard about what had happened, and how it was influencing my academic work: who did I want to become, and what did I want to write about? What fascinated me so endlessly about people's immigration stories? Why did Ilan feel so deeply that Israel was where he "belonged," despite his American Jewish identity, when to me Israel often felt alienating, frustrating, incredibly sexist, and profoundly militaristic?

These questions formed the kernel of what later became my dissertation proposal. I chose to compare women's and men's gendered experiences of immigration and how these folks create a notion of "home" in Israel, while simultaneously inventing different selves in the process.

Thankfully, I got a grant, packed my life into cardboard boxes, and arrived in Israel in August of 1998. Full of excitement and uncertainty, I questioned whether I could ever finish such an ambitious research project by myself. I was so far away from home—the sociology department, the bookstore, my friends, and Lake Michigan—that had provided so much meditative reassurance during those fitful, exhilarating steps toward dykedom and independence.

Not by accident, I decided to move to one of the most American neighborhoods in Jerusalem. The neighborhood, Kiryat Aron, is about ten minutes from downtown, on the west side of the city. It is flanked by the Jerusalem Theater on one end and a funky strip of coffee shops and boutiques at the bottom of the hill. The neighborhood has many synagogues, which span the religious spectrum and are known for their large contingent of American members. In the first few weeks after moving in, I frequently ran into lots of acquaintances from Camp Ramah and the American suburb of my childhood. I quickly realized that anonymity is an illusion in such a small neighborhood. Dense social networks overlap everywhere, and opportunities for invisibility are few. Even when I went running early in the morning, I saw at least a few people I knew on their way to work. Out of affection or claustrophobic frustration, I sometimes called the 'hood my "little American *shtetl*."

After living in Israel for a few months, I discovered that there are not one, but many thriving American immigrant communities in

Jerusalem. I am acutely aware that my neighborhood of choice, and my ethnographic project, are largely determined by my age (under thirty), my presumed heterosexuality (I was closeted to most people), my class background (upper middle), and my Jewish educational background based in the Conservative movement (years of Camp Ramah and United Synogogue Youth participation). If I had been married with children, I probably would have found my way into the older, more family-oriented American community that revolves around two shuls (one Reform, one modern Orthodox), known for their activism in religious pluralism and gender-egalitarian practices. Had I come to Jerusalem with an ultra-Orthodox (*Haredi*) background, I might have found an apartment in Sh'chunot Rivah, a stringently religious community on the other side of town that is also known for its American immigrant population. Or I could have chosen to live in one of the suburbs of Jerusalem, which are known for their very American and very national religious (*Dati Leumi*) character.

As they do everywhere else, the politics of identity matter fiercely in Israel. They have far more impact on major immigration choices like housing, education, and social networks than I had imagined before arriving. Plunking down into the center of Kiryat Aron yields a particularly rich slice of American immigrant life in Israel today, but only one of many possible slices.

I found myself living in the middle of a fascinating, loosely defined "community" of highly educated, mostly upper-middle-class, professional American immigrants (and to a lesser extent British, French, Canadian, Australian, and South African immigrants), who tend to work for high-tech companies or nonprofit and educational organizations that link Diaspora Jews to Israel. Many of these young, single (and predominantly heterosexual) American Jews came to Israel after spending their junior year at Hebrew University, and then again for a year or two at one of several yeshivas that cater to young Diaspora Jews searching for more religious study. In my dissertation, I call this a "gradual immigration" pattern, unlike other types of migration patterns where people move from one country to another for either economic incentives or political asylum. More often than not, these immigrants came without really knowing whether or not they wanted to make *aliyah*, but knew they wanted to spend more time in Israel. They were supported by the myriad of religious institutions and programs that encourage relationships between Diaspora and Israeli Jews. After finishing these programs, with nothing in particular beckoning them home (except their families and their own ambivalence about what to do in life), these immigrants decide to stay "just a little longer," which commonly stretches into another year or two. I've heard plenty of anecdotal stories of people taking a trip to the Interior Ministry to declare citizenship after already being in Jerusalem for two or three years. They figure they might as well reap the benefits of immigration, having already carved out a life for themselves with a job, an apartment, and a social life. While I certainly wouldn't call this pattern "aliyah by accident," it does appear that many young immigrants come to Israel unsure of, and quite ambivalent about, their future. They decide to make *aliyah* only after a couple of years of engaging in the tasks of making Israel seem like "home" through relationships, employment, and the mundane routines of daily life.

The English-speaking, young immigrant scene is diverse, but extremely small, depending on religious affiliation. Everyone seems to know everyone else. When I first arrived, I routinely played Jewish Geography with total strangers and discovered common acquaintances within one degree of separation. I played this game with my interviewees as well. Mutual acquaintances can smooth the initial anxiety of an interview. Based on that connection, I was considered somewhat of an insider. In fact, many of my research participants agreed to interviews based on hearing about the project from a friend.

The young American immigrants whom I interviewed came to Jerusalem in search of many things, but most often, they said they wanted to find a community where they belonged. They usually had little difficulty finding it, despite the fact that the romantic patina of belonging to that community had worn off. Most immigrants found themselves earning far less money with fewer opportunities for upward mobility. These immigrants were willing to trade their class privilege and material affluence for community (although some were more reluctant than others). Most of the folks said the rich friendships, religious atmosphere where "Shabbat is really Shabbat," and a sense of belonging in Jerusalem were worth the trade-off. Unlike in the United States, where there are tons of different choices for how to spend one's leisure time, young immigrants tended to structure their social lives around English language lectures (mostly organized by religious institutions), hikes, Israeli dancing, movies, coffee chitchats, and a growing poetry slam scene organized by active members of *Hakehilah*. Because of the conservative social character of Jerusalem, barhopping, theater-going, and organized sports aren't nearly as popular or plentiful.

Most importantly, the Kiryat Aron singles scene revolves around the weekly round-robin routine of sharing Friday night meals and Shabbat lunches at each other's houses. The "social economy" of Shabbat meals is the foundation of the immigrant community. It is a complicated web of obligations and reciprocal relationships, where immigrants invite friends (and often friends of friends and even strangers), to solidify and widen their social network. The guest list at most of these meals depends on who the meal organizer wants to "repay" for having invited them to a meal previously, so as to extend the circle of exchange and reciprocity. Communal meals are the preeminent way to meet new people in a relatively small community that is constantly replenished by visitors from the Diaspora and from students studying in Jerusalem at various institutions. It also serves multiple purposes by fulfilling a religious commandment, providing a sense of routine and structure to the week, and organizing time for social interaction. Shabbat observance leaves little downtime on the weekend for doing much else except praying, eating, drinking, and talking.

After several months of feeling guilty for constantly eating at other people's tables without any gesture of reciprocity, I became enmeshed in this social economy by organizing meals of my own. I remember pulling off this event for the first time: shopping, cooking, and cleaning my apartment on a frantic Friday afternoon to create a meal for fifteen people. After everyone left, I sat in exhaustion at a table filled with dirty dishes, challah crumbs, and half empty wine glasses. It occurred to me that an enormous amount of invisible labor goes into the creation and maintenance of this entrenched social ritual. To participate in the process of communal meal making, an immigrant has to decide when to do it (so that guests will show up and it won't conflict with other people's prior obligations), plan the menu, invite all the guests, shop for food, cook, and clean their tiny rental apartment. Depending on how many people attend, meals can cost a significant amount of money, which cuts into people's less than bountiful salaries. I've never seen anyone offer to pay for the meal, which would be considered extremely rude and in violation of the principle of *hachnasat orchim*—the "welcoming of guests" (although several jokesters seem to consistently sing for their supper). However, to help defray the costs incurred by hosting a meal, immigrants often bring "incidentals," like wine, challah, and dessert, as a gesture of thanks for the invitation and to prevent the meal organizer from blowing their week's salary on food expenses.

In Kiryat Aron, it seems like there's a relatively equal gendered division of labor among the single men and women who create these social gatherings: perhaps as a way to curry favor among the plethora of single women looking for partners, young single men create meals of their own on a regular basis as do women. In more religious American communities of married couples, the gender inequality in the division of labor is far more pronounced. At the meals I've attended given by married religious couples, the women have consistently scurried back and forth from the kitchen to organize, serve, and clear while the men sit contentedly, discussing the Torah portion of the week or talking about the latest political imbroglio in the news. This is not a surprising finding, but it is quite a stark contrast to meals I attended that were hosted by the young singles.

When I first began attending these meals during the fall holiday season of Rosh Hashanah, Yom Kippur, and Sukkot, I was stunned by the extent to which conversations focused on the politics of gender and sexuality. At first, I thought it was just me, that my decade long obsession with gender, sexuality, and feminist theory had rendered me unable to think through any other lens. But after postmeal analysis with several of my research participants, I realized that people would much rather talk about the micropolitics of intimate relationships than potentially divisive topics of public debate, like the intermittent peace process or strained relationships between religious and secular Jews. Almost as sport, everyone exchanged information and gossip about who is dating whom, who might be a good match for a friend, and what to do about the lopsided gender ratio between the scores of available women and the noticeably fewer men.

I knew instinctively, before I came to Jerusalem, that part of the process of immigration was about reinventing one's sense of self and identity. But I had no idea that one of the central aspects of that process revolved around the tangled issues of gender and heterosexuality, which in that setting meant the task of finding a partner with whom to marry, build a life together, and have several children (preferably in that order and as soon as possible).

During my time in Israel, a typical Friday afternoon looked like this: I would wake up from a brief nap around four-thirty, just as the sun was setting. In cramped apartments everywhere around me, young women and men would be showering, primping, perfuming, and rouging for the impending singles highlight of the week, otherwise known as *Kabbalat* Shabbat. I would quietly put on a demure sweater, long skirt, tights, shoes, and a little bit of makeup. That was my usual outfit for rounds of Shabbat dinners among modern Orthodox religious immigrants in my neighborhood. Inevitably, I wouldn't feel like schmoozing, so I'd skip *Hakehilah*, a.k.a. "singles central." Dalia, my roommate from Johannesburg, would wake up a bit later, and we would leave the house together with our entrance tickets for the evening meal at a friend's house: chocolate cake, wine, and *rugelach*.

We would walk past a shaded beige stone apartment building, and past the large green plastic garbage bins. All around us, people would be walking out of the many shuls in the neighborhood, dressed in their neatly pressed clothes. Down the street, we would turn into a narrow stone passageway, a gently sloping alley past a natural health clinic with a beautiful garden filled with cypresses, a large cactus tree, aloe plants, and jasmine bushes. Then we'd make another right turn onto a quiet residential street, toward the intersection where the *Hakehilah* building stands at the corner.

Within a few minutes after the services end, the street would be packed with hundreds of freshly showered young people chit-chatting, kissing each other, saying "Shabbat Shalom," and cruising the scene. It's an intense, if brief, social setting. Several young singles I interviewed said that they always feel like they're commodities on display. Even though it makes them feel uncomfortable, they force themselves to go, because it's the social moment of the week. It is a time when flirtations are begun, massaged, or broken; it is when plans for Shabbat meals are solicited, offered, and finalized. I often just parked myself next to the metal guard rails on the sidewalk to observe this cruising, watching people maneuver to place themselves in the best ogling position. The sexual headiness and tension would literally ooze down the street, the air thick with the perfume and aftershave lure of possibility.

The crowd would reach a huge swell within ten minutes. Any car that mistakenly or deliberately tried to drive down the hill past the synagogue would be forced to creep forward slowly. It would be impossible to drive down the street that was so clogged with people engrossed in cruising and conversation. On several occasions, I watched people in their cars curse in frustration with their inability to pass. Some drivers would lean on their horns, honking incessantly. That makes people especially angry, because it's a blatant violation of religious observance of Shabbat, when you're not supposed to be in a car in the first place. I'd make eye contact with the driver, and nod, shrugging my shoulders sympathetically. At least in my neighborhood, people wouldn't bang on the hood of the cars yelling *"Shabbes!"* or throw shit from the garbage bins, like people do in the more stringently religious neighborhoods in Jerusalem.

After about a half an hour, the meet-and-greet would slowly dissipate. Public religious cruising would be over until Shabbat morning after *davening*, when the whole process repeated itself. People walked up or down the hill in clumps, some carrying bags they brought with them to shul, filled with dishes or wine for the meal they're about to attend at someone's house. The singles scene in the neighborhood again retreated to the pseudoprivate sphere (nothing is every really private, let alone anonymous). Communal Shabbat meals took place behind closed doors, where gossip, schmooze, and wine flowed freely until the late hours of the evening.

At these Shabbat meals, I learned that the immigrants in the neighborhood often feel a relentless, nagging pressure to find a heterosexual partner. This was especially the case for those over thirty, who left the United States in disappointment over the Jewish dating scene in the major urban areas. Their anxiety was fueled by the noticeable gender inequity in the Jewish singles scene; there are far more single American women than men searching for a partner.

Given all the complaints about dating I've heard, and the plethora of *shadchanot* (matchmakers) who ply their trade in this city, I've wondered if there's a marriage panic occurring. Israel is a very publicly family-oriented society (though only specific kinds of families are recognized as ideal and valued). I think that American young singles quickly internalize the notion that creating their own version of the ideal Jewish family is not simply an individual life task. Their own autobiographical projects become folded into larger discourses centered around the imperative of continuing the "Jewish people and the Jewish nation." Rhetoric about finding a partner and having kids, which is embedded with nationalism, peoplehood, and Jewish existential survival, serves as the linchpin of society, and the definition of adulthood. It seems that national citizenship and participation in the future of the Jewish nation of Israel, hinges upon the ability of individuals to participate in the narrowly defined parameters of *sexual* citizenship and by reproducing patriarchal families. All these pressures exist simultaneously with the dilemmas and challenges of carving out identities as emerging adults and as Americans in an Israeli cultural landscape.

Not surprisingly, a few immigrants told me that they hoped to find an Israeli partner, to help them feel more like they belong. They wished to develop close ties to an Israeli family and to have Israeli children. A small number of Americans actually do accomplish this. Many more of the Americans I met were reluctant to get involved with Israelis, either because of their lack of Hebrew language skills, their perceptions of cultural differences, and/or their preference to socialize only with other Americans. Some feel a profound ambivalence about absorption into Israeli society because of their prejudice against Israeli manners, styles of social interaction, and cultural miscommunication.

As a result, many American singles wind up confining themselves to the relatively small community of fellow immigrants where speaking English is a relief, where everyone already knows each other, and where people publicly gripe about finding a suitable partner. Or, conversely, folks get extremely excited when "new blood" moves into the neighborhood because it increases the pool of available people to date. Little did I know that my arrival on the scene constituted "new blood."

Not only are gender and sexuality central preoccupations of my research participants, but these dilemmas form the nexus of my own experience as well. I knew that coming to Jerusalem as an out dyke would be hard, but I didn't imagine how hard it would be. Nor did I ever imagine what might happen to my ideas of sexuality and sexual identity in the course of doing fieldwork, especially among more religious American immigrants. To them, notions of queer visibility and equality are an anathema, an abomination forbidden by Torah.

During my dissertation proposal hearing, I tentatively raised the question of whether to come out to research participants. In unison, my three advisors shouted, "NO, NO, NO! You don't want to jeopardize your relationships with your informants!" Cowered by the forcefulness of their response, I steeled myself for a year in the closet. I wasn't happy about the prospect, but clearly, not claiming the privilege of heterosexuality would pose some knotty (albeit interesting) problems in the field. I reluctantly left a thriving queer/lesbian community in Chicago, and I arrived in Jerusalem knowing no lesbians personally, but aware of a few groups here and there, who met on a regular basis for social gatherings.

The Jerusalem queer community is tiny, fragmented, and relatively invisible to the public eye (although this is slowly changing with the establishment of a fledgling community center in the downtown area). The Jerusalem Open House opened in March 1998, as the first lesbian, gay, bisexual, and transgendered community center in Jerusalem. The center houses social and political programs, a community resource center, and a speaker's bureau. In a conservative, polarized, and religious city such as Jerusalem, I hope the center will become an important symbolic step toward a more pluralistic society in Israel.

It was hard feeling so invisible, so isolated, and so repressed—something that I struggled with from the moment I stepped off the plane. I couldn't walk into a bookstore and find any queer magazines on the display rack, let alone any queer books on the shelf. There wasn't one bar in the entire city where lesbians can hang out, cruise, dance, and be affectionate in a public place without fearing harassment. The notion of a queer business district—like the Castro in San Francisco or Andersonville, i.e. "Girlstown" in Chicago—doesn't exist. Most of the Israeli lesbians I met were much older than I was. Many were deeply closeted (both at work and to their families), reluctant to get involved with English-speaking lesbians, and a little resentful of temporary-resident Diaspora dykes who come for a year, look around at the state of queer culture, and compare their experiences of relative freedom to the homophobia and invisibility Israelis live with on a daily basis.

Playing it straight as a sociologist also had its emotional costs. I constantly felt duplicitous and dishonest. I was completely unprepared for how fully my assumed heterosexuality would be taken for granted and incorporated into the deepening levels of attachment and intimacy that I developed with my research participants. This made it even harder to explain why I initially lied to or hid from the few people I eventually came out to, including my roommate.

Early on in my fieldwork, new acquaintances asked if I wanted to be "set up" with available single guys in the neighborhood. I politely declined without saying why, sometimes using the cover of: "I don't date potential research participants; it's too unethical." I went running with an American woman in the mornings, who constantly complained about her dating troubles, and expected me to commiserate in turn about my own life. I tried to change the subject. When I interviewed more stringently religious people in other neighborhoods, they often assumed I was already married, and wanted to know "how my husband feels about this research project."

Long before coming out, I had grown uncomfortable with straight folks' ease in navigating the social world with a sense of entitlement, privilege, and "normalcy." When I arrived in Israel the issue of queer identity left me feeling uncomfortable in casual conversations at Shabbat meals with straight folks, where conversations about "homosexuality" took place in the abstract, as if the reality of queer people sitting in their midst couldn't possibly exist. In these situations, I confronted the ethical and political dilemma of whether to come out in a melodramatic flourish and potentially alienate my research informants, or suffer through the conversation in silence and fume at my own complicity in queer invisibility and heterosexism. I am acutely aware that my silences and fears of being out catered to, and served the interests of, the dominant forces of conservatism and religious fundamentalism in Jerusalem. I learned the hard way that lying is not an admirable research skill to develop for ethnographic fieldwork.

I also constantly debated which personal details to divulge and which to hide when meeting new people, regardless of their religious affiliation and identity. What should I tell about my own story of why I was in Jerusalem and how I decided on my research topic? I usually gave the briefest synopsis possible, without elaborating too much. People always seemed surprised by the casual revelation that I'm divorced, not only because they thought that I was about four years younger than I actually was, but also because I didn't seem to be ashamed. And always, the next question was, "So when are *you* going to make *aliyah?*" My stock reply became, "I'm here to *study aliyah*, not to make it." I learned that by telling my story of getting divorced (without the attendant part of coming out), I revealed myself to research participants as a vulnerable human being, which created a degree of intimacy and made them more comfortable telling their own stories.

Asserting my marital status, without sharing the crucial part about my coming out, also reinforced people's assumptions of my heterosexuality. They assumed that I was looking to get married again. Several times, I was asked out for a date at the end of an interview: "You listen so well; it's really nice to talk to a girl like you." Or even worse, I was unwittingly set up by well-intentioned interviewees who invited their neighbor in for coffee, to meet "the eligible young professor." These absurd moments produced hysterically funny field-notes, but at the time, I found myself silently screaming inside: "I'M NOT WHO YOU THINK I AM! STOP ASSUMING THE WHOLE FUCKING WORLD IS STRAIGHT!" I learned that it takes a lot of energy to silence the self with a smile.

The biggest paradox of my fieldwork experience (and by far, the most salacious) was the unintended, unfolding drama of getting briefly involved with someone: with a modern Orthodox man, of all people. Yes, you read that correctly. A man. It was an accident, an unintended surprise. I assure you, I didn't mean to! Being in a new, if brief, relationship with a man who wanted to build a committed, heterosexual relationship and family life forced me to reexamine all the questions I thought I had answered by coming out in the first place. In any case, I remain thoroughly unconvinced that the "heterosexual project" is what I want to do with my life. He and I are no longer together for precisely that reason.

I had to wonder if the relationship was an episode of "situational heterosexuality," in response to the overwhelmingly heterocentric atmosphere of Jerusalem's social climate. I fretted endlessly about what it all meant, and how it changed the course of my fieldwork. Did I now have to rescind my membership in the Lesbians of America club? Should I simply write this off as a "passing phase" and wait to revert to my jolly queer self upon my return to America? What the hell was I getting myself into? And how could I negotiate this without hurting myself and/or anyone else I care about in the process? In short, how could I have the chutzpah to get involved with another man after all the rigmarole of coming out, and how could I act like a mensch in the process of negotiating this weird, unexpected turn of events?

My parents, needless to say, were ecstatic. They felt much more comfortable asking me about my personal life. They clamored for details about the "nice doctor." My father asked if he could scrape the rainbow flag sticker off the back of my car that sat in his garage. I laughed at his joke, but felt deeply hurt afterward by his implicit devaluation of who I am. (The answer was no, because even if I came out yet *again* as straight, I would still be an outspoken advocate for queer equality and visibility.) My extended family exhaled a huge sigh of relief. Even with their support after leaving a bad marriage and coming out, this heterosexual relationship fueled my American Jewish family's not so subtle desire to see me "get over the queer thing already."

Being in a relationship with a man (however fleeting or impermanent it was), had its privileges and rewards, which were even more pronounced in Israel. There, assumptions about gender and heterosexuality are so seamlessly woven into the fabric of everyday life that they are naturalized, invisible, and deeply entrenched. This was ideologically hammered home to me in ways too numerous to count, and made all the more transparent after my initial struggle in the closet. I was extremely aware that I could be seen in public, holding hands with this man, without thinking twice about being harassed or physically assaulted. Research participants routinely inquired about "how things are going" and confessed their envy at how I had so easily "found such a mensch" while they're still single, lonely, and looking. I could read erotic poems at the poetry slam without having to deal with the issue of gendered pronouns if I so chose.

The public recognition of being invited to dinners and parties as a couple was pervasive and yes, I admit it, seductive. It's just so easy to play it straight. I could "forget" about all the work that needs to be done in the world to make it a better, safer, more just place for queers if I wanted to. But I don't want to, and I can't forget. In my mind, it didn't matter that I had a brief relationship with a man. I still love women, and I'm still queer.

In the end, it wasn't so much because of the privileges of heterosexuality that I left both the relationship and Israel. It was the nagging sense of not being honest with myself. I realized that there was no point in continuing a relationship that had no future in a place that never felt like home. It was impossible to imagine myself becoming more religious, wanting to move to a suburb outside of Jerusalem, and raise lots of children. I grew frustrated trying to explain basic concepts about feminism and gender inequality to this well-intentioned guy, who struggled to understand why *davening* behind a *mechitzah* and using masculine god-language create such profound alienation for me.

As a liberal Jew, I believe that to a certain extent, life is all about choices. But as a political leftist, and through my training in sociology, I know that sometimes the choices available to us are severely limited by our imaginations, not to mention all the obvious "big" things like racism, class inequality, gender stratification, and heterosexism. What I'm trying to do in life, in fieldwork, and through writing this essay, is to imagine as many choices as possible. I want to push and blur the boundaries of what's considered "acceptable." To call into question where "home" and the "Diaspora" are located. And to discover where my research participants and I ostensibly "belong" as American Jews. I want to make a home for myself: an intellectual, political, social, and erotic home of my own. In my work and in my life, I also strive to link, integrate, and write about how personal relationships and sexuality influence the process of writing so-called academic theory.

The delicious challenge in life is to meld a gutsy combination of chutzpah and *menschlekeit*. In other words, I want to do good for and with others, maintain a sense of honest integrity and ethical responsibility, and have fun in the process. In my mind, this is what being an American Jewish woman/feminist/queer is all about. I relish that challenge, with all of its attendant hopes and dilemmas.

19

Passages

LEAH BERGER

First born, my brother was
self-proclaimed—
the one who broke a lightbulb
in the delivery room
with the geyser of my mother's
waters breaking
as he emerged from her womb.

Second born, to the tune of
revolutionaries
I began kicking the night
they spoke of Marx the Jew
around the dinner table at the rabbi's house.
Seems I wanted to add a commentary
on the commentary,
my first *drash* a reminder to the comrades,
this is all very interesting
but what have you to say
about women's labor?

20

Meeting in the Middle

LYNNE MEREDITH SCHREIBER

I never dreamed that dating a Catholic man would lead me to orthodoxy. In the secular world where I grew up, I learned to believe that everyone was the same. I learned that hard work and love could lead anyone to a happy ending. I always knew that I was Jewish, but I never understood exactly what that meant. So, for two and a half years, John and I professed our love for each other, broke up, and got back together again. It wasn't until John asked me pointed questions about my religious beliefs that I began to wonder about them myself.

We met during the fall semester of my junior year in college. My friends and I were dressed up to go to a party on a Friday night, in light makeup, flannels, and our favorite jeans. John and I met at the party, and we ended up talking until six in the morning. He was five feet seven inches, with brown hair and brown eyes. He was wild and energetic, and his voice folded around my ears like melted chocolate.

And so it began. We played tennis, rented movies, and he became the first love of my life. At first, I rationalized that nothing would come of this liaison, simply because he wasn't Jewish. It was the carefree time of college, and I figured we'd have an intense, intimate affair with a dramatic, tearful good-bye. He'd be a note in the margins of my history. Nothing more.

In the beginning, we questioned each other about our respective religions. He produced enticing answers about Jesus and church and all of the Apostles. I confessed my inability to explain the Jewish belief system, traditions, or rituals. Despite a dozen years of Hebrew and Sunday school, I didn't know enough about my religion to answer even the simplest questions. I repeatedly picked up the phone and dialed my grandparents, who provided answers for both of us.

All along, John and I agreed that if we got really serious, we would have "the talk." Yet, throughout our relationship, we never stopped talking about our religious differences. If our relationship were to get to that elusive, more committed stage, we'd choose one religion, we reasoned: his. He had little interest in Judaism; he looked at Christianity as "Judaism plus," so it was up to me to leave my religious identity behind.

On the surface, our backgrounds weren't so different. Our families prized education and family togetherness. They taught us to be motivated and hardworking. Yet his parents knelt on padded benches in a church affixed with crucifixes while mine spent two days a year standing and sitting in a cavernous temple and eating honey cake. Their values were the same, but their beliefs were miles apart.

When I was growing up, Jewish observance was an obligation, not a joy. My mother came from a *Conservadox* clan: Grandpa was a first-generation American from New York, the product of Orthodox Polish immigrants, while Grandma was raised Reform in Detroit. When they married, my grandparents followed the stern instructions from my grandfather's father to "meet in the middle."

Meeting in the middle meant that Grandpa walked to shul on Saturdays and Grandma drove with the kids. Like many 1950s Jewish families, they hung red felt stockings on the mantle on December 24, because they didn't want their children to feel excluded from American culture. Their upbringing led my mother and aunts to choose Reform Judaism and my uncle to become a Buddhist. Only one aunt lights Shabbat candles quietly in her home.

Growing up, I didn't understand that Judaism was supposed to be a personal relationship with G-d. All I saw was men in white robes on a distant stage, lifting their hands and lowering them, indicating when we should stand and sit. Our words—our prayers—were in italics in the prayerbook. We knew to recite our part after the rabbi droned his part into the microphone. I'm embarrassed to say that my sister and I took frequent bathroom breaks during services, because we really weren't essential to the pleas. The rabbis did our davening for us. They didn't need us to reach G-d on our behalf.

I'm a product of the fast-paced, USA Today world of sound bites and quick bits. Even my religion came with Cliff's Notes. Like a backpack of rocks over my shoulder, I carried my Judaism with me everywhere. I wanted to set it down, but caught reproaching glances and raised eyebrows when I tried. I thought "mitzvah" meant "good deed," not "commandment." I had no idea what being Jewish meant, only that there was a smaller pool of boys available to date and an obligatory bris if I ever gave birth to a baby boy.

My journey toward becoming religious started inside of me. Even in high school, I was fascinated by the complexities of religion. When my tenth-grade English teacher assigned my first term paper, I chose to research and write about birth control and the Catholic Church.

Despite my early interest and passion in the subject, people who knew me years ago still comment about how funny, how strange, and how unexpected my choices are. To them, it looks like two very different extremes: once, I was in love with a Catholic man and now, I don't drive in cars on Saturday. For me, it is all part of a journey to infuse my life with meaning.

If ever I wanted to make it work with someone, it was John. We discussed religion all the time, and found striking similarities between the stories of the Last Supper and the Passover Seder. I loved the way his family had regular rituals. They went to church on Sundays and had lunch afterward at a New Jersey country club. With peaked fingers and bent knees they recited G-d-fearing prayers before bedtime. During Lent they ate no meat on Fridays.

For me, religion meant being dragged behind my parents to boring services on the High Holidays, when I would have rather stayed home in front of the TV. I loved matzo ball soup and gefilte fish, but beyond that, being Jewish just made me feel different from all of my friends. Being with John gave me a glimpse of what it would be like to fit into the mainstream.

We agreed that two adults can practice conflicting religions without feeling pressure from one another to change; it's only when kids come along that it gets tricky. Once I fell in love with John, I couldn't disentangle myself from that coupling. I couldn't be objective, or realistic, or honest with myself. So we were stuck, in love and uncertain. What we believed in our hearts was intrinsically different, even opposing. We agreed that a family has to be cohesive, solid—not Mommy doing Judaism and Daddy at the Catholic Church. We knew we couldn't do two religions. And he never wanted to learn about Judaism.

I sometimes had visions of the life we could one day have to-gether. I saw us living in a country-style house on the East Coast, with green fields reaching out behind our property. Inside, the house would smell of baking cookies, roasting meat, and drying laundry. I would be writing at an antique, rolltop desk. Then I imagined a black cross—like the one in John's parents' house—nailed to the wall. I realized that I didn't want crosses or other Christian symbols in my house. "I can do everything else," I told him, "just nothing overtly Christian." John didn't understand: If I were willing to marry him and raise my children in a non-Jewish environment, why wouldn't I be comfortable with non-Jewish symbols?

Then, he popped The Question: "How can you be so Jewish when you don't know anything about it?" I recoiled defensively. I looked him in the eyes and replied: "Because of the Holocaust. So many Jews were killed; how can I voluntarily kill some more?" He nodded si-lently. All I could think to add was that it would kill my parents and everybody who came before if I had Christian symbols in my house. My legacy would end right there, forever.

In that dingy apartment with the deep-throated lyrics of Queensryche softly throbbing from the stereo, John pushed me to think about my insistence on being Jewish, despite my lack of educa-tion and religious commitment. At first, I folded my arms across my chest and pursed my lips defensively. But I knew he was right. John's questions challenged me to commit myself to a search for a substan-tive religious identity of my own. I posed questions to priests and rabbis, and sat silently in huge churches and benign temples. It was the best, boldest gift anyone has given me, though at the time I just felt deeply embarrassed by my ignorance.

The religion issue never got easier. When we tried to project our separate ideas of happily-ever-after onto our relationship, our religious differences became the source of heartfelt frustration and bittersweet agony. We would often sit on the tattered carpet of his tiny college apartment and shoot questions at each other. Years of Catholic school and church attendance put him in a strong position to issue immediate answers. With each of his questions about Judaism, I drew a blank. I picked up the phone and called my grandparents.

I struggled to subscribe to my parents' age-old dictum. It was the one family tradition that had been passed down from generation to generation: whether or not they chafed against the hard armor of religious rules, they married within the faith. I broke up with John

dozens of times. We dated on and off for years, through graduations
and moves to different cities. Regardless of how far away we moved,
we always found each other again, driving across miles of calm country, toward the imagined magic once again.

My parents never accepted my relationship with John. It was
usually our family *minhag* to invite non-Jewish friends to Passover
meals, but John was not welcome at my grandparents' seder table. My
parents dangled threats before me: If you marry a Catholic man, we
won't pay for a wedding. If you have a Catholic wedding, we won't
attend. After hearing doors slam again and again, I began to finally
turn away from John.

Despite the tumult and turbulence, knowing John was a gift that
inspired me to search for my own religious identity, and for that I am
grateful. In the end, I realized that I couldn't be anything other than
Jewish. What I liked about Christianity was the regular ritual, the
belief in a Higher Power, and the way that values and integrity bound
John's family together. But I couldn't sign onto Jesus, couldn't stom-
ach bowing before a porcelain statue of a bearded man. What I liked
about Christianity was its Jewish roots.

So I set about figuring out what I wanted Judaism to mean to me.
I was living in New York, and the last time I had seen my family, my
mother pressed a ten-dollar bill in my hand and said, "I know movies
are expensive in New York. Please see *Schindler's List.*" I saw the
movie with a non-Jewish friend, and I cried like floodgates had opened
on a rising river. My friend sat helpless beside me at the movie and
in the cab afterward, uncertain how she could help, if at all. At home,
I called my mother, the tears still flowing. "I'm sorry," I said. "I will
always be Jewish."

Looking back, I cringe at the thought that I initially stayed Jewish
out of a frightful persecution complex, because of the Holocaust. Today,
I marvel at my initial motivation to hold onto my heritage, and I thank
G-d repeatedly for leading me to a more concrete Jewish identity.

On the day that I realized I couldn't not be Jewish, I also realized
that I had to educate myself. I needed to figure out how Judaism could
be significant to me. The years of Hebrew and religious school at the
Reform temple where I grew up didn't cut it, so I vowed to find
something that would—before I fell in love again, and way before I
had children.

After John and I broke up the most definitive time, I delved into
Judaism, looking for a place where I belonged. I moved to Washing-

ton, D.C., where I taught Sunday school at a suburban synagogue. During that year, I had to teach my ninth-grade students—half of whom came from intermarried families—about interdating. I told them to figure out what they believe before falling in love. It's such easy advice, but it's so hard to follow.

In Washington, I worked as a staff writer for the *Washington Jewish Week* newspaper. As with any reporting job, I had to know my subject better than my readers in order to provide compelling explanations and context. This posed a problem: I'd been careening through my Jewish life on autopilot, and my grandparents were not always available when I had a deadline dilemma. That job forced me to learn more about my Jewish identity. I was challenged to question my heritage and to make my own choices.

During my early days at the newspaper, a colleague named Debbie harangued me with questions about what I believed. She had been raised Reform, married a man with a Conservative background, and over the years they became modern Orthodox together. Her synagogue intrigued me. When I visited, I met religious Jews who defied the stereotypes I had once believed. I thought men held women in disdain, and I expected the women to be frumpy. I found a group of stylish, dynamic, and intelligent Orthodox Jews who were committed to Torah. I discovered that Orthodox Judaism was not the oppressive regiment I had imagined. Instead, it was a passionate attempt to derive meaning from the mundane.

I didn't find this community until seven months after my move to Washington. Throughout those months, Debbie constantly challenged me about my beliefs. Late at night, in the privacy of my two-bedroom Bethesda apartment, I thought about her questions.

"The Reform movement doesn't even believe in *halachah!*" Debbie spat at me one day. "Yes, we do!" I threw back, quickly thumbing through a glossary of Hebrew terms to learn the meaning of "*halachah.*" Later, I learned that the Reform movement, in fact, does not subscribe to the generations-old canon of Jewish Law.

Debbie was eager to invite me to her home for Shabbat. It would be a real Sabbath celebration, without music or television or cars. We would walk under the silent moon to the synagogue and stay up late drinking wine and coffee, talking and debating. I put it off repeatedly until a Friday in December, when I finally agreed to be her guest.

The night before, I wrestled with anxious anticipation and contemplated ways of canceling diplomatically, without offending her. I even called my father, thinking he'd be on my side and would provide a plausible reason why I could cancel on such short notice. But he told me canceling would be rude, and advised me to go with an open mind. In the end, my not-very-interested-in-Judaism father was the one who encouraged me to explore my own beliefs.

I arrived at Debbie's house around four on that winter day. I was terrified that I wouldn't know what to do, that I'd make a mistake. I didn't know what I'd do without the constant company of television, radio, telephone, and my computer. I had even erroneously thought that Orthodox Jews were forbidden to flush toilets on Shabbos. I was afraid that my ignorance of Judaism would be obvious to everyone.

Yet, I fell in love with Judaism that Shabbat. I loved the idea of family togetherness over a decorated table. The house was warm and well lit, the sweet aroma of homemade challah filling the front hall, and a carrot kugel steaming in the oven. I learned the prayer for hand washing and listened to her family *bentsch* after the meal. Saturday morning, I watched, my mouth opened in awe, as "cool" people swayed to the lilting voices *davening* in Hebrew. It wasn't the oppressive and restrictive world I thought existed behind the cloak of Orthodoxy. It was something modern and doable and attractive, and I wanted it for myself.

For the past eight years, I have taken small steps forward and smaller steps backward, in an effort to make my life observant. I traveled to Israel where I *davened* at the Wall in Jerusalem's Jewish Quarter, with the Shabbat sun setting in pinks and oranges behind heavy blocks of ancient stone. I learned to nap on Saturday afternoons, endured the dark when friends in Petach Tikvah lost power during a cold February Shabbat. I came to accept and even enjoy concepts of modesty and discipline. I have traveled through various Orthodox communities. I've seen it all, and I like so much of it.

It has not been easy to become observant. For a time, seemingly simple strictures were impossible for me to take on, like giving up sleeveless shirts and short skirts, or turning off the radio on Saturdays. In the years since that first Shabbos, I have gone back and forth. I went from no Jewish observance to an ambiguous place between religious commitment and personal independence.

A few summers ago, I hiked up a thousand feet of elevation in the Big Horn Mountains of Wyoming, with a non-Jewish friend at my side. Pale yellow light streamed between branches of tall, thick trees. Except for the quick intake of breath and the crunch of leaves underfoot, I heard nothing. Surrounded by bushy fir trees and drastically sloping hills, I began a one-sided conversation on the merits of a religious life. Eight hundred feet above flat land, I described why I loved the seemingly confining life of Orthodox Judaism. I told him in detail about the beautiful *Shabbatot* I had spent at my rabbi's house. Far up in the clouds, with snow-covered peaks a quick thousand feet away, I finally accepted that religious Judaism is where I belong.

Now, Judaism is something I hold close, like a bunch of freshly picked flowers tight in my closed palm. I know now that if I unfold my fingers, the flowers will fall to the ground. Time and again, I had to turn completely away from my community to find that it's exactly where I fit. Today, I am fully Orthodox. More than anything, I believe that the Torah came from G-d and is immutable, and I let that guide my actions. I am trying to observe every little detail, while still forgiving myself when I don't, and allowing the patience that is necessary to make such drastic life changes.

My memories keep me calm in the times when I struggle with religion. I think about a particularly beautiful Shabbat in Jerusalem. Twilight descended on the city, washing a soft orange light onto the pink stones of the *Kotel*. I prepared for Shabbat, and tucked my backpack into a bottom bunk bed at the Heritage House in the Old City. That youth hostel is a nesting place for wandering Jews who want a genuine Sabbath in the geographic heart of our world. A dozen young women lit tiny tea-light candles on a deep windowsill and covered our eyes one after the other, breathing the syllables of the blessing through soft lips.

When we walked to the Wall to pray the evening service, we joined the waterfall of people down the steep steps to the flat plaza, where brush grows between the stones and softly smiling faces wave and shake in rhythmic *davening*. Across the partition, a few men sang a melodic Carlebach tune to *Kabbalat* Shabbat, and I shared a prayer book with a red-haired woman from Chicago, who pointed to the parts I was supposed to say in English. Later that night, I sat drinking steaming coffee from a Styrofoam cup with women in flannel pajamas, and we talked about the worlds we had willingly left behind for the promise of the flickering candles on our mantelpieces.

The next morning, we poured down the stairs to join the thick sea of praying people, and then ascended to homes where celebratory food snuggled in ovens. I stopped at a top-floor apartment, the home of a mythical rabbi who wore a *streimel*, a round, dark fur hat, even in the heat of the day. When he arrived home from *davening* that Shabbat morning, we all hushed into silence in the tight space of his living room to hear his words. He spoke in Hebrew, and I picked at the noodles of the *Yerushalmi* kugel he made himself for the occasion, knowing that one day I would understand fully what he was saying.

I am not proud of some of the steps backward that I have taken along my journey. I have slipped on muddy paths, rebelled like a child in a screaming tantrum. I bought a house within walking distance from the synagogue, but after the mortgage was approved, I spent a year eating cheeseburgers. I never walked to shul—never even went to shul—even though I lived so close. I have spent so many months growing near, and then doubling back. I wish it had been easier for me to become *frum*.

I am living the life of the Orthodox Jew, an individual who stands alone before my Creator: my desires and passions, my sins and whims, in full view of Him only. I love walking to synagogue on Saturday morning, calling out "Good Shabbos" to the people I pass. I even say hello to the little boys who, in their black pants and white shirts, mutter "Good Shabbos" to the sidewalk in response. Even in the coldest weather, I don't mind the walk. It's the only time I stop rushing and notice the peaceful quiet outside my suburban home.

Interdating remains a complicated issue. American culture is enriched as individuals trace their roots and share the idiosyncratic qualities and traditions of their heritage. There is nothing unlovable about Gentiles. I've realized that the non-Jewish men I've dated are wonderful, caring individuals, but they're not who I want to spend my life with.

One of my best friends (who was born and raised in Detroit by American-born parents) spends Friday nights doing Irish Celie dancing at the Gaelic League headquarters. As friends, we can appreciate and respect each other's individuality, without really confronting our differences.

When I last saw John, I told him about the *mezuzahs* that I have nailed to every doorframe in my small house, and the two sets of dishes I keep in facing cupboards, the separation I insist upon between dairy and meat. I wondered what he would think of this very Jewish person that had blossomed out of the helpless and uneducated Jew I used to be.

That last time we met, it was after three years of silence. We got in our cars and met in the middle, between Chicago and Detroit in

Paw Paw, a small outpost outside Kalamazoo. As I drove west on I-94, I wondered about who he and I had become in the years since we had loved each other. Over the phone, he told me that he was six months out of an intense breakup and called himself "an emotional basket case." I was years away from anything emotionally challenging. In fact, he was the last person I had truly loved. I called him because I wanted closure and a chance to move beyond the memories of our hands interlaced. I also wondered if perhaps I had let go of something beautiful that I should have kept.

It was a crucial test from G-d, and I'm thrilled to have passed. I arrived first and sat in the warm car, the engine humming and the radio blaring. I watched every car that passed, looking for his black Acura. Finally, a compact with a bike rack on the roof turned in. It was John, with the same lean, pointed face and strong hands. The hair on his slight sideburns had grayed and he was skinnier than ever, but other than that, he was the same guy I could never fully leave.

I had rounded into a woman confident in her femininity. We hugged nervously, then slid into a restaurant booth, starving but unable to eat. We perused separate menus and decided on pizza. Casually, I asked, "thin or thick crust?" He shot me a look, and I knew immediately it would be thin crust, remembering his East Coast aversion to thick, midwestern pizza. When we ordered his pizza, without my input whatsoever, I knew that it was finally over. The yearning that I felt was for closeness and caring, not necessarily for John.

We reminisced jovially, but whenever I attempted to talk about my life—what I had become in the absent years between us—he clammed up. That night, I realized that if I had married John (or any of the men with whom I had brief relationships), I would have never fully found my own religious identity. That day was a homecoming of sorts, a melancholy growing-up. John's life didn't include me anymore and I realized I wanted mine free of him. I told him softly that it's okay if all we have now is history. We cried as we parted once again, this time for good.

If it had been different in Paw Paw, if the electricity we used to feel would have resurfaced and encircled us in its cocoon, maybe I would have tried to make it work. But I know in the depths of my soul that it never could. Today, I'm not a person who can abandon my beliefs for another. I have come to accept that my beliefs have not necessarily followed a straight path, but when I look back, I see that each step has brought me closer to loving Judaism.

My story is the story of the exile of the Jews: a story of discovery, of picking up and discarding, of mending the worn fabric of a life, and sometimes throwing away the sharp shards of identity found in the back of a dark closet. I'm glad I chose to stay Jewish. I come from a beautiful tradition of candles and wine and fresh-baked bread, of quiet conversations with my Creator in the angled sunlight of the morning. My ancestors smuggled brass candlesticks out of countries where they were hated, and set them on dusty countertops in a land where they didn't speak the language. When I step into a Jewish sanctuary, I am immersed in the hush of carpet and colored windows, amazed by the dark lightness of the Ark and the scrolls it keeps carefully inside.

21

Secret Weapon

AMY ELISABETH BOKSER

Our temple was just
off the service road—
walls adorned with tin
menorahs, parking lot
overgrown with weeds.

My brother said
if I went there by myself
he would kill me:
I believed.
He was old enough
to go to Hebrew school.
He told me about something
called the Holocaust.
I knew that, like Christmas
it wouldn't happen
to people like us.

We would walk there
five whole blocks
to "gather hay"—
picking grass
wild onions
and a leaf
that smelled so noxious
we took it home and dried it
for our Secret Weapon.

He said that Jews
were killed in showers.
Gas came out instead of water.
I took baths.
Kids were burned in ovens.
A fat man came down the chimney
across the street.

I helped my brother
make more Secret Weapons
in the coffee cans
rusting in our backyard.
He said one whiff of that
and the Nazis would have run
in an instant.

He also told me there were
dragons in the world
monsters in the desert.

Our temple is now
an insurance office
aluminum rectangles
nailed over the menorahs.
They paved the parking lot
of course. I would not
go there by myself.

So it's a good thing
my brother planned ahead.
The coffee cans are waiting
in my parents' yard
more potent with each season.
I have seen the Gila monster
the Komoto dragon
and that everything he told me
is true.

22

Ira Glass, Where Are You?

TOBIN BELZER

Once a week, I have a date with Ira Glass. For one glorious hour on Saturday afternoons, he talks and I listen. In the sanctuary of my living room, I'm completely engrossed, drawn in by the gentle lilt of Ira's Chicago accent and his contemplative pauses. Each week, he invites guests to talk about their lives. Ira weaves his own thoughtful comments through their narratives, drawing out a theme, even when the stories seem to have nothing in common. The tales are sometimes sentimental and poignant, other times outrageous. I lie on my couch as I listen, grateful for the opportunity to think about issues and people outside my own reality. I let my mind wander as I inhale the scent of perfumed oils from the bath I've just soaked in, and I think about Ira Glass: my dream guy.

During our weekly liaisons, I've cultivated a detailed fantasy about Ira. He is introspective and communicative, funny and kind. He is incredibly handsome, in a very Jewish-looking way. He has a circle of close friends; is self-confident and charming. He is smart and sensitive. Most importantly, he and I adore each other.

The real Ira Glass is the host of a radio show called *This American Life* (on WBEZ in Chicago). Each week, with millions of other National Public Radio listeners and devoted fans, I tune in to hear the show. Listening to Ira makes me feel hopeful and safe. For one hour every Saturday, I concentrate on the sound of his voice while I picture a future for myself with a wonderful Jewish husband.

Ira has lent his name and voice to my fantasy; I've filled in the rest with my imagination. Sometimes on his radio show, Ira mentions

177

details about his own life. He shares his opinions and occasionally he discloses an intimate detail or two about his personal life. These are the moments that I both cherish and dread. I want to know everything about Ira, but at the same time, I don't want to know anything. By creating a fantasy about Ira's identity that is solely based on my fantasy of him, I am learning about my values, passions, and priorities.

Ira is the most recent in a long series of crushes. Since shortly after I hit puberty, I've been almost exclusively attracted to Jewish men. I am drawn to their intelligence, sensuality, and Dustin Hoffman-esque vulnerability. Since high school, I've dated Davids, Aarons, and Daniels. I've lusted after Mandy Patinkin, Jeff Goldblum, and Matthew Broderick for years. I believe a man looks more handsome when he is wearing a *tallis* and *kippah*.

In retrospect, I know that I developed my proclivity for Jewish men as a form of adolescent rebellion. I grew up in a secular Jewish family. Throughout my childhood, my family celebrated Hanukkah and Passover, and Christmas and Easter as social events. My father acted as though any practice of Jewish tradition or custom constituted religious fanaticism.

When I was fifteen, I rebelled by joining a synagogue, enrolling in Confirmation class, giving myself a Hebrew name, and becoming a bat mitzvah. I was angry with my parents for denying me a Jewish childhood. I wanted a mother who would light Shabbat candles and a father who would lead a real Passover seder. I wanted them to raise their hands above my head to bless me, and to rejoice in my love of Jewish learning.

At dinner one night, I told my mom that I wanted our family to be a Jewish family. She replied: "When you have a family of your own, then you can do things exactly how you want to." Since then, I've been determined to find a partner with whom I can cultivate a Jewish life.

At fifteen, finding a wonderful Jewish husband did not seem like such a formidable task. That, however, was before I discovered the Jewish singles scene. After college, I took someone's advice and tried to "meet a man while doing something I enjoy." Since then, I've been to countless concerts and lectures. I joined book clubs and attended Shabbat dinners, participated in challah-baking workshops and annual Israel fairs. With other twenty-something Jews, I painted a school for deaf children and walked to raise money for breast cancer research.

From these experiences, I learned one thing with certainty: singles events are the loneliest gatherings in the world. Each event is essentially the same. We stand around, drinking cheap wine and eating kosher cheese, trying to ignore the fact that there are three times as many women as men. Our interactions are tinged with an inevitable hint of desperation, because none of us are completely satisfied being single. The women end up commiserating in clusters. We don't hide our disappointment: most of the guys, we agree, seem like total losers. We try not to turn competitive in the climate of scarcity.

After meeting at least two women who will most likely become my friends, I allow myself to leave these functions a little early. Driving home, I give myself a pep talk about how great it is to interact with so many interesting women. I try to stay hopeful about meeting a man who I'd want to have an intimate relationship with. And I remind myself to avoid dwelling on the "relationship" topic.

Despite my efforts (or maybe because of them), the topic feels impossible to avoid. Anytime I turn on the television, thumb through a magazine, peruse an advice column, or listen to the radio, I encounter relationships everywhere. This is especially true since I have chosen to pursue a career as a professor of sociology, a field that is based on the examination and explication of the social world.

There are almost two million web sites about relationships. I just turn on my computer and everything I never wanted to know is at my fingertips. With one click, useless advice, quizzes, horoscopes, quotes, and humor flood my screen. Between the wedding industry, the beauty industry, and the sex industry, the topic of mating dominates the cyber-world.

I recently read a *New York Times* article called "Who Says You Can't Hurry Love? 8 Minutes in the Life of a Jewish Single: Not Attracted? Next!" The article describes a new fad among Jewish singles called "speed-dating." This new practice is traditional matchmaking with a modern twist. In the usual scene, singles are left to fend for themselves. In speed-dating, the organizers systematically pair up each participant with eight potential mates, for eight minutes each. Eight minutes, claim the organizers, is enough to discern whether chemistry exists between two people. Speed-dating is part *yente*, part sorority rush. The practice, invented by the Aish HaTorah Foundation in Los Angeles, has become enormously popular among twenty-something Jews, and has spread to fifteen cities and five countries including Australia and South Africa.

I think the motivation to find a life partner in eight minutes is fueled by the shame that remains attached to being single. The "old maid" archetype is alive and well in the twenty-first century. She is still being held over the heads of young women to remind us that it is unacceptable to stay single. We all have an unmarried family friend or relative whose image is evoked, by well-meaning advice givers, as an example of who not to become. We're also reminded that the longer we stay single, the worse off we are.

Being single has turned me into a veritable advice magnet. It seems like half of the people in my life are having the experience of being young, Jewish, and single, while the other half are offering advice about it—solicited or otherwise. The combination of my marital status, and the fact that I am still a student at age twenty-nine has nearly cemented my status as "not quite adult." As such, my love life (or lack of it) is open for discussion. Privacy, apparently, is earned under the wedding canopy.

When I decided to attend graduate school to study sociology and women's studies, my parents warned: "You won't find a husband hanging around women's studies." Others were encouraging, heartened by the mistaken belief that Brandeis University would be teaming with eligible Jewish men. My recently married friend told me: "Marry someone who loves you more than you love him." My grandma suggested that I cultivate a love of sports, and urged me to attend a hockey game, because "men like hockey." Similarly, a cousin urged me to make more male friends, so that I can "get inside male culture." My mom's friend raved about personal ads, and a woman at my gym couldn't say enough about her dating service experience. Five different friends encouraged me to try Internet-matchmaking through *jdate.com*. My aunt suggested that I take matters in my own hands by hiring a professional. But really, is a matchmaker's office any place for a Jewish feminist?

There is a very fine line between being open to the possibilities of love and being desperate. To me, the shame that accompanies being single does not feel half as bad as the shame of admitting that I want to get married. For a few years, I refused to acknowledge that marriage was even a considerable option for me. I didn't want to be one of those pitiful women actively searching for a husband.

My fears have been intensified by the entertainment industry, which offers particularly offensive images of Jewish women. We are overwhelmingly portrayed as loud, pushy and completely undesirable. Jewish men on television are never attracted to Jewish women; the rate of intermarriage and interdating on television is 100 percent.

Despite my feminist awareness, it takes tremendous energy to disregard those harmful stereotypes. Most of the time, I remember that I am dynamic and desirable. But when I am feeling particularly vulnerable, I tend to believe that all the nice Jewish men are either married or gay. At times, I become thoroughly convinced that smart women intimidate men. I am also prone to believe that Jewish men, on a very fundamental level, don't like Jewish women at all. Sometimes, I completely forget that it is possible to be happy without a husband. It is a particularly low moment when I find myself relating to the characters on *Ally McBeal.*

I forgive myself for these moments of weakness and regression, since my life has been flooded with that romantic ideal since I can remember. I learned from an early age that my fundamental role in life would be as someone's wife. At five, I had already internalized that expectation. During kindergarten, I participated in the annual Halloween costume-parade wearing a tiny white gown and proudly clutching a fake bridal bouquet.

Growing up, I learned that making friends was important, and that having a job I liked would be desirable, but that my ultimate happiness depended on finding a man. I believed that falling in love and being a part of a couple would provide the most important kind of connection and validation. I dreamed that someday I would live my own romantic happily-ever-after.

Like most girls who grew up in Los Angeles, I began to cultivate my appearance at a young age. Only beautiful, thin women (I believed) were worthy of men's desires. In junior high, I thought that wearing the right clothes would make me popular with boys. I quickly discovered that my body was wrong: the right clothes didn't fit. I went to a nutritionist to learn that small portions of low-fat food would make me thin. Which meant desirable. Which meant happy. I was desperate to be happy, so I lost thirty pounds. For good measure, I made one additional adjustment: I got my nose "fixed." The less Jewish I looked, the more beautiful I felt.

I have learned a lot since I began dating fourteen years ago. Becoming a feminist and working with a great therapist has helped to dissuade much of my angst about relationships. I have worked hard at cultivating a sense of self-importance and self-worth beyond my appearance, and have struggled to stop judging myself based on my attractiveness to men. I am learning that to have a true partnership with a man, I must take time to develop a strong sense of myself. And

I know that I am happiest when I surround myself with friends, when I do work that I value, and when I take care of myself.

I am now sensitized to the heterosexism that dominates the relationship discussion across media. As I studied sociology and feminism, I began to envision a life for myself outside of the white, middle-class, heterosexual ideal I had grown up coveting. It was both terrifying and exhilarating to think of my life on my own terms. Instead of a nuclear family unit, I extended my vision of family to include a community of friends.

I expanded my life possibilities so much that I dated a woman. For a while, I became part of a loving and supportive all-women community. Once I liberated myself from the competition for the scarcest resource (Jewish men), I felt free. But I had the same relationship with my girlfriend as I had with all of my Jewish boyfriends. I learned that dysfunctional psychological patterns emerge in relationships regardless of gender. Self-awareness, I discovered, matters more than anything.

I have long since rejected the idea that I need a partner in order to be happy, but my desire for partnership remains compelling. Recently, my soon-to-be-engaged friend and I went browsing for rings. Between my "oohs" and "aahs" at the sparkling rocks in the glass cases, I wondered if I would ever wear such a ring.

I never exactly envisioned myself as a traditional bride. I was an aspiring nonconformist during my late teens, and I had elaborate plans for an unconventional wedding. I decided that my gown would be made of live flowers, and that my lover would wear a suit made entirely of cake. We would pledge our love to one another, and eat lots of cake. At eighteen, I proclaimed that I was searching for the man who would appreciate that ceremony. I enthusiastically set out to find "cake man."

Eleven years later, it is difficult to muster that same enthusiasm about finding my partner. Acquiring a feminist lens has helped assuage the fear that I will never find Him, but it has also in some ways, inflamed it. Many of my worries have been confirmed. I learned that many of the qualities that I want in a life partner are discouraged in males. From an early age, boys are shamed for being emotionally effusive and communicative. Men who exhibit those qualities are stigmatized and disparaged for being emasculated.

While my education has heightened my understanding of gender politics in relationships, it has also interfered with my ability to engage in those politics on a personal level. Statistically, I know that the more highly educated I am, the more difficult it will be to find a partner. Although my education will enable me to avoid relying on a relationship with a man for financial stability, I know that to have a truly equal marriage partnership would be exceptional, not normative.

Still, I understand the allure of marrying young. My mom was married before she was legally allowed to drink the champagne at her wedding. By my age, she was living in a charming little home in the suburbs with my sister, my dad and me. Like many women in her generation, she moved directly from her parents' house into a home with her husband.

Since I left that home to go to college eleven years ago, I have moved twelve times in six cities. Feeling transient is getting really old. I'm not sure if I want a house in the suburbs, or even if I want to have a child, but it would be wonderful to feel settled. It is practically impossible, and absolutely exhausting to maintain hope and confidence in a situation so full of unknowns.

I would love to be able to throw away my moving boxes. It would bring me great pleasure to fill my cupboards with fabulous kitchen gadgets, which for some reason, are only acquired as wedding gifts. It feels incredibly unjust that I must find a husband before anyone will buy me a Kitchen Aid mixer. I recently decided that when I finish my doctorate, I am going to register for that wonderful kitchen stuff I've wanted forever. After spending years working to earn my Ph.D., it will have been well worth the wait.

In most every other aspect of my life, I have the self-confidence and wisdom to feel in charge of my successes and failures. But when it comes to dating, I foster a lot of magical thinking. Sometimes, I wish someone could tell me that my life will definitely have a happy ending. I love to get my tarot cards read and I decorated my apartment according to the rules of Feng Shui. With candles, crystals, and wind chimes, I created an environment promoting positive relationship energy. (It can't hurt, anyway).

When I'm feeling pessimistic, my friends are reassuring. Their "you'll find him" speech really does help. I have every confidence that my friends will find wonderful partners, because they are successful, interesting, and witty single women. So, I reason, this must also be the case for me. I spend a lot of time thinking about how to be ready and how to least expect it (because, I'm told, that's when I'll meet him).

The rational, sociologist side of me wonders: how can I simultaneously believe that sexuality and gender are socially constructed, and
still long to find my *bashert*? Intellectually, I know there is nothing to
worry about, and I feel comforted by the statistics. I know that 90
percent of men and women eventually marry, and more than 70 percent of divorced men and women remarry.

Unfortunately, my investment in the romantic ideal is not rational. As a result, my level of anxiety is easily manipulated. I know that
a woman over thirty-five has a better chance of getting married today
than she did in the 1950s, but I am still upset by media scare tactics.
When a national news magazine contended that once a single woman
reaches forty, she has a better chance of being struck by lightning
than finding a husband, I panicked despite myself.

As a Jewish sociologist, it has been hard not to be discouraged by
the grim statistics surrounding the growing rate of intermarriage. As
a member of a Conservative youth group, I was successfully indoctri-
nated to be disdainful of those who "marry out." During the years I
participated in United Synagogue Youth, I engaged in numerous discussions, attended workshops, and heard lectures on the topic of Jewish continuity. My Jewish peers and I pledged to one another that we
would save the Jewish people by never, ever marrying non-Jews.

It seems that the indoctrination of my male Jewish counterparts
was not as successful. I am repeatedly struck by the overwhelming
lack of male twenty-something participation in Jewish life. At almost
every Shabbat dinner I attend, the conversation tends to linger on
the single question: where are all of the interesting Jewish men?

That same question has echoed in my head at the numerous
conferences I have participated in as a Jewish academic. I have spent
days on end, sitting in uncomfortable conference chairs with hundreds of middle-aged Jewish academics, talking about nothing but
Jewish continuity. I am frequently one of the only young people present
at such conferences. The only men present are invariably over fifty.

The ever-increasing intermarriage rate among young Jews is always a hot topic. I've been to entire conferences devoted to the in-
reach versus outreach debate. The intellectual and political views of
academics are invested with the spiritual fervor of religious doctrine,
so sessions on the subject of intermarriage tend to take on the intensity of rabbinic sermons. The more conservative scholars argue that
the Jewish community must set a standard for a Jewish lifestyle that
reflects their ideal (which is implicitly white, middle-class, and het-

erosexual). Their model rarely includes any alternative versions of family and is often myopic to the reality of blended families, intermarriage, and single parenthood. In this view, I am only relevant to the Jewish community when I marry a Jewish man. The age-old message persists: it is not possible to be fulfilled living as a single Jewish woman.

Liberal scholars argue for increased inclusion and an expanded vision of Jewish life that allows access to those who don't fit the traditional model. Their remarks usually include class or race consciousness, and even an acknowledgment that not every Jew is heterosexual. As a single woman under thirty, I am accounted for in the liberal model, but my input is rarely included in the discussion.

While Jewish scholars and community leaders from across the political and religious spectrum purport to be fundamentally concerned about the next generation, they consistently talk about young Jews, instead of with us. For me, those conferences are a site where my intellectual and my emotional life combine, or rather, collide.

I feel pulled in every direction by the conflicting proclivities of my multiple identities. As a Jew, I learned that my true love has been predetermined by God, and that I will find Him according to a higher plan. As a girl growing up in Los Angeles, I believed that I would have a Hollywood-style romance. Is it possible to maintain political consciousness, spiritual faith, and intellectual integrity while still holding onto my girlhood fantasy?

Rationally, the limitations of love are obvious. I know that to expect happiness, security, personal value, self-fulfillment, and a meaningful life from one relationship is optimistic at best. Yet despite all of my knowledge to the contrary, part of me continues to believe that my life will feel more secure, more meaningful, and less lonely when I find Him. But how can I find a Jewish man to marry when I can barely find one I'd want to date?

My search is complicated by the fear that He doesn't exist. When I meet someone who seems interesting, the tremendous feeling of relief makes it almost impossible to see him clearly. I know that no one is perfect, but it is hard to recognize the difference between someone who is not perfect and someone who is not right for me. It is difficult not to get caught up in trying to "make it work" with the wrong guy, because the thought of ending a relationship is laced with the fear and shame of being single again. And the prospect of being set up on another series of blind dates is enough to make anyone a little panicky. The sorrow and loneliness that accompanies a breakup makes a relationship hardly seem worth the effort. It is no wonder that the thought of going through another relationship makes me feel emotionally exhausted.

My parents' input is also difficult. I have not emulated their lives with my decisions to live Jewishly or to become an academic, but a heterosexual relationship is a topic about which we can actually bond. I resent the homophobia embedded in their relief and enthusiasm at my heterosexual choices, but at the same time, I enjoy their attention. It feels great to relate with my parents about an issue they value and understand.

It is easy for me to get caught up in the tremendous internal and external forces that drive heterosexual romance. Following the social mores in a relationship with a man requires little creativity; roles are predetermined and boundaries are clearly defined. But the strict confines of romantic love also make it easy to lose myself. I find myself trying so hard to be the perfect girlfriend that I forget to assert (or even to notice) what I want and who I really am.

Even though I know that married life is far from perfect, I feel envious of my friends who are married. Many have found relationships that I would like to emulate. I try to keep those couples in mind, so that I will recognize my own when I find it. Mostly, I can't wait for a time in my life when I am not fretting about finding a relationship.

A few of my friends have found their own wonderful Jewish men, but the majority is just like me—still looking. Some of them have given up on finding a Jewish man, claiming they don't find Jewish men attractive. They urge me to stop limiting myself, that I am being too picky, or even prejudiced. But dating someone who isn't Jewish does not feel like an option for me: I need to be with somebody who shares my values and beliefs. (I wouldn't date a Republican either.)

Jewish women in my mom's and grandmother's generations seem to have had a much easier time meeting marriageable men. When I talk with older Jewish women about my difficulty finding a desirable man, they react with disbelief. They act as though they just showed up at a B'nai B'rith mixer and a few weeks later, they were engaged. By my age, they explain, they'd already been elected president of their temple sisterhoods and were volunteers in their kids' Hebrew school classrooms. They do not recognize how much social life has changed since they were young, single Jewish women.

During the course of the twentieth century, normative rules for intimate relationships have changed dramatically. Social, religious, and legal dictates aimed to uphold the ideal of heterosexual marriage have eroded, and a more liberal climate has emerged. More than ever, the existence, content, and length of coupled relationships are determined by individual desires rather than by external regulation. Divorce laws have been liberalized and advances have been made in the effectiveness of contraception. Arranged marriages are long gone. Now, unmarried couples often live together, and it is no longer shameful for children to be born to unmarried parents. It is no longer illegal to be gay. Despite all of these advances, we are still not really free to love happily, intimately, and equally ever after.

Today, young Jews are getting married later than ever. Members of my generation are constantly on the move. Some of our most intimate relationships are long distance. Telephones and e-mail have made it possible for some of our closest relationships to occur without being face-to-face. But the privatization of relationships has also made it more difficult for young people to find each other.

Though much about relationship politics has changed, the economic reality of partnership has remained constant. As women in past generations have discovered, finding Him doesn't guarantee a happy ending. Having both a career and a family is only a privilege for families with the financial wherewithal to make that choice. For many women, "having it all" is an economic reality with which they must contend. Only one in ten of all North American women will escape having to take care of herself economically.

Despite the economic disadvantages embedded in the normative model of heterosexual relationships, few socially sanctioned alternatives exist. I have found no model or external validation for the happiness I have found as a single, Jewish woman. I profoundly enjoy and cherish the expansive, self-guided rhythms of my life. I have learned invaluable emotional, intellectual, social, and financial life lessons while living alone. My life feels full: I spend hours each week making meaningful connections with friends and coworkers; I practice meditation with a Jewish women's spirituality collective; and I invest my time, money, and intellectual energy in Jewish and feminist communities. I am constantly in relationship: with my family and friends, with myself, and with God.

On Saturdays, I've created my own version of Shabbat. I have brunch with someone I love, take a long walk, and linger in a bath before settling on my couch to listen to *This American Life*. I put aside the contradictions in my life, temporarily pausing the work of trying to integrate my often contradictory spiritual, intellectual, political, and emotional selves. I listen to Ira Glass, and for one hour, I luxuriate in the experience. I enjoy the wholeness of the present moment and feel grateful for the lessons of the search.

Reference

Williams, Monte. "Who Says You Can't Hurry Love? 8 Minutes in the Life Of a Jewish Single: Not Attracted? Next!" *New York Times*, March 5, 2000.

23

Stepping Eastward

DAVEENA TAUBER

I visited New York for the first time when I was twenty-four. Growing up in a smallish town on the northern California coast, I had always imagined that real Judaism existed in the East. To me, New York was my bubby's stories about how her father sold pickles from a stand, and how they kept a Shabbas carp in the bathtub. It was the setting of the *All-of-a-Kind Family* books that I loved. New York was the site of heroic labor struggles and the Triangle Shirtwaist Fire; and it was where Emma Goldman became radicalized. New York dominated my perception of Judaism, despite the fact that only one of my grandparents was born and raised there.

When I traveled to New York for the first time, I looked forward to tracing the footsteps of people and stories I had only read about. I expected to find a sense of homecoming and a deep connection with the place and people. Instead, I discovered just how deeply my Jewish experience had been influenced by the four generations of my family who had moved westward, away from the established centers of Jewish life.

Unlike my Jewish friends from the New York area, my childhood was not filled with Jewish neighbors, friends, or businesses. Judaism was not my primary source of identity or community. As a child, I fiercely claimed my Jewish identity in reaction to Christianity, which was overwhelmingly present in my elementary school. I never learned how to feel Jewish in a Jewish community. That only became clear once I moved East.

My Judaism sometimes feels like a garment that I haven't worn for a long time, but cannot bear to discard. There are times when

189

it feels unfathomably large, and other times when it feels too tight to wear comfortably. When I wore my Judaism on the West Coast, I almost always felt overdressed. When I wear it on the East Coast, I feel naked.

I grew up in Petaluma, a farming community about fifty miles north of San Francisco. My hometown has only two claims to fame: it was once the chicken capital of the world; and it was the all-American town that Hollywood chose as the setting for films like *American Graffiti* and *Peggy Sue Got Married*. With the kidnapping of a young girl named Polly Klass, Petaluma was portrayed by the media as the paradigm of the white, middle-class dream destroyed. I didn't know, until years after I moved away, that there had once been a thriving radical Jewish community in my hometown.

My mother and I moved to Sonoma County after my parents' divorce when I was two. We were part of a wave of progressive and alternative folks who settled in Sonoma County in the early '70s, looking for new ways of life. Many of our friends converted beautiful old barns into living and working spaces. We made our home west of town in a former chicken ranch, where my mother set up a pottery studio, and her partner had a woodworking shop. An older Jewish couple, who had survived the Holocaust, owned our first long-term home in Petaluma. Retired from chicken farming, Anne and Walter rented out their big house, Springhill House, to a group of graduate students and lived in a smaller house out back. We moved in when I was four, and lived there for most of my early childhood. Anne was a surrogate bubby to me. She likes to remind me that she's known me since I was pishing in my pants.

Most of our housemates at Springhill House were Jewish, but like many in their generation, they were busy rejecting the institutionalized structures in which they were raised. My memories of our huge solstice parties are much stronger than my recollection of any Jewish holidays.

The fears I grew up with were not Jewish fears. I was afraid that the sun was going to swallow the earth. Skylab was going to fall on my house. When my mother's antinuclear affinity group met at our house, I hid. My mother didn't discuss her activism on this issue with me because she didn't want to scare me. I had learned about the Holocaust, and the idea of being rounded up and shipped off to death camps frightened me, but it didn't seem as immanent as nuclear war.

What I didn't know was that there had been a radical Jewish culture long before we arrived in Petaluma. Though it speaks of a different age, Kenneth Kann's ethnography, *Comrades and Chicken Ranchers*, describes images that reflect my own memories of the Jews in my area.

Like the women mentioned in the book, many of the women I knew growing up were the hitchhiking, vegetable-eating, nonmarrying kind—including my mother. I knew plenty of farmers, anarchists, longhairs, and escapees from the East Coast. The folks I knew were neither ardent Zionists nor Communists like the Jews described in the book, but they had a communal vision of their own.

My mother had always been interested in country life. She told me that her earliest memories involve watching the ladybugs at a park in the Bronx. Later, when she moved with her family to Santa Monica, my mother decided that she only liked her new house after finding tiny insect eggs on the hedge in the yard. Although the suburbs of Santa Monica seemed positively pastoral to my bubby, my mother's childhood dream was to live on a horse farm like her best friend.

Her journey to the rural area where I grew up was a circuitous one. She met my father at a Jewish summer camp and they met again on a kibbutz in Israel. They were married in Santa Monica, served a year in the Peace Corps, and then settled in San Francisco. But their marriage did not last long; they divorced two years after I was born.

My mother moved away from her family to create a different kind of life than the one she had known. The hallmark of the community my mother and her friends created was that it was based on affinity rather than blood. My early childhood was spent living communally with adults who were not related to me, but who functioned very much like family. We lived in a house with several other adults and children. Two of my mother's women friends are aunt-mentors to me. They supported and advised me through the difficult years of adolescence, when I didn't feel that I could confide in my mother. One of our housemates eventually became my mother's partner.

As a child, I attended a parent-run school called "Children's Workshop." My friends were from married, divorced, single-parent, lesbian, gay, adopted, and "blended" families. I was not conscious of growing up in a non-normative family until the year I turned nine. We had moved with my mother's new partner onto a larger chicken ranch west of town, so I started at the local public elementary school. For the first time, I became conscious that I was "alternative," and from a "broken" home. At the new school, students were anchored to desks, instead of being able to move around. We sat in rows instead of circles and had to call teachers by their last names. There was no daily singing or drawing mandalas. Our teacher encouraged boys to play football and girls to cheerlead. Once, the teacher sent me out of the room for asking too many questions. I was miserable.

I was also different from the other students because I was Jewish. At my new school, making Christmas presents and dyeing Easter eggs was a regular part of the curriculum. When I told my mother, she sat me down and explained the concept of the separation of church and state. That was all the ammunition I needed: I spent the remainder of my public school education engaged in a struggle with teachers and school administrators over that issue. I was infuriated by their evoca-tion of the word *American* when they really meant "Christian."

My teachers agreed that my holiday should be represented, since Hanukkah was the "Jewish Christmas." But that wasn't my point. I didn't want to perform my Jewishness for them by making latkes and singing Hanukkah songs (by myself, of course). Nor did I want to go through the motions of celebrating their holidays, religious or not. My suggestion—that we remove religious holidays from the school alto-gether—did not go over well.

My family responded with both humor and anger. When my jun-ior high school chorus teacher threatened to fail me if I didn't sing at the Christmas concert, my father sweetly volunteered to burn a bagel on her lawn.

My alienation from the mainstream white culture of the West Coast took its toll on my self-esteem. I began to dislike my ethnic features. I hated my nose so passionately that my friends teased me about having an olfactory fixation. I was also self-conscious about my olive skin.

I desperately wanted to belong. When the Girl Scouts started a Brownie chapter at my school, I enlisted immediately. I loved the uniform. And I especially loved the fact that my mother, who hated department stores, had to take me shopping. But when I put my two fingers in the air and swore to help God, the country, and the troop, I wondered if the God they mentioned was my God. I had my doubts, and so did my Girl Scout leader, who felt that there was something vaguely un-American about a Girl Scout who wouldn't sing Christ-mas carols or make Christmas tree ornaments out of wooden shower curtain rings. My desire to belong to *something*, the absence of my culture, and all of that emphasis on God, made me want to explore my own traditions.

Both of my parents had religious training, but neither attended shul or observed more than the major holidays. So my decision to give up ballet lessons and attend Hebrew school was a surprise to them. My grandparents were delighted. I entered Hebrew school a year late, and became a bat mitzvah at fourteen. I tried my hand at Sunday school, but stopped going when I discovered that we were not going to read the Bible. Instead, my mother and I commenced reading a few chapters a night at bedtime.

My bat mitzvah was an incredibly important rite of passage for me. It was one of the few gatherings in my life that included both sides of my extended family, as well as my friends (both Jews and non-Jews), who had supported me since childhood.

The event was low-key and homemade. We had the reception in the temple social hall and made all the food ourselves, which involved the time consuming task of *kashering* our kitchen. I convinced my mother to buy me a new, white Gunney Sac dress, but she held out against the heels I wanted. My stepmother, however, was happy to oblige. When we rehearsed carrying the Torah scroll around the sanctuary, I panicked. I had never worn heels before, and the scroll was so heavy, I was sure I would fall. But when the moment came, God must have carried the scroll for me; I didn't feel a thing, even in my four-inch platforms.

My haftorah portion was from Judges and I gave my speech about how justice had failed in the trial of Dan White, who had recently been sentenced to only five years in prison after assassinating San Francisco Mayor George Moscone and gay, Jewish city supervisor, Harvey Milk.

Those years were the most intensely religious of my life. I kept as kosher as I could, given that no one I knew was kosher. I fasted on Yom Kippur, even though I nearly fainted after a demanding dance rehearsal. And because my first visit to Disneyland fell during Passover, I refused to eat any junk food. I furnished my dollhouse with a tiny clay menorah, a Passover plate, and a kiddush cup modeled after the exquisite set that my mother had made. I also made tiny *haggadot* and an embroidered three-layer *matzah* cover.

Between my bat mitzvah and leaving for college, I moved away from Jewish involvement. But in my first few years of college in Portland, Oregon, Jewish rituals and observances became increasingly important to me as I moved out of the community I had known in my early childhood. I began to think again about my connection to Jewish tradition, this time through the lens of feminism. I was determined to figure out how I could call myself a "feminist" and still claim my Jewish identity.

After my sophomore year, I received a scholarship to explore the connection between Judaism and feminism through poetry. I spent that summer immersing myself in writing by and about Jewish women. I began with the wonderful anthology *The Tribe of Dina: A Jewish Women's Anthology*, which led me to Anzia Yezierska and other Yiddish women writers. I was incredibly moved by Irena Klepfisz's remarkable collection of essays, *Dreams of an Insomniac: Jewish Feminist Essays, Speeches and Diatribes* as well as her remarkable poem "Keeper of Accounts." I read Esther Broner's *A Weave of Women* and Melanie Kaye/Kantrowitz's *My Jewish Face and Other Stories*. I subscribed to a Jewish-feminist journal, *Bridges: A Journal for Jewish Feminists and Our Friends*, which was the first publication to reject and, many years later, the first to publish my work. These resources gave me access to a community that was unavailable to me in my own life: a community of Jewish women who were thinking openly about the delights and difficulties of being Jewish and feminist.

That summer, I baked bread, wrote poetry, and was trained to work at a battered women's shelter. I wrote midrashic poetry about Shabbat, about Esther, and about *Havdalah*. In the fall, I presented the poems to my friends, schoolmates, and most importantly, to my mother, who flew up to attend the reading. Reading Jewish feminist writers provided me with a community of sorts, but it was not a local community. All of the writers seem to have close connections to the East Coast. So during my junior year of college, when a professor offered to share a research grant that would send me to the East Coast, I jumped at the chance.

The work I was doing was in Washington, D.C., but I decided to spend a week in New York. A friend who my mother had known since she was nineteen graciously invited me to stay in her Upper West Side apartment. I went to New York expecting to find my roots, to follow the "Walking Tour of Radical Jewish History" from *The Tribe of Dina*, to feel an instant kinship with the place where my mother's mother had sold pickles on the street. Instead, I felt culture shock.

My mother's friend lived in a tiny apartment that received no natural light. I missed my spacious, sunny apartment, on the top floor of an old house that I rented in Portland for less than three hundred dollars a month. I felt like Heidi in the children's story: cut off from the natural cycles of day and night, claustrophobic and confused.

My mother's friend threw a small soiree to introduce me to Jewish women my age. I felt the cultural differences between the East and West, expressed in their body language, eye contact, conversation, and relative formality. The cosmopolitan young women, who had gone to Ivy League schools and had internships at magazines like *Ms.* and *Lilith*, profoundly intimidated me.

Sitting there, in that circle of Jewish women, I felt aware for the first time that my best friends (in fact, most of the people and places in my world) were not Jewish. Sharing my Jewish culture with my non-Jewish friends is a real source of pleasure for me. In fact, one of my favorite Jewish experiences was a Shabbat ceremony performed at a friend's house in San Francisco where seven women, Jewish and not Jewish, stood in a circle and knotted our shawls together in a circle that held us all.

I returned to Portland breathless with relief. I had expected to find a sense of Jewish connection, but instead I felt more culturally identified with my West Coast-ness than with Judaism. I was sure that I could never live on the East Coast, until I applied to graduate school. The only university that offered me sufficient financial support was smack in the middle of the Garden State; I now live an hour from New York.

I have learned a lot since I moved to New Jersey. When I first visited New York, my head was filled with images and stories of working-class struggles. I had once believed that the stereotype of the wealthy Jew was not only malicious, but also false. I didn't know any Jews (or non-Jews, for that matter) who were wealthy. So I was unprepared for the level of Jewish commercial success I witnessed: I saw children being picked up from Hebrew school in limos on the Upper East Side, visited the expansive Jewish museum, and glimpsed the massive workings of the Jewish philanthropic apparatus. For the first time, I saw that segments of the Jewish community have economic power, and that some Jews have succeeded according to the capitalist ideals of mainstream America.

My own class background makes it difficult for me to appreciate their financial success. My parents and their friends conscientiously chose their lifestyle based on ideology rather than on economics. They pursued their passions rather than their pocketbooks. I know now that our ability to make such a choice was a privilege. My mother and I never experienced deprivation, but we also never owned a home, took vacations, or participated in other tokens of middle-class identity. I was able to attend college through a combination of federal and school grants, loans, and work-study.

I have a hard time identifying with people's urban values and interests and it's been difficult to find a community because, for the most part, I have internalized my mother's Thoreauvian values about voluntary simplicity and creative subsistence. When I was young, my mother and I had bitter arguments in the aisles of supermarkets. Why couldn't I have bologna? (Nitrates); Ramen? (Japanese whaling); soda? ("I don't want you to put that crap into your body!"). Sometimes, I still feel the internal tension between the child who wanted name brand jeans, and the adult who has chosen to prioritize other things. And I expect that I'll revisit these struggles if I have children someday. As I affirm my own commitment to creative minimalism and low-impact living, I also try not to forget that it is a privilege to be able to choose my way of life.

I am still learning how to communicate with East Coast Jews. At first, I completely avoided talking about Israel and about the Holocaust because I knew that those were highly flammable topics. I am still a little hesitant to talk to Jews about those issues, because I'm afraid that I'll be told that I can't really understand, because I didn't live through the Holocaust, or because I haven't been to Israel. I want to tell them I'm not the malicious child at the seder; I'm just the one who doesn't know.

My relationship to the physical features that once marked my difference has begun to change on the East Coast. On the West Coast, white men at folk dances would frequently ask where I was from. When I answered, "northern California," they clarified, "No, I mean, what's your ethnicity?" They guessed that I was Latin American, Indian, Italian, Native American, or Middle Eastern. They almost never guessed Jewish. In rural northern California and in Oregon, I felt ethnically "marked" in ways that I don't in the mid-Atlantic.

I find that white people on the East Coast are more closely connected to their ethnic heritage. A block near my house is lined with Catholic churches: Hungarian, Czech, Polish, and Latin American. In my various West Coast communities, many people of European descent migrated from other places, leaving family baggage but also ethnic richness behind.

My friends from the West Coast and I come to our own traditions through processes of rejection, experimentation, and appropriation. We have de-essentialized culture and ethnicity. While this process can be wonderful in its potential for sharing, it can also be problematic in its potential for misuse. I'm troubled, for example, by the New Age appropriation of Native American spirituality, which continues a long tradition of cultural oppression. Still, I recognize the importance of experimenting with spiritual traditions other than one's own. And I value the fact that Jewish culture is not the only culture I claim as my own.

Since living on the East Coast, I've noticed people seem to have closer ties to their families than anyone I knew in northern California. For the first time, I've seen how strongly Judaism is centered in the traditional conception of a family. That has had a profound impact on my ability (or inability) to feel at home in mainstream Judaism, since I grew up valuing a different kind of family. My ambivalence about my Jewishness is connected to my misgivings about my extended family and about traditional family norms.

Growing up, I absorbed the feeling that extended family was a difficult but necessary part of life. Visits to my mother's family were short, and we left feeling relieved. My mother and I have only recently begun to rethink our connection to our extended family, who sometimes seem related to us only by the most fantastic accident of fate.

Since moving East, I have been hungry for knowledge of my family history. When I go West for vacations, I have begun to spend time with my grandparents, listening to, and taping, their stories. That way of relating has helped to build a new bridge between us.

Living on the East Coast has been the hardest transition of my life. I had expected to find a sense of homecoming and a deep connection with the Jewish community, but it has been difficult to find a Jewish community where I feel at home. Instead, I found my home-away-from-home in a small town in Vermont. While my colleagues here go to "the city" (which will always be San Francisco to me), I escape to Vermont. There I write, grow a garden, volunteer on an organic farm, work at the food co-op, and intern at a progressive nonprofit. That is my idea of heaven.

References

Broner, E. M. *A Weave of Women*. Bloomington: Indiana University Press, 1985.

Kann, Kenneth L. *Comrades and Chicken Ranchers: The Story of a California Jewish Community*. Ithaca, NY: Cornell University Press, 1996.

Kaye/Kantrowitz, Melanie. *My Jewish Face & Other Stories*. San Francisco: Spinsters/Aunt Lute Book Co., 1990.

Kaye/Kantrowitz, Melanie and Irena Klepfisz, eds. *The Tribe of Dina: A Jewish Women's Anthology*. Boston: Beacon Press, 1989.

Klepfisz, Irena. *Dreams of an Insomniac: Jewish Feminist Essays, Speeches, and Diatribes*. Portland, OR: Eighth Mountain Press, 1990.

Klepfisz, Irena. "Keeper Of Accounts." *Nice Jewish Girls: A Lesbian Anthology*. Ed. Evelyn Torton Beck. Watertown, MA: Persephone Press, 1982.

Spyri, Johanna. *Heidi*. Philadelphia: McKay, 1922.

24

Making Love on the Deutsche Bahn

RUTH A. ABUSCH-MAGDER

It was the last night of our last trip, and David and I were determined to make the most of it. We arrived at the train station late at night, tired but satisfied after four days of visiting museums during the beautiful Parisian fall. We stood by the window and watched the station disappear, and the city lights soon followed as we sped through the countryside. We savored kosher cold cuts, and over dessert, we talked with excitement about our future. Full of whimsy, we made love with the curtains open. My very pregnant body was silhouetted by the night. We fell asleep in our first-class sleeping car, happy and secure, headed for home, speeding toward Germany.

I will not tell you that we were unaware of the ironies, nor will I tell you that we thought of them at every moment. The past was the backdrop on which we built our six months in Germany. But in living everyday life, some acts forced us to be in the present and allowed us to let go of the past. Some acts were mundane, others glorious. There was garbage to sort into recycling, drinks shared with friends at parties, the birth of our son. In all of these acts, all that mattered was the moment. For it to be otherwise would have been suffocating. But two years later, I cannot recall that night on the train without simultaneously calling to mind other memories, both personal and collective, which give it meaning far beyond romance.

The first time I took a night train, I was twenty. I was traveling around Europe with my parents and brother: London, Paris, Vienna, and Amsterdam, a few days in each city. My parents refused to go to Germany. There was no reason to go, and every reason not to. Vienna was different. My mother's family was from Vienna. We had addresses to look up, graves to visit. We saw nothing that was not directly connected to our family. My parents imagined Nazis in every doorway, around every corner. They invoked the past so often that by the second night, I too heard goose-steps in my sleep.

We left as soon as possible, making our way to Amsterdam on a night train. My brother and I bunked in a third-class sleeping car. The beds were narrow benches, stacked three high, up to the ceiling. They were hard and uncomfortable. There were no sheets, only thin dirty wool blankets. In these surroundings, my sleep was restless and shallow. I woke when the train stopped and went to the window to see what had happened. I rolled up the blinds and a station sign filled my view from the window. I was confronted face-to-face with the word "Nuremberg." There was no escape: not from the train, nor from the images of deportation, concentration camps, and suffering.

It is not surprising that trains feature prominently in my German and Austrian experiences. Trains are a major means of transportation in Europe. What is surprising, given my general attempts to avoid the subject of the *Shoah*, is that travel in Germany and Austria have featured prominently in the last few years of my life. I have never read *The Diary of Anne Frank* or seen *Schindler's List*. In more than twenty years of formal Jewish education, I have never written a paper on the Warsaw Ghetto. I have made a conscious effort not to initiate involvement with history and memory of the destruction of European Jewry.

In reality, these are mere tokens of protests, personal attempts to clear breathing room amid the pervasiveness of the Holocaust in my life. When I first brought my future husband home to meet my family, David observed that not a meal went by without some mention of the Shoah, Hitler, or Nazis. This was a complete surprise to me. It was of course obvious, but I had never really noticed. In its omnipresence, the destruction of European Jewry was part of the white noise of my childhood home.

My mother, born in Palestine in 1940, grew up with almost no family. The few lucky ones were spread over the face of the earth after treacherous clandestine escapes from Europe. The rest (the majority), perished in cattle cars, ghettos, camps, and in other ways that we are left to imagine. My father's family (both sides of which came to Canada in the 1880s and 1890s), was left untouched by the tragedy on a personal level. Nonetheless, my father has made the Shoah his personal obsession. He buys every book written about the camps, Nazi cruelty, and righteous Gentiles, in an attempt to try to understand how human beings could both endure and inflict such suffering. Over the years, our discussions of Judaism and theology never escaped the topic of good and evil, as exemplified by the Shoah. On Yom Kippur, when I was fourteen, my father entered my room to share a thought: "To bear Jewish children," he told me, "is to damn them—if not in that generation, then in the next—to an untimely painful death." Then he left me alone to ponder.

At the Orthodox school I attended, there was no escape either. God and anti-Semitism shared central stage in the loosely defined curriculum designed for inculcation. Hatred of Jews was proof of our chosenness. Stories of expulsion and immolation were used to teach us about the precarious nature of Jewish survival. Horrible fates befell those that did not obey God's law. Repentance and righteousness were always redeemed, if not in this world then in the world to come. Our education highlighted the sanctity of martyrdom. We heard tales of maidens dragged through the streets rather than submit to an immoral act or conversion.

The Shoah, with its celluloid images and reams of written testimony, provided ample affirmation of this vision of Jewish history: pious rabbis who had kept their faith in the camps, parents who had sacrificed themselves for their children, Gentiles who had suffered horrible fates as punishment for friendship with Jews. They lived among us, not just on Holocaust Remembrance Day, but also throughout the year. The mantra in the Jewish community is "never forget." Forgetting is not an option to me. The challenge for me is to not always remember.

When they showed a film about children my own age being loaded into a truck and being gassed to death, I could close my eyes. But I could not escape seeing, hearing, and knowing. I worked hard to keep at bay the fear that the child in the film could be, should be, will be me. I attempted to suppress the urge to wonder what I would have done, how long I would have survived, how I would have died.

As a child, I collected other people's memories. I found most of my schoolwork tedious and troublesome, but lessons about pioneer sewing bees and barn raisings were intriguing. I read the *Encyclopedia Judaica*. I asked questions. I listened intently. I was particularly interested in family stories: Grandma Rose's tales of going to school by horse-drawn sleigh, and gliding over packed ice; Grandpa Harry's rags-to-riches tribute to hard work and family life.

I spent many hours curled up in my Oma Lizzi's bed late at night. We were content for hours, going over the details of the layout of her childhood apartment, or the story of her sister's birth. In her youth, she took hiking trips with the Maccabi youth group, went on strolls with suitors along the Danube, and made visits to the opera. She told me of food shortages during World War I, and of her escape from death by bombs in pre-state Palestine.

There were many stories that Oma did not tell me. Born and raised in Vienna, she was an ardent Zionist; she went to live in Israel at age twenty, in 1931. But she returned often to visit her mother and sister. She was there on November 9, 1938, to witness Kristalnacht, when "good" Austrian citizens destroyed Jewish businesses, schools, and places of worship. I knew about Kristalnacht, her vain attempts to convince her mother to leave, her sister's escape by walking over the Alps, and her mother's death at the concentration camp at Theresienstadt. But these were things that my mother told me. Oma never spoke about the Shoah.

By trade I am a historian, trained to remember. In my twenties, I made my way to graduate school to pursue a doctorate in Jewish history. The decision to become a Jewish historian was not simply an opportunistic, professional choice. I believe that an inclusive future can only be built on a reading of history that values the diversity of women's contributions throughout time. It was largely the feminist idea of a usable past that fired my imagination. The courses I chose, and the papers I wrote reflected my belief that an inclusive approach to the past held the potential to transform the future. My feminism and my Judaism motivated me to study modern Jewish history. The Shoah figured nowhere in my conscious decision to become a Jewish historian.

Several weeks into my first semester, a friend asked me why I was in graduate school. I told her that contrary to my day-school education, I did not believe in resurrection; nevertheless, in my mind, death did not mean the end. We achieve immortality in the deeds and in the legacy that we leave on this earth, I told her. My Oma, for example, lived on in the stories and lessons she passed onto me. To achieve this immortality, one needs to be remembered. As an historian, I can restore the memories of people whose lives had unjustly been forgotten. I can rescue their souls.

Despite my attempts to avoid the Shoah in the early years, when choosing a field of specialization, I decided to write about the domestic lives of German Jews in Europe and America before World War I. Focusing on a pre-Nazi era allows me to avoid immersing myself in the documentation of the destruction of European Jewry. But the topic can hardly be escaped when working on any aspect of German Jewish history. Such endeavors mean learning German history, being in contact with German scholars, traveling in Germany, and learning to master the German language. My choice of the dissertation topic was consciously rooted in my family background, and it allows me to confront the legacy of the Shoah on my own terms.

German is my Israeli-born mother's first language. It was the language my mother and grandmother spoke for convenience and privacy. *Oma* had tried to teach me, but as a child I resisted, seeing no use for a language of a people whom I had learned were innately evil, and of a place I had no intention to visit. As an adult, I spent a summer in my boyfriend's apartment in Cambridge, Massachusetts, taking a course called "German for Reading." My grasp of German, however, remained superficial and inadequate. The best solution, in my mind, was immersion. I spent the following summer in Salzburg studying German.

This was not an uncontroversial decision. My parents said nothing. But before I left, other Jews asked how I could bear to spend any time in that country. How could I give them my money? I too had some doubts. What if my occasional deportation nightmares became a regular nightmare during my stay in Salzburg? On the whole, however, I looked forward to the summer. Austria was both the forbidden and the Promised Land. A morbid sense of curiosity propelled me to believe that this was a pilgrimage I needed to make.

The process began on the plane. Before landing in Munich, the woman sitting next to me noticed my guidebook and struck up a conversation. Realizing we were both taking the same train south, she offered to help me find my way. She told me about her vacation in London and a little about her life in a small town on the border between Germany and Austria. She asked me about my travel plans, and I was forced to decide what to reveal. Saying that I was studying history was fine, but when she asked me about my specialty, what should I tell this frail woman in her seventies? She was quick to tell me that she was originally from Czechoslovakia and had come after the war to escape the Communist regime. Did I believe her? Should I believe her? I don't remember what I told her. I only remember that conflicts boiled inside of me as we talked.

Throughout that summer, my encounters with older Austrian women were a source of internal tension. On our family vacation to Europe a few years earlier, I had broken with my family and visited a Jewish friend in Berlin for two days. One afternoon, I sat in the garden of a palace and watched Germans stroll in the park. I was amazed at the hatred that filled me. When older people passed by, I thought about breaking their legs. I actually envisioned what it would be like to break their legs and let them bleed to death in slow, agonizing pain. I silently wished their children and grandchildren dead. They had all been too willing to perpetuate (or at best to overlook), the extermination of generations of Jews. What did they do to deserve a life and a legacy? In Salzburg, I encountered older women all the time. Taking the tram from the school to the center of town, I often had to decide whether I was willing to give up my seat to someone in their seventies or eighties. As a child, my Oma had taught me that this was the proper thing to do. What had their Omas taught them as children? Were they taught to spit on Jews?

Giving up my seat allowed me to feel self-righteous. When I did, I felt morally superior to the very people I was helping. It was a small action, one that in the 1930s, Christian Germans would have easily overlooked. Now, seventy years later, I was willing to relinquish my seat and transcend my own justifiable prejudices. I glared at a recently seated elder, wanting her to appreciate the sacrifice I had just made. I wanted her to understand that her acceptance of my chair signaled Jewish moral superiority. On the days when the anger was too overwhelming, I averted my eyes and waited to see if someone else would be as generous as I wished I could be. I knew that what others saw was simple rudeness, not the paralysis of history.

Two years later, when I was pregnant and showing, I was amazed at how infrequently people gave me a seat on a bus or subway in Munich. In Bavaria, where rules and regulations are the foundation of the society, this courtesy was extended only rarely, and then usually by dark-haired Turks or East European foreigners. I tried to accept this as a cultural difference. David took offense. It was hard not to agree with him sometimes.

One day, near term, when I was feeling particularly ill, we waited for the subway in the fashionable district near the university. The seats on the bench were all taken. I did not want to make a scene, but David knew I needed to sit. Standing in front of the bench, he held my hand and asked loudly, in English, if I was feeling well, and if I wanted to sit. It was a scene with which I was already familiar. David became more indignant and more vocal. I was embarrassed. No one moved. Perhaps, I reasoned, the women in their fifties and the non-German-looking types seated on the bench did not understand our discussion, or did not realize I was pregnant and not just fat.

The actions of one man in his late twenties, however, left little room for question in our minds. He sported a well-cut suit, expensive eyeglasses, and a stylish haircut. Instead of the shopping bags or backpacks others held, he had only a smart leather briefcase tucked securely between the ankles of his well-polished shoes. He was engaged in reading a newspaper, not a popular tabloid, or even the local high-minded paper, but a northern journal: the equivalent of a Bostonian reading *The New York Times*. Wealth and education made him stand out from those seated around him. When we arrived on the platform, the partially folded paper had rested comfortably on his knees. When we argued directly in front of him, he raised and unfolded the paper so that it formed a complete barrier between us. It's very possible that he heard and understood every word David said. By not looking at me he also averted his conscience. This way he could avoid the impropriety of his act. We could not help but wonder if this was how Germans and Austrians in the 1930s and 1940s managed to convince themselves that they did not know what was going on in their own Reich, country, and apartment building.

My time studying German in Salzburg was not only about anger; it was also about love. Set alongside the banks of a river surrounded by Alpine mountains, the town is picturesque and serene. The downtown is crowded with historic, colorful, old buildings, and cobblestone streets. The outlying areas are modern with beautiful gardens. The city has all the amenities—theater, cafés, boutiques, department stores, music, and a university—without the haste of a large city. To my surprise, I could easily imagine life in a place such as this. That thought was both comforting and disquieting. From afar, it was easy to hate Austria and everything associated with it. From afar, I could see no appeal. Living in Salzburg, I began to viscerally understand my family's love affair with that land.

For my great-grandfather, that love meant fighting for the Kaiser during World War I. It was a love that earned him medals of courage and an early death. For my great-grandmother, it was a love that made it impossible for her to leave. When the Nazis came for her the first time, she stalled them with bribes and tales of her husband's sacrifice.

Even then, she could not imagine the treachery that lay ahead. Hers was a blind love. My great-grandparents' love of Austria, while perhaps naive, was untainted by knowledge of future savagery. I have the privilege of hindsight. How is it possible to love the towns, foods, and mountains that nurtured and fed such gross inhumanity? In my family, the avoidance of the Germanic was an attempt to distance ourselves from the enemy. My joy while in Austria and Germany could not exist without a lingering sense that it was an affront to the memory of those who had suffered and perished.

Falling in love with the sights and sounds of Salzburg made me feel the betrayal of European Jewry all the more keenly. As I walked on the now *judenrein Judengasse* to my favorite stationery shop, the absence of Jews was profound. I passed the old home of family friends, and found that it was now a clubhouse for fascist youths. If the setting, the street, and the house were not so beautiful, there would be no jealousy, no longing to be part of such a place. But the longing did exist. Desire only makes the sense of betrayal all the more acute.

My infatuation, despite the guilt and anger, was inevitable. Salzburg was also a homecoming. There was much that was unexpectedly familiar. The old women who caused me so much consternation also conjured nostalgic visions of my grandmother. Until the end of Oma's life, she belonged to a kaffeeklatsch of Viennese women, who met regularly in Tel Aviv for cakes, coffee, and German language discussion. The fashionable women who gathered in Salzburg cafés bore a strong resemblance to my great-aunts in dress, manner, and to my uneducated ear, even language. When an older woman passed close enough for me to smell her perfume, I was reminded of the loose pink powder that my Oma applied with great care before going out. The architecture that I had always associated with the stylish towns surrounding Tel Aviv was almost identical to that of the modern neighborhood where my language school was located. I had thought this style was Israeli. Now I saw the Germanic influence.

I had always been aware of my family's German roots, and some of the strongest connections I made to that heritage were in the kitchen. My growing academic interest in cookbooks and food-ways made me aware of food as a means of cultural transmission. Even so, I was unprepared for the extent to which Austrian food provided insight to the past. Yogurt, for example, had loomed large in my childhood. It was one of the special treats we ate on trips to Israel. The Israeli yogurt was different from the Canadian kind. It was creamier, fresher, and never had to be stirred from the bottom. Best of all, Israeli yogurt came in flavors like mocha, butterscotch, and even chocolate. The lack of available kosher food reduced me to a vegetarian diet while in Austria. I suspected that yogurt would be a staple, but I did not anticipate the degree to which the taste and texture of Austrian yogurt would invoke my memories of Israel. Walking through the dairy section of the supermarket in Salzburg, I was delighted to discover my favorite chocolate yogurt from Israel, the kind with the tuft of whipped cream on the top. There in the aisles of Salzburg's supermarket, "Julius Meinel," I was transported back to the SuperSol supermarket on Tchernischovsky Street in Tel Aviv.

As a child, I knew that some of the foods we ate were German. Schnitzel appeared regularly on our family table. It too was a staple of my mother's childhood diet in Israel. The name Wiener schnitzel left little question about its Viennese origin, but more often than not, I did not consider the national origin of the foods that arrived on my plate. I did not notice, for example, that other Canadian families did not regularly use chives as a garnish. I attributed food to the people who had taught me to eat them. I ate kohlrabi and red currents because my grandfather Otto (who was also from Vienna) ate them. Oma ate dark bread with butter, salt, and chives, so I did as well. When my mother refused to buy white bread, preferring instead dark whole grain loaves, I had mistakenly understood her tendencies as purely Israeli.

Eating in Salzburg and later in Vienna, Munich, and throughout the German-speaking world left no question as to the national origin of my family's culinary traditions. Chives and kohlrabi are abundant, showing up in every garden and at almost every meal. Tart, red currants, which are rarely seen in North America, made their way into all sorts of sweet and savory dishes. The bakeries are filled with dense, multigrain loaves, and pastries that were unmistakably familiar. At beer gardens, plates of cheese are served with a slice of dark bread, spread with butter, chives, and salt. Although the German language remained largely a mystery, food was familiar and surprisingly comforting.

The following summer, David and I took a vacation to another place with beautiful mountains, picturesque villages, and significant history. In contrast to Austria, however, nothing in Venezuela was familiar. We marveled at the strange sights and sounds. We reveled in the exotic flavors of the mango and the fresh cocoa seeds. I had no preconceived ideas. In Venezuela, I was unencumbered by my personal involvement with its past. This freedom was somewhat disconcerting. I was only a visitor, unsure how to understand all that I encountered. Used to the burden of the past, I felt some guilt at experiencing unfettered pleasures. In Austrian and Germany, history weighed on my soul, but it also helped me to define my place, my connection. Even as a visitor, I had a relationship to the place, the society, and the people.

As difficult as it is to confront a past that includes joy and creativity as well as depravity and betrayal, that confrontation allowed me to live in the present. Knowing that the place and people will never let you forget, eases the burden of always remembering.

Two years after my summer in Salzburg, David received an Alexander von Humbolt Award from the German government, allowing him to spend six months working at a German university. We did not hesitate to take it. Just a week prior, a pregnancy test had confirmed that we were indeed expecting a child. We did the calculations and realized that the baby would be born during the six months we would be in Munich. Ignoring the irony of traveling to Munich to give birth to a Jewish child, we concentrated on the benefits of such a plan, and went ahead to book our tickets.

Living in Munich for six months was different from spending six weeks in Salzburg. Obtaining a visitor's visa demanded an understanding of bureaucracy worthy of an advanced degree. Simple tasks like shopping for breakfast cereal turned into adventures in language, culture, and taste. The German system of needing to reserve the washing machines in our building required us to schedule our lives around our whites and darks. Day to day, David had experiments to run. I had German classes to take. We enjoyed social engagements and all the regular pleasures of living in a city: museums, cafés, and parks. Our lives were full and fulfilling. Much of our time was spent in the present, not dwelling in the past.

This is not to imply that we escaped history or remained unaware. The Holocaust was everywhere. The main plaza at the entrance of the university is called "Geschwister-Scholl-Platz," named after the brother and sister team of Hans and Sophie Sholl. In 1943, they had thrown anti-Nazi pamphlets off the gallery in the university entrance. It was a brave act, one that earned each of them an untimely death at the hands of the Nazis. It was a small act, merely a token protest. Nonetheless, in this city, which was the original seat of Hitler's power, such an act was so remarkable that it earned the Sholls a central place in the geographic memory of Munich.

The Hofbrauhaus, where Hitler launched his first, failed putsch is still a popular drinking place at the center of town. Buildings such as the music school exist in the shadow of their past roles as centers of operations during the Nazi regime. In vain, I searched for a hairdresser who had experience cutting my thick curly "Jewish" hair. The Nazis were highly successful in ridding the city of Jews. Overwhelmingly still *judenrein,* such tresses are not commonly found or cut in Munich.

The Holocaust was also nowhere. In contrast to Geschwister-Scholl-Platz, the memorial that marks the place where the synagogue once stood is a muted affair. It is not marked on most maps, nor have the streets been renamed to memorialize what once stood there. The colorful Movenpick restaurant marque and the constant flow of nearby traffic dwarf the black statue. The Jewish museum in Munich occupies two tiny rooms and is run privately by a non-Jewish individual. Hopelessly underfunded, it is tucked away in a small flat and not easily found.

Everyone who knew us with even a casual level of intimacy knew we were Jewish. I am a Jewish historian, we keep kosher, and we speak exclusively in Hebrew with our son. Yet the Holocaust never came up in conversations with non-Jews. Even Judaism was rarely discussed. Like the subject of race in the United States, the Shoah in German lands is taboo. Sidestepping certain subjects protects people from looking at the personal faces of the perpetrators.

Only once, when in Salzburg, did I discuss the Holocaust with a native, and then, only under the influence of a moderate amount of alcohol. One night, after drinking with some classmates and our Austrian teacher, I ventured into the forbidden territory by saying that I did not want to know what her family had done during the war. She was defensive but vaguely understanding. In the morning, with a clearer head, I regretted my faux pas. If I didn't want to always remember, I realized that there were topics that I shouldn't broach.

Since returning from Europe, I have realized that despite all my attempts, I will not find a way to make sense of the destruction and savagery of the Holocaust. In each of the last four generations, members of my family have attempted to deal with the reality and the memory of the Shoah. Growing up, I instinctively knew that none of their approaches worked for me.

My approach is indirect. I spare myself the worst nightmares. I look not at the horrors of 1933-1945, but rather at what came long before and what remains after. I have the advantage of distance. I can ask questions and go places where others could not. Writing a dissertation on

German-speaking Jews, studying and living in German-speaking lands, and working with and befriending Germans: these are all means through which I confront our tortured legacy. I have found some peace. Studying the lives of nineteenth-century German-speaking women allows me not only to fulfill a feminist mission by restoring women's memories, but also to recall to life Jews, whose legacy was taken from them.

To make love on a luxury train headed from Paris to Munich is also my own way of coping with the past. With the background of cattle cars and death camps, the romance of the moment was transformed into a statement of defiance and protest. Taking pleasure in tastes, feelings, and emotions are the privileges of being alive when so many no longer breathe. These are the burdens and irony of survival.

Reference

Frank, Anne. *The Diary Of A Young Girl.* New York: Paper Books, 1952.

Glossary

aba: Father.

Adonai: one of many ways to refer to the most sacred name of God.

Aleinu: prayer that closes every service in which Jews make a special obligation to make God's greatness known to the rest of the world.

aleph-bet: first two letters of the Hebrew alphabet. This phrase is used to refer to the Hebrew alphabet in general.

aliyah: "going up." Also means to move to Israel, or to make blessings over the Torah.

Amidah: standing prayer in intimate communication with God that is the center of every Jewish prayer service.

Asherah: Semitic name for a Cannanite goddess, once worshipped by ancient Hebrew women. She is associated with groves and trees.

Ashkenazi: Jews and their descendents from Eastern Europe.

Ashrei: song of praise, based on Psalm 145.

Avinu Malkeinu: "Our Father, Our King." Prayer recited during the ten days of Repentance between Rosh Hashanah and Yom Kippur. Emphasizes a twofold relationship to God, the Jews as both the children of God and God's subjects.

Aytz Hayyim: "Tree of Life." Often used to refer to the Torah.

baalat/baalei teshuvah: "master(s) of repentance." A Jew who becomes more observant, usually one who adopts an Orthodox lifestyle.

Bais Yaakov: a network of Jewish schools for girls founded by Sarah Schenirer in 1918, in which secular and religious subjects were taught.

bat/bar/bas mitzvah, bath/bar mouswa: "daughter/son/children of the commandment." The age (for boys 13, girls 12) at which one is expected to take on the responsibilities of an adult Jew.

Baruch Hashem: "Praised be God." Exclamation of joy or thankfulness.

bentsching: Yiddish. To recite a blessing.

bimah: elevated platform in place of worship from which the Torah is read and sermons are delivered.

binah: knowledge, wisdom.

brachah/brachot: blessing(s).

Bris: ceremony in which a baby boy is circumsized. Takes place when the baby is eight days old.

bubby: Yiddish. Grandmother.

bulbe: Yiddish. Potato.

chometz: food that is forbidden to eat on Passover, such as leavened bread, wheat, spelt, rye, oats, and barley. Also refers to objects such as dishes that may have contained or been used to contain unleavened products.

challah: braided bread, eaten on Shabbat and on festivals.

charoset: a mixture of wine, chopped apples or dates, and nuts eaten at the Passover meal as a symbol of the mortar Jews manufactured when they were slaves in Egypt.

Chumash: Five Books of Moses.

chutzpah: Yiddish. Guts, spirit.

Cohane: one who is descended from the priestly class.

Conservadox: Slang shorthand for Jews whose observance levels and political leanings are a mix of denominations.

Dati Leumi: Nationalist Religious Party in Israel. "Dati" refers to Orthodox Jews.

daven/davened/davening: Yiddish. Pray, prayed, praying.

Deutsche Bahn: German train system.

drash: biblical commentary.

dreidel: spinnable top used in games played on Hanukkah. The Hebrew letters on each side of it spell out the phrase "A great miracle happened there," referring to the miracle of this holiday.

Eheyeh Asher Eheyeh: "I am what I am." God's secret name, revealed by God to Moses in the Book of Exodus.

El: one of the many ways to refer to God.

Fir Kashes: Yiddish. The Four Questions asked at the Passover seder by the youngest child present. The answers to the questions explain the significance of the holiday.

frum: Yiddish. Religious.

gabbai: congregant member of a synagogue who assigns honors and leads different parts of the service.

galut: exile. Refers to Jews living in the Diaspora, not in the land of Israel. It is also used to refer to a condition of oppression and persecution.

gefilte fish: stuffed fish served on Shabbat and on other holidays.

gimulut hasidim: "deeds of loving kindness." One of three pillars on which the rabbis claim that the world rests.

goy/goyim: "nation(s)." Refers to non-Jews.

Haftorah: specific section of the biblical prophets read in the synagogue after the corresponding Torah reading.

haggadah/haggadot: book(s) used at the Passover seder, containing the story of the Exodus and the rituals commemorating its events.

hakehilah: "the community."

Halachah: "the way you go." Jewish law, the roots of which are found in the Torah, as codified in the Talmud and in other Jewish sources.

halachic: in accordance with Jewish law.

hamantashen: jelly-filled triangular shaped pastry eaten on Purim.

Hamotzi: blessing recited over bread, literally "who brings forth."

hannukah/iot: candelabra(s) used during Hanukkah.

Hanukkah: Festival of Lights, lasting eight days, commemorating the military victory of a small group of Jews over foreign enemies.

Haredi: ultra-Orthodox Jews in Israel.

Hashem: "The Name." Used to refer to God in lieu of using the sacred name.

Hasidic/Hasid: one who is part of the movement within Judaism founded by the Baal Shem Tov (lit. "Master of the Good Name") in 1736, emphasizing prayer, joy and kabbalah, or Jewish mysticism.

Havdalah: "Separation." The service marking the end of Shabbat and beginning of the new week.

Hillel: international foundation for Jewish campus life consisting of regional centers, campus foundations and student organizations, which aim to provoke a renaissance of Jewish life. Hillel was one of the great Jewish rabbis.

Hineh Ma Tov: "How Good It Is." Popular Hebrew song and folk dance.

Ir Hakodesh: "The Holy City." Refers to Jerusalem.

Judengasse: German. "Jew's alley." Refers to areas of a city to which Jews were segregated.

Judenrein: German. "Free of Jews." The initial aim of Nazi policy was to rid Germany of Jews, first by forcing them to emigrate by making life unbearable and then by exterminating them.

Judeo-Arabic: version of the Arabic language with influences from Hebrew.

Kabbalat Shabbat: a service which welcomes the Sabbath.

kasher: to make or be kosher, according to Jewish dietary laws.

kashrut: Jewish dietary laws, found in the Book of Leviticus.

kavannah: "intention." Implies the feeling accompanying or behind an action.

kedushah: holiness.

kehilah: community.

ketzeleh: Yiddish. Little kitten, term of endearment.

Kiddush: prayer sanctifying the Sabbath, said in Jewish homes before Shabbat, during holiday meals, and in the synagogue, so that strangers spending Shabbat away from home will be able to hear it.

kippah: also called a "yarmulke," a skullcap worn by Jews during prayer, and at all times by observant Jews.

kol isha: "The voice of a woman." According the Talmud, it is it not permissible for women to sing, since our voices could distract men from concentrating on prayer.

Kol Nidre: a prayer service on the eve of Yom Kippur.

Kotel: also called the "Wailing Wall" and the "Western Wall." The remains of the Second Temple located in Jersualem, where Jews from around the world come to pray.

Kristallnacht: German. "Night of Broken Glass." On November 9, 1938, there was a major organized pogrom in Germany in which Jewish property was destroyed and Jews killed.

kugel: Yiddish. Noodle pudding.

latke: Yiddish. Potato pancake eaten on Hanukkah.

L'cha Dodi: liturgical poem sung as part of the Friday night service, a symbolic welcoming of the Shabbat, personified as a bride.

L'dor v'dor: "from generation to generation." Refers to the passing of the Torah down to each generation of Jews.

Lilith: the legendary predecessor of Biblical Eve, who insists on equality with Adam.

Lubavitch: Hasidic sect of Judaism, which focuses on outreach to unaffiliated Jews, and on the coming of a messianic era.

Maariv: evening prayer service.

Maimonides: Rabbi Moises Ben Maimon, also called the "Rambam." Twelfth-century philosopher, rationalist, and Torah commentator, author of the *Guide to the Perplexed*.

maror: bitter herbs, served at the Passover seder and symbolic of the bitterness of slavery for the Israelites in Egypt.

Masada: a fortress on the top of a mountain in Israel where a group of zealots committed suicide rather than convert from Judaism.

matzah: unleavened bread, eaten to satisfy the biblical commandment to commemorate the Jews' hasty departure from Egypt.

matzah ball: dumpling made of ground matzah meal, served in chicken soup.

mazel: luck.

mazel tov: good luck; congratulations.

mechitzah: separation between men and women's sections in some traditional prayer services.

Megillah: scroll containing the Book of Esther, which tells the story of Purim, read on Purim morning and evening.

Melech: king.

menorah: a candelabra, typically used on Hanukkah.

mensch: Yiddish. One who demonstrates personal integrity and moral correctness.

menschlekeit: Yiddish. Humanity, humaneness.

meshuggeh: Yiddish. Crazy.

mezuzah: small box affixed in the doorways of Jewish homes containing important Jewish prayers.

Midrash: parable or explication of biblical text.

mikvah: ritual bath used for purification, conversion, or rebirth. Most often used by married women after menstruation and childbirth. Men also immerse this before getting married and before holidays.

mincha: afternoon prayer service.

minhag: custom.

minyan: quorum of ten adult Jews, which is necessary in order to recite certain prayers.

Miriam's cup: modern addition to the Passover seder. The cup is filled with water and placed next to Elijiah's cup, a reminder of the story of Miriam's Well, which brought water to the Israelite tribes in the desert.

Misheberach: healing prayer.

Mishnah: Jewish oral tradition.

Misnagdim: non-Hassidic Orthodox Jews who stress rational and intellectual approaches to Jewish practice.

mitzvah/mitzvot: commandment(s). There are 613 commandments outlined in the Torah that Jews are instructed to undertake.

Mizrahi: Jews who are indigenous or descendents of Jews from the Middle East and North Africa.

Modah Ani: "I give thanks." A short prayer recited immediately upon waking in the morning.

Musaf: additional prayer service for Shabbat and holidays.

Navi: prophet.

neshamah: "soul" or "breath."

niggunim: wordless melodies often used in Hasidic music and prayer.

Omer: "A sheaf of barley." An offering brought to the temple during Passover. In modern times, this is symbolically counted each day during the seven weeks between Passover and Shavuot.

payes/peyes: curls worn by ultra-Orthodox men.

Pesach: Passover.

punim: Yiddish. Face.

Purim: Feast of Lots. Commemorates the biblical story of the deliverance of the Jews in Persia via Esther and her cousin Mordechai.

putsch: revolt or revolution; a coup.

Rebbe: "Grand Rabbi" leader of Hasidic communities, believed to have mythical spiritual power. Sometimes used as a term of endearment.

rebitzen: wife of a rabbi.

Rosh Chodesh: "the head of the month." The first day of the new month, celebrated with special liturgy. Midrashic sources site this as a special holiday for women. In modern times, it has been revitalized as an occasion for groups of women to celebrate the new moon together.

Rosh Hashanah: "the head of the year." The Jewish New Year, marking the beginning of the Days of Awe.

sambousak: Middle Eastern style pastries eaten on Purim.

Satmar: sect of Hasidic Judaism.

schach: any plant material that grows from the ground (branches or corn stalks), used to cover the sukkah.

schmooze/schmoozed: Yiddish. Talked intimately with someone familiar.

seder: the ritual Passover meal.

Sephardic: Jews and their descendents from Portugal or Spain.

Shabbat/Shabbes/Shabbos/Shebbath: seventh day of the week, Saturday, observed as the day of rest and worship by Jews.

Shacharit: morning prayer.

Shavuot: "weeks." A harvest festival that also commemorates the giving of the Torah to the Jews on Mount Sinai.

Sh'ma: Call to listen. The central Jewish prayer, affirming the oneness of God and the centrality of God in the lives of the Jewish people.

shidduch: "match." An arranged date.

Shechinah: Divine Presence, described by mystical literature as a female aspect of God.

Shehechianu: blessing recited on the first night of all holidays and on moments of celebrations and thanksgiving. Expresses personal gratitude for being alive and well and able to celebrate the occasion.

shlep: Yiddish. Drag, carry, or haul, particularly unnecessary things, parcels, or baggage; to go somewhere unwillingly.

Shmonah Esrei: "Eighteen" (actually nineteen) blessings; also known as the Amidah.

Shoah: "destruction by fire." Another name for the Holocaust.

shofar: ram's horn blown on Rosh Hashanah and Yom Kippur; call to repentance.

shomer negia: one who follows the custom of some traditional Jews of not having any physical contact with members of the opposite sex, with the exception of family members, until marriage.

shpiel: Yiddish. Talk.

shtetl: Yiddish. Small Jewish village where Eastern European Jews lived in the beginning of the eighteenth century.

shul: Yiddish. House of worship.

siddur: prayer book.

smicha: rabbinic ordination.

snioot/tzniut: modesty.

streimel: round fur-trimmed hat worn by some Hasidic men.

Sukkah: "booth." A temporary shelter built and used during Sukkot.

Sukkot: harvest festival celebrated for seven days, during which Jews erect and dwell in a sukkah.

tahor: typically, but controversially translated as "pure."

tallis/tallit: a four-cornered garment with tzitzit worn during morning prayers.

tameh: typically, but controversially translated as "impure."

tefillah: prayer.

tefillin: phylacteries; black leather boxes containing scrolls with passages of scriptures.

tikkun olam: healing the world.

Torah: the first five books of the Hebrew bible.

treif: something (food or object) that is not kosher.

Tisha B'av: "the ninth day of Av." A fast day commemorating the destruction of the Second Temple and other tragedies that occurred throughout Jewish history.

tzedek: justice.

tzitzit: fringes attached to the corners of garments as a reminder of the commandments.

USY: United Synagogue Youth, the youth group of the Conservative movement.

yente: Yiddish. Matchmaker.

Yerushalmi: from Jerusalem.

yeshivah: center of Jewish learning.

yichud: "seclusion." Time spent apart by the bride and groom immediately following the wedding ceremony, in which they were to have consummated the marriage.

yiddishkeit: Jewishness; Yiddish culture.

Yizkor: memorial prayer.

Yom Kippur: "Day of Atonement." A fast day, considered the most sacred day in the Jewish calendar, in which Jews ask God and one another for forgiveness for our sins.

zayde: Yiddish. Grandfather.

Contributors

Editors

TOBIN BELZER, Ph.D. is a Postdoctoral Research Associate at the Casden Institute for the Study of the Jewish Role in American Life and the Center for Religion and Civic Culture at the University of Southern California. She earned a Ph.D. in sociology and a joint master's degree in women's studies and sociology from Brandeis University. Tobin is the founder and director of The Chutzpah Network for Young Jewish Leaders, and was awarded a Joshua Venture Fellowship for Jewish Social Entrepreneurs.

JULIE PELC is studying to become a rabbi at Hebrew Union College—Jewish Institute of Religion in Los Angeles. She is a recipient of the Wexner Graduate School Fellowship and has a master's degree in rabbinic studies from the Ziegler School of Rabbinic Studies at the University of Judaism, and a master's degree in education from the Harvard University Graduate School of Education. Her writing was recently featured in the magazines: *Spirituality and Health* and *Lilith*. She loves rollerblading by the Pacific Ocean, writing, dancing, doing chaplaincy work, and volunteering at Planned Parenthood. Julie is currently recovering from brain surgery after suffering a brain aneurysm. She is now on an intensive path of healing.

Contributors

RUTH A. ABUSCH-MAGDER is currently a graduate student in modern Jewish history at Yale University. Her dissertation, "Homemade Judaism: Domestic Jewish Culture in Germany and America: 1850–1914" deals with the role of food in Jewish life. She has lived in Canada, Israel, the United States, and Germany. She resides in New Jersey with her husband David and their children, Oren Aryeh, who was born in Munich in 1997, and Aliza Yona.

CARYN AVIV, PH.D. currently directs the Program for Collaborative Care at the University of California, San Francisco Breast Care Center. Dr. Aviv's dissertation, "Home-making: Gender, Emotion, and American Immigration to Israel," investigates the gendered dimensions of transnational migration and American communities in Israel. She has written articles on the politics of breast cancer and women's health, global immigration, feminist theory, gender, and sexuality. She is the co-editor of *Queer Jews* with David Shneer (NY: Routledge, 2002).

LEAH BERGER is a resistance writer of poetry, prose, and song. She makes her home in the rapidly growing border town of Tucson, in the Sonoran Desert bioregion, where she spends time writing, painting, singing, dancing, planting seeds, and praying for rain. Her work has appeared in *Bridges: A Journal for Jewish Feminists and Our Friends* and *The Soronran News*. She can be reached via e-mail at rootwumun@yahoo.com.

AMY ELISABETH BOKSER is currently teaching English in Mexico. She really likes cookies as well as a few other things.

SHOSHANA M. FRIEDMAN grew up in Newton, Massachusetts and is now an environmental studies major at Oberlin College. Her loves include singing, hiking, journaling, environmental activism, and poetry. She wrote *Singing Praises* when she was sixteen years old.

ANDREA GOTTLIEB wrote the poem, "Orange," at age 15 for a high school English class. She is currently at the University of California in Santa Cruz studying sociology and mathematics. She is very passionate about the connection between Judaism and social justice, and intends to work for radical change by following the tradition of Jewish activism. Her favorite activities include off-roading, star-gazing, and processing. She also eats a lot of tofu.

VERED HANKIN, an internationally acclaimed storyteller, has been named "the leading Jewish storyteller of her generation" *(The Jewish Week)*. Vered was the recipient of the National Security Education Project Grant to study Midrash at Hebrew University in Jerusalem and research grants to study Midrash at University of California, Berkeley and Graduate Theological Union. Her publications include contributions to *The Complete Guide to Storytelling for Parents* (Norton Press, 2000) and interviews in *Response* and *New Voices*. She was commissioned by Mayan and Jewish Women's Archive to create performances annually for their Women of Valor project. Vered's CD recording, "The Day the Rabbi Disappeared: Jewish Holiday Tales of Magic," has received the prestigious Award of Excellence from the Film Advisory Board and the Gold Award from NAPPA (National Association of Parenting Publication Awards).

Residing in Manhattan, Vered is currently exploring the healing power of stories through doctoral work in clinical psychology at the City University of New York. For information and show updates go to: www.veredhankin.com

JESSIE HELLER-FRANK is an award-winning poet and an internationally published author. Her work has most recently appeared in *Hot Chocolate for the Magical Lover's Soul* and *Magical Souvenirs*. She is a University of California, Davis graduate and a M.F.A. candidate at San Francisco State University.

CHARLOTTE GREEN HONIGMAN-SMITH is a writer and activist living in San Francisco. After growing up in the Soviet Jewry movement of the 1980s, she attended a year of rabbinic school at Leo Baeck College in London, and has worked for Jewish National Fund, Congregation Sha'ar Zahav in San Francisco, Tikkun Magazine and too many insurance and health-care administration offices to count. At the moment, she is taking a leave of absence from the board of directors of the Bay Area Council for Jewish Rescue and Renewal while she finishes editing an anthology of writing by Jewish women from mixed families, and publishes *Maydeleh: a 'zine for nice Jewish grrrls*.

GABRIELLE KAPLAN-MAYER is a writer, performer and educator. A 1993 graduate of Emerson College with a B.F.A. in performing arts and a 2001 graduate of The Reconstructionist Rabbinical College with an M.A. in Jewish Studies, Gabrielle uses the arts to explore both sacred texts and contemporary Jewish issues. Her books *The Magic Tanach and Other Short Plays* and *Extraordinary Jews: Their Lives on Stage* are published by A.R.E. Publishing, Inc. Kaplan lives with her husband Fred and their two beautiful black cats, Lila and Ebenezer.

LOOLWA KHAZZOOM has done ground-breaking work in the field of Jewish multicultural education, offering workshops and founding organizations throughout the United States and in Israel for the past decade. Two years ago, she founded the Jewish Multicultural Curriculum Project, creating the first-ever children's curriculum that covers all the Jewish communities around the globe. She is the editor of an anthology, *Behind The Veil of Silence: Middle Eastern and North African Jewish women Speak Out*. In addition, she has published numerous articles in women's magazines internationally and is the author of *Consequence: Beyond Resisting Rape*. She also has a band, Grrrl Monster, for which she writes, sings, and plays bass, and they just put out their first CD, *Fed Up*. This year, Loolwa hopes to record her first CD of Mizrahi songs for Shabbat and the holidays. For more information about her work go to: www.loolwa.com.

MELANIE LEITNER, PH.D. is currently an American Association for the Advancement of Science Diplomacy Fellow at the U.S. Agency for International Development in the Bureau of Economic Growth, Agriculture, and Trade. She is working in the Middle East Regional Cooperation Program, which funds collaborative research projects between Israel and its Arab neighbors. She spent the past year as a Congressional Science Policy Fellow in the office of Illinois Senator Richard Durbin working on health policy issues including bioterrorism, cloning, and dietary supplements. She grew up in Brookline, Massachusetts and graduated *magna cum laude* from Brown University in Providence, RI in 1993 with a Sc.B. in neural sciences. She spent the year after graduation in Israel as part of the volunteer/ leadership program Project Otzma, co-sponsored by the Jewish Federation and the Israel Forum, before heading to St. Louis for graduate school. In graduate school, Leitner's research focused on identifying the biological roles of a newly discovered family of survival protein for brain cells. While a graduate student, she was very active in student leadership and advocacy, especially on behalf of women in science. She received her Ph.D. in neuroscience in 2000 from Washington University in St. Louis. This is her first published poem.

LEANNE LIEBERMAN was born in Vancouver, Canada in 1974. Since graduating from McGill University, she has lived in Japan and Israel and traveled throughout the Middle East and Asia. Leanne is an elementary school teacher, but is currently working on her master's degree in English and creative writing. Her fiction and poetry have been published in *Fireweed*, *Pottersfield Portfolio*, and *Antigonish Review*. Leanne is also the author of the novel *The Plum Rains*.

DEBORAH PREG'S poetry has appeared in the literary journals *Midwest Poetry Review*, *Wisconsin Review*, and *Anthology*. "The Kibbutz," her first publication, appeared in *Bridges: A Journal for Jewish Feminists and Our Friends*. She formerly served as the fiction editor of *Northeast Corridor*. Deborah, who has a bachelor of arts in English literature, pursues many creative endeavors in addition to writing. A gallery of her photography work is on display at www.FieldandForest.com.

EVE ROSENBAUM received her M.F.A. in creative writing from American University. Her poetry and prose have appeared in literary journals, including *Potomac Review*, *Caprice*, *Brooklyn Review*, and *For Poetry*. Her essay, "The Word," appears in the anthology, *Yentl's Revenge: The Next Wave of Jewish Feminism* (Seal Press, 2001). She currently lives in Washington, D.C.

LYNNE MEREDITH SCHREIBER is a freelance journalist, poet, and college instructor who has taught at Wayne State University, Oakland University, Oakland Community College, and through the Writer's Voice program of the YMCA. She has written four books, including *Driving Off the Horizon: Poems by Lynne Meredith Cohn* (1996), *In The Shadow of the Tree: A writing workbook for kids with cancer* (2001), *Residential Architecture: Living Places* (2002) and *Hide and Seek* (2003). Her work has appeared in the *Detroit News*, *Chicago Tribune*, *Home Magazine*, *Woman's Day*, *Better Homes and Gardens*, *Hockey Digest*, *Tennis Magazine*, *Poets & Writers*, and others. Lynne lives in Oak Park, Michigan with her husband Avy and their son Asher Melech.

ALEZA EVE KAUFMAN SUMMIT grew up outside of Boston. After graduating from high school, she spent a year traveling, living, and working in Ecuador and Israel. Aleza now attends Tufts University, where she majors in international letters and visual studies, and recently spent a year studying at the University of Buenos Aires.

ALANA SUSKIN was ordained as a Conservative rabbi in 2003. Her work has appeared in numerous journals and anthologies.

ANNA SWANSON is a queer Sephardic Jew from Vancouver, B.C. Her poetry appears in literary journals including *Grain*, *Prairie Fire*, and *The Malahat Review*. She works in community arts and loves her rubber boots.

DAVEENA TAUBER is a graduate student in English Renaissance literature at Rutgers University. Her dissertation explores the seventeenth-century tension between English reliance on Jewish imagery and English ambivalence about whether to re-admit the Jews themselves. She currently lives in Portland, Oregon with her partner and a little red hen named Paprika.

CLARA THALER is a law student in Boston. Her short fiction has appeared in *Pillow Talk II* and *Friday the Rabbi Wore Lace: Jewish Lesbian Erotica*. This is the first nonfiction piece that she has published.